# A PREFACE TO *THE FAERIE QUEENE*

# A Preface to *The Faerie Queene*

by

GRAHAM HOUGH

**DUCKWORTH**

*Third impression 1983*
*Second impression 1968*
*First published 1962*

© GRAHAM HOUGH 1962

ISBN 0 7156 0270 5

*Printed in Great Britain by*
*Biddles Ltd, Guildford, Surrey*

# PREFACE

I WOULD have called this book "Spenser and the Romantic Epic" except that I have already written two books with the word "romantic" in the title, and I should like to break the habit. My purpose has been to study *The Faerie Queene* in relation to the *genre* to which it belongs, and to see how far it represents an individual variant of the type. In the course of doing so I hope to provide a general introduction to the poem. Systematic study of Spenser has been going on for over two hundred years, so one can hardly hope for any extravagant novelty; but the rich and admirable Italian literature that Spenser drew upon is now little read in England, and I do not know of any single study of *The Faerie Queene* on just these lines. There is possibly some virtue in digesting a mass of scattered and voluminous material that is not altogether easy for the ordinary reader or student of Spenser to bring together.

The Spenser bibliography is very large and I am indebted to a great deal of it; indeed the soil is so well cultivated that it would be difficult to trace the original propagators of many current topics of discussion without making a complete survey of previous work, which was not my intention. Specific obligations are recorded in the notes, but I should like to acknowledge here the more general and pervasive debts. The first is to the superb Variorum Edition of Greenlaw, Osgood and Padelford (Johns Hopkins, Baltimore, 1932–49). This provides a whole library of Spenser scholarship from the earliest times to the date of its appearance. Where books and articles are quoted or abstracted in its pages I have frequently given references to this edition (cited as *Works* in the notes) as well as to the original place of publication. I have made extensive use of the existing source-studies, never for their own sake, but always with the idea of elucidating Spenser's intentions. The most important articles

5

# PREFACE

are those of Koeppel, R. E. Neil Dodge and H. H. Blanchard; and Miss McMurphy's *Spenser's Use of Ariosto for Allegory* put me on to the allegorizers of the *Orlando Furioso*. I have also found much relevant material in Professor Renwick's *Edmund Spenser* and Dr. Tillyard's *The English Epic*. J. A. Symonds' *Renaissance in Italy* is still the fullest and most interesting account in English of the lives, works and background of the Italian poets that Spenser knew, and I used it widely at the beginning of my reading. By far my greatest debt in general criticism of *The Faerie Queene* is to the writing of Professor C. S. Lewis. Like so many others I found my first real guide to the reading of the poem many years ago in his *Allegory of Love*, and his work both here and in the history of sixteenth-century literature has been present to my mind throughout.

There are many places in *The Faerie Queene* where any judgement or interpretation must be controversial, and it is not possible in a book of this scope even to outline the contending opinions. The fact that I have settled for one does not imply that I am unaware of others. It seemed best to give translations of the passages of Italian poetry quoted, and I should have liked to use the delightful older versions of Harington and Fairfax. But though they are excellent reading on the large scale they proved not to be accurate enough for this purpose. The nineteenth-century translations are close, but unpleasing poetically; so in the end I made plain prose versions intended only to be used as cribs. Chapter VI on the allegory of *The Faerie Queene* has a theoretical introduction. I have never been very happy about the current views of allegory and symbolism, their relation to each other and to other aspects of literature; and this is offered as a suggestion towards clearing the matter up.

Christ's College,                            G.H.
   Cambridge.

# CONTENTS

# Chapter I

## SPENSER AND THE ROMANTIC EPIC

### I

To Milton the poet of *The Faerie Queene* was "our sage and serious Spenser, a better teacher than Scotus or Aquinas": to Hazlitt it was equally clear that "the love of beauty and not of truth is the moving principle of his mind". Spenser's poetry, he says, is all fairyland, and if you do not meddle with the allegory it will not meddle with you. I cannot think that I am writing for those readers with whom it is quite natural to take Spenser in either of these ways. Those who have found a better teacher than Scotus or Aquinas will hardly come to me for further directions; and those who are happy with Spenser as a pure teller of fairy tales will not be asking for directions at all. But most readers and students of poetry today fall between these two classes, and their enjoyment of Spenser has been hindered by extreme views. More rewarding standpoints were open all the time, and they have been recommended; but the two excessive ones have in fact, and half unconsciously, exercised the greatest attractive force. Either it has been didacticism—for readers have been induced to believe that *The Faerie Queene* is uniformly allegorical and that allegory is uniformly didactic—or it has been pathless wandering through an enchanted forest. And though either or both of these might have been attractive to former ages they have not been to our own. To give some clues towards another way of reading Spenser might help to restore a source of poetic pleasure that to many has been missing for too long.

There can be no doubt that it has been missing. Spenser has been the most neglected of all our great poets in this century. His traditional position is among the greatest of our elder writers—with Shakespeare, Chaucer and Milton. That is the sort of company he keeps, and it is in the belief that he belongs there that these pages are written. Yet anyone who is familiar with the taste of students and general readers of poetry today can testify that he is remarkably little read. People who would think it quite impossible to leave *Paradise Lost* unfinished will admit that they have never finished *The Faerie Queene*. It is not that Spenser's ancient fame has been attacked: it is by no means an unmitigated misfortune to a poet when this occurs. Since Milton's celebrated 'dislodgment' some thirty years ago I suppose that he has been more closely read and perhaps more genuinely appreciated than ever before. Controversy generates interest, and the interest outlives the vulgar dust-storm. But some time since the Romantic age when his position in general esteem was very high Spenser's reputation has quietly slipped away from him; or it has remained as an empty reputation. The shrine is undefaced, but remarkably little visited.

Some reasons can be suggested. A gulf divides us from Spenser; but because his language is not difficult and his manner unaggressive we are not clearly aware of it. Christian, heroic, chivalrous, romantic—our world is none of these things. In entering Spenser's world we enter a foreign country; we must learn a different language and a different set of conventions; and this we often fail to see. We expect Spenser to satisfy more of our twentieth-century expectations than he does, and feel a sense of failure and disappointment when this turns out not to be the case. It will be said that Dante's world is more foreign still, and yet we succeed, more or less, in making the necessary translations. But Dante's flinty face opposes itself to ours with such uncompromising rigidity that we can do nothing but change all our expectations or give up reading him altogether. With Spenser it is different. There is so much that is easy, familiar and English that we expect more; and do not notice how utterly removed he is in most of his assumptions from our secular, unhierarchical, utilitarian world.

Other reasons are more technical. Modern poetic theories, tacitly or openly, have been centred on the lyric; they have notoriously had difficulties with the long poem. And the difficulties have been greatest with the long poem of relaxed and unobtrusive structure like *The Faerie Queene*. The taste for diffuse narrative has been so abundantly satisfied in our day by the novel that little new narrative poetry is written and old narrative poetry hardly contrives to get itself read. There is also a special difficulty with Spenser. His poem belongs to a forgotten kind, at least as far as England is concerned. The theory of *genres*, poetic 'kinds', is never likely to be revived in its old form. The idea of a fixed number of pre-ordained poetic types, each with its own laws, has been too rigid a scheme to accommodate the actual diversity of poetry since the later eighteenth century. However, regarded not prescriptively but heuristically, not as a framework but as a map, it can still be extremely useful. The traditional kinds—tragedy, comedy, epic, pastoral and the rest—do form a rough map of the main areas of human experience; and the special types of rhetoric traditionally assigned to them do furnish a rough scheme of the varied possibilities of expression. And with older literature where the concept of a kind was actually a constitutive factor in the production, to know to what kind a work belongs is often a necessary preliminary to understanding it. *Lycidas* would remain obstinately opaque to one who knew nothing about the pastoral, and Spenser is not easily approached with the critical do-it-yourself kit supplied for use in colleges today. The procedure of tackling everything with a meagre outfit of contemporary ethical prejudices does not work well in this case.

We said that *The Faerie Queene* belongs to a forgotten kind. It has been forgotten in England for about a century, and its disappearance from the English reader's memory coincides with the beginning of the silent decay of Spenser's fame. Until the middle of the nineteenth century the romantic epic, which is the kind to which *The Faerie Queene* belongs, was a living part of the English reader's literary experience and had been for two hundred and fifty years. Spenser's work had a context and did not appear, as it often does today, as an isolated sport, unrelated to other poetic experience. In the letter to Sir Walter Raleigh prefixed to the first three books of *The Faerie Queene* Spenser, besides his discipleship to Homer and Virgil, cites Ariosto and Tasso as his masters. The debt to the ancients is distant and general, and the acknowledgement of it is perhaps little more than that formally expected of any writer of a long poem in the Renaissance. The debt to the modern Italians, Ariosto and Tasso, especially to Ariosto, is specific and pervading. *The Faerie Queene* simply could not have the structure and atmosphere that it has without the *Orlando Furioso*. Some of its most famous passages are plain borrowings from *Gerusalemme Liberata*, and I believe for myself that its general moral temper has been much affected by Tassonian influence. Of all this more hereafter; the point at the moment is that the educated reader at any time for over two centuries from Spenser's death would have been quite aware of these links. Or if this is to overstate the case, would have been aware of having read poetry of the same general type elsewhere. Today, though an influence from Dante would not be lost, one from Ariosto or Tasso would probably pass quite unnoticed.

It is worth pausing for a moment to illustrate the currency of the romantic epic in England from the sixteenth to the middle of the nineteenth century.[1] The best testimony is the number of translations. Sir John Harington translated the notoriously bawdy twenty-eighth canto of *Orlando Furioso* for the delectation of Queen Elizabeth's court ladies, and the Queen made him do the remaining forty-five as a penance. His version came out in 1591 and there were two reprints of it in 1607 and 1634. In the eighteenth century a new translation was made by J. Hoole and this ran through at least six editions between 1773 and 1806. Between 1823 and 1831 W. S. Rose, a friend of Scott, made yet another (and by far the closest) translation; and this was reprinted in 1858 and 1864. The destinies of Tasso were similar. A partial translation of *Gerusalemme Liberata* was made in 1594, by one R.C.; and this was succeeded in 1600 by the famous and charming version of Fairfax, reprinted in 1624. Hoole, besides his work on Ariosto, translated the *Gerusalemme* in 1763 and this ran through nine editions between that date and 1807. New translations were made by Hunt in 1818, by Wiffen in 1824, and by Lesingham Smith in 1870; and there are doubtless others that

---

[1] On this see Mario Praz, "Ariosto in England" and "Tasso in England", in *The Flaming Heart*, New York, 1958.

# SPENSER AND THE ROMANTIC EPIC

I have missed. So apart from the fact that Italian was more widely read up to the late nineteenth century than it is now, the works of Ariosto and Tasso were always generally available to English readers.

Literary references to their work are numerous—often of the casual and unpremeditated kind that are most evidential. Scott's love for Ariosto finds its way into his novels. The romantic and poetical ambitions of Frank Osbaldistone, hero of *Rob Roy* are illustrated at the beginning of the book by his making a translation of the *Orlando Furioso*, and parts of it are actually read aloud by the heroine Diana Vernon in a later chapter. Darsie Latimer, the rather similar hero of *Redgauntlet*, describes to his prosaic friend Alan Fairfax the incident where he is taken up on the crupper of Redgauntlet's horse (letter IV), and can find no better illustration than a reference to Ariosto:

> It reminded me of the magician Atlantes on his hippogriff, with a knight trussed up behind him, in the manner Ariosto has depicted that matter. Thou art, I know, matter-of-fact enough to affect contempt of that fascinating and delicious poem. . . .

Hazlitt discusses both Ariosto and Tasso in the *Edinburgh Review*. Wordsworth was a reader of Ariosto, and introduced Coleridge to his work. Tasso appears with Homer, Virgil, Milton, Shakespeare and Spenser in Keats's *Ode to Apollo*; and Byron of course devoted a poem to the Tasso legend. In the mid-nineteenth century Tasso seems to have been a part of refined feminine education. Gwendolen Harleth in *Daniel Deronda*, not a particularly intellectual young woman, says (Chap. V) "I dote on Tasso", and goes on to speak of the *Gerusalemme Liberata* (she uses the Italian title) "which we read and learnt by heart at school". Samuel Palmer, the painter, writing to Miss Julia Richmond in 1866 "Let me recommend you Fairfax's Tasso, even though you may have read the original".[1]

By now this sort of familiarity has quite disappeared, and

---

[1] And there is a charming period piece discovered for me by Dr. Barbara Reynolds, a Victorian song called 'Ruby' whose heroine is seen "with her deep-fringed eyes/Bent over the Tasso upon her knee".

a whole area of poetical experience has slipped out of general awareness. It is an area in which the heroic, the supernatural, the romantic and the merely fantastic are curiously mingled. There is a rapid succession of different tones and levels, switches from politics to religious devotion, history to allegory, geographical particularity to wild fantasy, human moral action to pure enchantment. This is a peculiar note of the romantic epic and when the modern English reader finds it for the first time in Spenser he seems to have no set of expectations ready to meet it. Recent literary taste has been formed far too largely on realistic literature, on the novel, and often on a pedestrian moralism to which criticism of the novel has given rise. This is the worst possible preparation for reading a kind of narrative where psychological probability counts for little, correspondence with any particular state of affairs in the actual world for nothing at all, and the moral *significatio* is not arrived at by the coherent working out of a consistent chain of events but is approached in half-a-dozen different ways—by allegory; by romance that falls short of allegory yet seems to have a typical value; by pictorial imagery of various kinds; besides by the universal narrative method of giving to characters and actions the sort of value we should ascribe to them in actual life. The heavy brow-knitting, the pressing of the plough down into the furrow that accompanies much critical reading today seem hardly the appropriate method for the romantic epic. A certain agility, an almost careless adroitness in adapting to the shifts of tone and temper, is a more useful way of approaching the total meaning. (This is not the same thing as Hazlitt's contented acquiescence in the absence of total meaning.) And for Spenser it is certainly most useful to restore an earlier situation and to have some idea of the tradition in which he was working. To set *The Faerie Queene* in its proper place in the epic tradition is the main purpose of this book.

II

The romantic epic of Italy has its distant ancestry in the *chansons de geste* of France, but in form and spirit it belongs to such a different world that it could fairly be described as a complete perversion of these austere originals. There are several cycles of these old French epics all having for their theme or for the background of their adventures the struggle between Christendom and the Saracens. The Italian poems are derived from the central Carolingian cycle which has as its main characters Charlemagne and his peers. Happily this takes us back for purposes of illustration and contrast not to the subsidiary *chansons* such as *Le Charroi de Nimes* or *Le Couronnement de Louis*, but directly to the oldest, the grandest and the most famous of the French epics, the *Chanson de Roland* itself.

*Le Chanson de Roland* is different in almost all points, material, structure, style and temper, from the Italian poems that are derived from it or from its fellows (for the descent is doubtless not direct); and *a fortiori* different from Spenser. But to say something about it at the beginning is not altogether pointless. Spenser's romance-world is an ancient and well-cultivated soil, with the débris of many civilizations beneath its surface—more even than Spenser knew himself. There is interest and value in looking briefly at the remote origin of the literature that Spenser drew on. And the Carolingian cycle has I believe left one legacy of fundamental importance to all its successors.

The *Song of Roland* purports to have been composed by one Turoldus. It probably dates from the early years of the twelfth century. It is, as everybody knows, a tale of tragic heroism, told with bare passionate simplicity. There are no digressions from the tragic outline: and as for style there is but one simile, which takes two lines. The characters are warriors and heroes, royal and venerable, like Charlemagne, wise and temperate, like Oliver, or passionate and brave to the point of recklessness, like Roland; loyal, like Archbishop Turpin, or treacherous, like Ganelon. But none of them engages in irrelevant adventures, or falls in love, or is distracted in any way from his heroic and tragic destiny. The plot is essentially the ample treatment of a simple idea. Charlemagne and his host are returning from Spain after a successful campaign against the Saracens. In crossing the Pyrenees Roland is given the rearguard. He refuses the offer of half the army and will take only twenty thousand men. But he has been betrayed by Ganelon who hates him; and arrived at

Roncesvalles he finds himself ambushed by a huge Saracen army. Against the advice of his comrade Oliver he refuses to blow his horn to summon help from Charlemagne, and stands to fight it out. They make a heroic defence but it is hopeless. At last Roland does blow his horn; the sound carries thirty miles; Charlemagne hears it and turns back; but it is too late. Oliver dies, Roland dies, and Charlemagne arrives only in time to take revenge for the slaughter of his peers.

What has this heroic legend, in its noble simplicity, to do with the fluid intricacies of Ariosto or Spenser? Only this—that the blast of Roland's horn in Roncesvalles echoes through all medieval Europe, and gave rise to a whole new literature. The *Chanson* dates, as we said, probably from the early twelfth century. The events it describes are perhaps partly historical, but largely legendary. Charlemagne advanced into Spain and had his rearguard cut off in the Pyrenees on the return, in 778. But other parts of the Carolingian cycle tell of his being besieged in Paris by the Saracens; and of this history knows nothing. What we have here, however, is a picture of Christendom militant against a surrounding pagan foe. That Charlemagne actually accepted and identified himself with this idea is indeed historical. But that it has entered so deeply into *The Song of Roland* has another cause. The end of the eleventh century is the time of the first Crusade, when the idea of a holy war against the infidel again filled the mind of France. When Roland, after having struck the first blow in the first battle, cries out

Nos avons dreit mais cist gloton ont tort

it is doubtless the spirit of the first Crusade that speaks as much as that of his assumed historical period. And that crusading spirit, in which the mind of the eleventh century mingles with that of the eighth, is of great importance for later poetry: it means the beginning of the Christian epic.

"We are right and these miscreants are wrong." This is something new. The epic has always lived by conflict; but till now, simply by conflict between two sides; both perhaps protected by gods; both probably noble; one destined to prevail— but only by superior prowess, or the accidental support of an immortal conceived in essentially human terms. Homer writes from a Greek point of view, but he does not suggest that the Greeks were right and the Trojans wrong; or the Trojans right and the Greeks wrong. Virgil has moved perceptibly nearer to the idea of a hero with a divine mission; but neither does he suggest when his Trojans arrive on the Lavinian shore that they have a sacred and pre-ordained superiority and that the Latins are perverse to oppose them. It is a consequence of polytheism (one of its great blessings, to my mind): when both sides are supported by equally reputable deities neither can claim supreme supernatural sanction for its position. It cannot be suggested that one side is of the family of the faith, while the other is in outer darkness, representing only evil or perversity or blindness. There is a difference, then, between two kinds of conflict—conflict between two sides which merely happen to be humanly and historically opposed; and conflict between two sides one of which is eternally and supernaturally right and the other eternally and supernaturally wrong.

The second notion, that of conflict with a supernatural sanction, is original with the Christian epic, and in various forms and with varying degrees of intensity runs all through it. It is not quite absent even in the more frivolous Italian epics, and it returns with all its weight in the operations of Spenser's Red Cross Knight and Sir Artegall. It is of central importance in *The Song of Roland*, first by reason of the subject of the poem, and then by reason of the crusading age in which it was written. When the Carolingian cycle was diversified and romanticized in Italy it might seem that this august theme would altogether disappear; but this is never entirely so. The characteristic of the Italian versions is that they are filled out with extravagant adventures in the East in which one of the paladins, usually Rinaldo, is entangled with a Paynim princess. But however many fantastic episodes and irrelevant characters may surround them, Charlemagne retains his character as the Christian king, and Roland as the Christian champion. Roland is even turned into a Roman that he may more appropriately function as a defender of the Catholic world. And the tale keeps returning to Charles beleaguered in Paris by the Saracen hordes, Christendom surrounded by the forces of outer darkness. To readers of Ariosto who are struck only by the fantasy and irony it may seem an absurdity to make anything of this aspect of the *Orlando Furioso*. But there is a case to be made for it all the same. And with Tasso the case needs no arguing. Writing in the full tide of the Counter-Reformation and completely expressing its spirit, he takes the holy war as his inspiration and his theme. The first Crusade which contributed its spirit and its feeling to the *Song of Roland* is the actual historical subject of *Jerusalem Delivered*. We might add that neither in Ariosto nor in Tasso do the exigencies of the faith exclude chivalry and courtesy to those outside its bounds.

### III

French literature, including the Carolingian cycle, spread to North Italy about the end of the twelfth century,[1] and for the best part of a hundred years the north was a cultural province of France. But the influence was not confined to the courtly and the cultivated. The Carolingian tales were above all popular in their diffusion. The story of Roland and its various offshoots, notably that of Rinaldo, were sung in the market-places in a mixed dialect of Franco-Italian. They continued, proliferated and were elaborated throughout the thirteenth and fourteenth centuries; and finally, about the beginning of the fifteenth century, were combined into a huge prose compilation called the *Reali di Francia*, which performed much the same service for the Charlemagne legend in Italy as Malory did for the Arthurian legend in England.

However, at the very time the Carolingian cycle was gaining a new lease of life among the populace in Italy it was losing favour in courtly circles. It is of course pre-chivalric, and represents the manners of an earlier feudal age. The far more refined and sophisticated kind of courtly society that was growing up in the twelfth century had found its sustenance not in the rude and

---

[1] On the migration of Arthurian and Carolingian material into Italy, see J. A. Symonds, *Renaissance in Italy*, vol. 4, chaps. 1, 4, 7; Pio Rajna, *Le Fonti dell'Orlando Furioso*, Florence, 1876; E. G. Gardner, *Arthurian Legend in Italian Literature*, 1930; A. Viscardi, "Arthurian Influence on Italian Literature", in *Arthurian Literature in the Middle Ages*, ed. A. Loomis, 1959.

stern *chansons de geste* but in the mazy enchantments of the Arthurian romancers, of whom the type is Chrétien de Troyes. Love, hunting, tournaments, knight-errantry—the sentiments, pageantry and pastimes of courtly life replace the monotonous warfare of the earlier epics. And while the old Carolingian tales satisfied the people, it was this new matter, with its elaborate courtesy and refined sentiment, that was seized on by the courtly circles of northern Italy.

Arthurian literature is so vast and many-sided that it is important to realize just what it contributed to the Italian romance-epic. Like Charlemagne, Arthur was a Christian prince fighting against pagan enemies; but that aspect of his legend is of no interest for the tradition we are following. Already in Chrétien de Troyes the figure of Arthur has sunk into the background, and it is the exploits of the individual knights of the Round Table that provide the themes. And with the disappearance of the great theme of national and Christian war against a pagan foe these exploits are in the strictest sense individual—deeds of personal prowess, undertaken for love or personal renown. True, the knights of the Round Table sometimes fight against pagan or Saracen knights; but these are in no other way distinguished from the Christians; they are equally likely to be noble and brave; the code of chivalry embraces pagan and Christian alike. And failing a supply of suitable paynims the Christians are more likely to fight each other than to let their arms rust unused. There is no particular *point de repère* for the various adventures and this makes a further difference from the *chansons de geste*, where the siege of Paris or some other aspect of the continuing struggle against the infidel is constantly pulling us back towards an overriding central theme. And the disappearance of the holy war affects the supernatural no less than the natural events. They are no longer parts of a providential scheme, they are individual enchantments, infinitely various, and mysterious in means and motive, a parallel on the magical plane to the confused play of individual wills in the natural world. Ontological confusion no less: in the older layers of the Carolingian cycle the world is on two planes only—the will of God and the actions of men: but in the Arthurian world who would care to define the metaphysical status of Merlin or Morgan le Fay?

Above all it was the love theme that distinguished the Arthurian romances from the older epic. In the *chansons de geste* there are either no heroines or their rôle is restricted within the narrowest compass. Even if these tireless warriors could have found time for love the sternly limited emotional scope of the *Chanson de Roland* could hardly have admitted it. The style is perfectly adapted to stories of battle, heroism, treason and death: it could have done nothing with the elaboration of personal sentiments. In Italy it was above all the love stories, the stories of Lancelot and Guinevere, Tristan and Iseult, that represent the Arthurian cycle. It is curious to see the familiar northern tales in their Italian guise. *Qui conta della reina Isotta e di M. Tristano di Leonis; Qui conta come la damigella di Scalot morì per amore di Lancialotto del Lac*—these are two of the rubrics from the *Cento Novelle Antiche*. And the Paolo and Francesca episode in Inferno V—

> leggemmo insieme un giorno per diletto
> di Lancilotto e come amor lo strinse—

bears incidental but compelling witness to the way Arthurian romance could naturally be invoked as the predestined betrayer of gentle hearts. So a new motive enters Italian romance literature—love and the fatal power of the heroine. We are already within sight of Angelica and Bradamante. It is this grafting of the newer Arthurian romance on to the old Carolingian stock that brings the Italian romantic epic into being. It also accounts for the pervasive atmosphere of Arthurian romance in Spenser, with the absence of specific Arthurian tales or specific debts to Malory. We are right in feeling that the Arthurian element is there, but it has been filtered and transmuted through Spenser's Italian sources. And when a different and distinctly British Arthurian element enters into *The Faerie Queene* the ordinary reader probably fails to notice it.

IV

The comparison of the old romance literature and the new was made by Boiardo,[1] Ariosto's predecessor, the first great poet of the revived romantic epic:

> Fo gloriosa Bertagna la grande
> Una stagion per l'arme e per l'amore,
> Onde ancora il nome suo si spande,
> Si che al re Artuse fa portare onore . . .
>
> Re Carlo in Franza poi tenne gran corte,
> Ma a quella prima non fo sembiante . . .
> Perchè tiene ad Amor chiose le porte
> E sol se dette alle battaglie sante,
> Non fo di quel valore e quella estima
> Qual fo quell'altro che io contava in prima,
>
> Però che Amore è quel che da la gloria
> E che fa l'omo degno et onorato,
> Amore è quel che dona la vittoria,
> E dona ardire al cavalliero armato.

Britain the great was once glorious for arms and for love, whence its name is still spread abroad, and brings great honour to King Arthur. . . . Charlemagne then held a great court in France, but it was not like that former one. . . . Because it shut the door against Love and gave itself only to the holy war it was not of the same worth and reputation as that other one of which I spoke first. For it is Love that brings glory, and makes a man worthy and honoured; it is Love that brings victory and gives courage to the knight at arms.

(O.I., II. xviii. 1–3)

Matteo Boiardo, Count of Scandiano, wrote for the courtly society of Ferrara, a world already penetrated with the charms of Arthurian romance. We find members of the ducal house of Este bearing Arthurian names, Isotta and Ginevra; and the duke himself writes in 1470 to borrow as many French books as he can, especially those of the Round Table. Boiardo's poem *Orlando Innamorato* was roughly contemporary with Malory's *Morte d'Arthur*—begun about 1475 and first published in 1484. It inaugurates a new *genre*, and the principle of the new *genre* is a simple one—it is the fusion of the matter of Britain with the

---

[1] The best short account of Boiardo in English is in Symonds op. cit., vol. 4 chap. 7. See also C. S. Lewis, *The Allegory of Love*, 1936; and E. M. W. Tillyard, *The English Epic and its Background*, 1954.

matter of France. Some contamination of the Carolingian stories
with Arthurian material had already occurred sporadically in
the popular tradition; but it was left for Boiardo systematically
to infuse the spirit of chivalry and romantic love drawn from the
courtly Arthurian romancers into the older cycle of legend. The
very title of his poem indicates what he was doing. Who could
think of Roland in love, as long as he remained in the sphere of
the *chanson de geste*? Boiardo sets out to accept this challenge and
to place Roland in another light.

> Non vi par già, Signor, meraviglioso
> Odir cantar de Orlando inamorato,
> Che qualunque nel mondo è piu orgoglioso,
> E da Amor vinto, al tutto subiugato;
> Nè forte braccio, nè ardire animoso,
> Nè scudo o maglia, nè brando affilato,
> Nè altra possanza può mai far diffesa,
> Che al fin non sia da Amor battuta e presa.

Do not let it seem surprising to you, Sir, to hear about
Roland in love, for the proudest man in the world is conquered
and totally subjugated by Love. Neither strong arm, nor fiery
courage, nor shield nor mail nor sharp sword, nor any other
power can serve as defence against it; in the end they are overcome and captured by Love.

(I. i. 2)

His method is to take the characters, Roland, Charlemagne,
and the rest, and the general basis of the Carolingian tales, and
then to diversify them by love, magic and chivalric adventure.
The Arthurian tales are not used as such; their material and
spirit are taken, rearranged and placed in another setting. The
opening scene affords a good example. Charlemagne is in his
great hall holding the feast of Pentecost, to be followed by a
tournament. He is sitting at the *tavola ritonda* surrounded by his
peers; and into the hall comes a beautiful maiden, attended by a
single knight and guarded by four giants. She is Angelica.
Orlando and a number of the other knights incontinently fall in
love with her; and she brings a challenge which sets the whole
story in motion. But what is Charlemagne doing sitting at a
round table? And have we not met this scene before, or others

remarkably like it? Of course it is like the beginning of *Sir Gawayne*, or any one of half-a-dozen other Arthurian stories—the great feast at Camelot, the appearance of a stranger, and the beginning of a quest or a series of quests. *The Faerie Queene* was to begin in the same way, though Spenser, affected by later notions of epic correctness, plunged *in medias res*, left what was chronologically the beginning to the end, and so never got to it at all. The two fountains of Cupid and Merlin, the one inspiring love and the other hate, which play a large part in the story, are similarly removed from the Carolingian and akin to the Arthurian spirit. Above all there is the central importance of the heroine, the delectable Angelica, whose caprices and enchantments control the whole intricate web.

Boiardo is the creator of this new romance world, where the peoples of the earth are in motion, the hordes of the pagan East gathered together for the assault on Christendom, and Charles calls all the nations of the Christian world to combat; where the action centres in France and Spain, but ranges over Tartary, Cathay and Africa; and where the great historical movements are crossed, tangled and ultimately controlled by the caprice of individual romantic love. He is of course building on a large body of popular and bourgeois *rifacimenti* of the Carolingian tales already in existence. They had already complicated the old outlines with fantastic adventures, the entanglement of the Paladins with Oriental princesses, and so forth. They had already handled the heroic material in a spirit of adventurous levity. But the colouring of the whole with the spirit of chivalry, the idea of love and arms as the two poles on which the romantic epic should turn, is Boiardo's own.

His style is straightforward, easy and a little rustic. He tells his tale with a rather grand carelessness and an undertone of irony that is nearer to simple humour than to the finesse of Ariosto. And his admiration for the virtues of chivalry is wholehearted and perfectly genuine. Spenser read him—there are enough parallels to prove this, though they are not very significant[1]—and a certain old-fashioned simplicity of mind brings him in some ways near to Spenser. But more important

[1] See H. H. Blanchard, "Spenser and Boiardo", PMLA, XL, 1925.

is the fact that he created Ariosto's world, and therefore, at one remove, Spenser's world. He lays down the lines both of its adventures and its characters. All the principal characters in Ariosto are taken over from Boiardo. (There are slight changes in the forms of the names, and I will use the Ariostan ones to avoid confusion.) The principal heroes, Orlando, Rinaldo, Astolfo, Ferrau, all subject to the whims of Angelica; the faithful lovers Ruggiero and Bradamante, Brandimarte and Fiordiligi; the magician Atlante; the enchantresses Morgana, Alcina and Origille, with their beguiling gardens; the magic lance, the shield, the lions, the dragons, the hermits, the salvage men; all these that make up Boiardo's world are taken over bodily by Ariosto. And without them we should not have Arthur, Guyon, Calidore, Artegall and Britomart, Scudamour and Amoret, Archimage, Duessa and Acrasia. Intricate adventures proliferating into many episodes, feats of arms inspired by love, and a background, however treated, of religious conflict—these are the materials that Spenser was to inherit. It is even possible to find, besides one or two explicitly allegorical episodes, a general allegorical undertone to Boiardo's romance; and it is more than likely that Spenser read him in this way.

*Chapter II*

# ARIOSTO

Aᴙɪosᴛo simply enters Boiardo's world, takes over Boiardo's unfinished theme, and makes it the subject of his own poem. This must be one of few examples of a work that is a great achievement in its own right existing merely as a sequel to another. One of few examples in literature, that is; the situation is common enough in the decorative arts, where we find the greatest painters continuing schemes left incomplete by their predecessors. Such a procedure must necessarily sacrifice integrity and completeness of design; it is most likely to seek its effects by a brilliant elaboration of episodes and a harmony of atmosphere rather than structure. And this is an enduring legacy to the romantic epic. Even later, when as with Tasso and Spenser the need for a strong directing plan is felt, there is a tendency (more marked in Spenser than Tasso) for the episodes to take charge, to become sources of satisfaction on their own, without much recollection of the grand design.

In spite of his multiplicity of plot and motive Boiardo has a relatively firm command of structure. It is far easier to retain some sense of direction and general progress in reading the *Innamorato* than in reading the *Furioso*. At first sight Ariosto seems to have thrown all such considerations to the winds. The reader wanders through an endlessly varied landscape, continually meeting new characters; and when the old ones turn up again he forgets where it is that he saw them last. Further acquaintance reveals a few fixed points to which the narrative returns, and a few continuing threads, often obscured, which nevertheless run through it. The chief fixed point is Paris, where Charlemagne and his army are besieged. We first arrive there in Canto II. We return to it in XIV, XV, XVI, XVII, XXVI,

XXXI, XXXVI, XXXVIII, XXXIX, XLIV, XLVI; and many of the distant adventures are related to this central situation, as when Rinaldo goes to Scotland (II, IV, V, X) to summon aid for Charlemagne. The siege of Paris in fact serves much the same structural purpose in the *Furioso* as Gloriana's feast in *The Faerie Queene*. Another point of reference, this time not geographical, is the glorification of the house of Este: Ruggiero is one of its mythical ancestors, as Arthur is of the Tudors. The main continuing narrative threads are the loves of Ruggiero and Bradamante, paralleled in *The Faerie Queene* by the loves of Artegall and Britomart; and the caprices of Angelica, with all their effects on Orlando and the other paladins. Of this there is an echo in the story of Florimell in *The Faerie Queeen*. But it is safe to say that these elements of recurrence and stability are not easily held in the memory in the actual reading of *Orlando Furioso*; what we chiefly experience is a multitude of local effects.

It would be wrong however to say that there is no structural principle. There is one, and it is the principle employed in much medieval romance—in Malory and his French originals for example. The principle is to have a number of parallel stories which are kept going concurrently, one being broken off at any convenient point to take up another. After a number of these strands have been woven together and the gaps have become extensive the continuity of any one strand is hard to keep in mind —so hard that I can scarcely suppose we are meant to keep it in mind very distinctly. Certain general situations, such as the war itself, the continually interrupted and frustrated affairs of Ruggiero and Bradamante, the continual attraction of Angelica, the consequent derangement of Orlando, we do indeed retain. Beyond this we take the adventures as they come. The demand for local completeness is satisfied by interpolated novelle, some-times contained within a single canto, like the story of Ricciardetto and Fiordispina (XXV), or the host's tale (XXVIII), sometimes spread over several, like the tale of Ginevra and Ariodante in IV, V and VI. We can recognize this as a rough description of the narrative method of *The Faerie Queene* too; indeed if it were not for the letter to Raleigh and the far more widespread allegorical interest, it is probably all we should recognize. The interwoven plan with interpolated tales has its own charm. In a simpler form it survives in fiction as late as *Tom Jones*. But we have become unaccustomed to it; and it is clearly more suited to a romance, with its freedom from circumscriptions of place and time, than to a realistic narrative.

Profusion and variety of incident, then, is the keynote of the *Orlando Furioso*.

> Le donne, i cavalier, l'arme, gli amori,
> Le cortesie, l'audaci impresi io canto.

It is noticeable that in his opening lines Ariosto puts the ladies before the arms and the courtesies before the feats of daring. This may well be a pointer to his main interests; but on the face of it his story is one of knightly adventure, and we might begin by seeing how he handles the active, epic side of his work, the battles and single combats. It is clear at once that though the authentic heroic spirit may not be the mainspring of his work, Ariosto is immensely interested in the detail of war, tactics, and physical encounter. Take Agramante's attack on Paris in Canto XIV.

> Siede Parigi in una gran pianura,
> Ne l'ombilico a Francia, anzi nel core:
> Gli passa la riviera entro le mura,
> E corre, et esce in altra parte fuore;
> Ma fa uno isola prima, e v'assicura
> De la città una parte, e la migliora:
> L'altre due (ch'in tre parte è la gran terra)
> Di fuor la fossa, e dentro il fiume serra.
>
> Alla città che molte miglia gira,
> Di molte parti si può dar battaglia:
> Ma perchè sol da un canto assalir mira,
> Nè volontier l'esercito abarraglia;
> Oltre il fiume Agramante si ritira
> Verso Ponente, acciò che quindi assaglia:
> Però che nè cittade nè campagna
> Ha dietro, se non sua, fin alla Spagna.
>
> Dovunque intorno il gran muro circonda,
> Gran munizioni avea già Carlo fatte,
> Fortificando d'argine ogni sponda,
> Con scannafossi dentro e case matte:

Onde entra ne la terra, onde esce l'onda,
Grossissime catene aveva tratte;
Ma fece, più ch'altrove, provedere
Là dove avea più causa di temere.
(XIV. 104–106)

Paris is seated in a great plain, in the navel of France, right in its heart. The river passes within its walls, and runs and flows out on the other side. But first it makes an island, and so secures one part of the city, and the better part. The other two (for the great territory is divided into three parts) are girt round by the moat without and the river within.

The city which is many miles around might be attacked from many sides: but because he only plans to attack it from one side and is not willing to disperse his troops, Agramante withdraws across the river to the west, so that he might attack from there; for he has neither town nor country behind him that is not his, as far as Spain.

Everywhere within the circuit of the great walls Charlemagne had already made great provision, fortifying every shore with embankments, with drains and casemates inside; and where the river enters and goes out he had laid great chains; but had provided more strongly for those places where he had most cause to fear.

This interest in the strategic situation, the lay-out of attack and defence, has no parallel in Spenser. Compare the attack on the castle of Alma in *F.Q.* II. ix, where indeed we find a superbly created atmosphere of hungry revolt, terror and violence, but nothing specific, no soldier's detail of what was actually done. Paris is historically and geographically solid as nothing in *The Faerie Queene* attempts to be. It is the same even in purely fantastic episodes. Courthope[1] has aptly compared Orlando's destruction of the Orc (*O.F.* XI, 37–43) with the Red Cross Knight's dragon fight, to show how specific as to scale and detail Ariosto is, where Spenser is content with only so much concrete specification as will conduce to the moral effect. The single combats, so frequent in this kind of romance that they tend to a tiresome sameness, in Ariosto are all individual. Each has its

---

[1] W. S. Courthope, *History of English Poetry*, vol. II, 1897, pp. 269–74. I do not deduce from this, as Courthope does, that Spenser is inferior; simply that he has, without knowing it, a different purpose.

own quality and its own vicissitudes, from the half-comic one in Canto II between Rinaldo and Sacripante, where the Saracen is riding Rinaldo's horse and cannot make it do what he wants, to the climactic battle between Ruggiero and Bradamante in Canto XLV, conceived in a truly chivalrous and heroic vein, where all Ruggiero's effort is to defend himself without hurting his lady. Often Ariosto treats his heroic material in a spirit of levity; but not always; and even when he is half-mocking, he is always so much engaged with his actual events and images, his wheels grow so hot with rolling, that he extracts the maximum of life and interest from every individual adventure. The spiritless sequence of walloping and carving that we so often find in this kind of thing is transformed in his hands into a miracle of imaginative vitality.

When we come to the love motive the variety of mood and treatment is still more evident. The caprices of Angelica hardly come under this head; they are more a contribution to the plot than to the emotional atmosphere of the poem. In Boiardo the extravagant desirability of Angelica was the beginning of the whole action, and Ariosto continues her rôle. She is an enchanting heroine; her impertinent waywardness can always give the action a new turn; she drives Orlando mad, and the other paladins to lesser vagaries; but she is only the fleeting object of desire; we never see her from within. With Bradamante the case is quite different. Her constant passion for Ruggiero, her pride, her restless energy, and the femininity always retained under the warrior guise make her Ariosto's most individual creation. Iconologically she descends from Virgil's warrior-maiden the swift Camilla; she is the *virago* heroine, the woman who is as brave and effective as a man, an ideal, as Burckhardt informs us, much cherished in the Italian Renaissance. What makes her live for us more fully than any other character of Ariosto's is that we follow her emotions so closely—her longing for Ruggiero when he is absent, her passions of jealousy and suspicion when she believes he is attached to another woman, her devotion to her parents and the loving frankness that underlies her adventurous rôle. The scene where at last they meet and recognize each other (XXII. 32 seq.) is one of straightforward and happy tenderness; and against the picture of the flighty Angelica we can set that of the blushing Bradamante telling Ruggiero that he must seek her as an honest lover and ask her father Amon for her hand. The loves of Brandimarte and Fiordiligi are treated in a similar vein of tender seriousness, though here the outcome is a tragic one, and the lament of Fiordiligi over her dead lover (XLIII. 160–163) is one of the great scenes of pathos in the poem. English critics have sometimes expressed surprise that Spenser found so much in Ariosto to satisfy his own graver temper; but I think the surprise is misplaced, unless like Sir John Harington at the beginning of his Ariostan labours we deliberately choose to concentrate on the cheerful bawdry.

Of course the cheerful bawdry is there too. There are a few genuinely scabrous passages, such as that of Angelica and the hermit (VIII. 47 seq.). But Canto XXVIII about which so much fuss has been made, and which the *mauvaise honte* of Italian editors cuts out of most modern editions, is only a Chaucerian fabliau. And the entertaining tale of Ricciardetto and Fiordispina in *O.F.*, XXV evidently shocked Spenser so little that he adapted one of its situations to his own more modest purpose in the Malecasta episode of *F.Q.*, III. i. It is of course true that the unabashed hedonism of Ariosto is utterly alien to Spenser's temper; but it is also true that it is not as omnipresent in Ariosto as has often been made out. And none of it is much likely to have upset the Spenser who wrote the Paridell and Hellenore canto (III. x) of *The Faerie Queene*. What we find in the love passages of Ariosto is the whole range from a generous human passion and tenderness, through a civilized epicureanism, to the spirit of the fabliau or the novella. What we do not find is the element of Platonic (if that is the word) idealism about love that is so strong in Spenser. For that he went to other Italian sources; some of it he found in Tasso, some of it outside the romantic epic altogether.

Just as there is a humane and generous ideal of love to be found in Ariosto, so there is a humane and generous ideal of loyalty and friendship. Brandimarte loves Orlando "as much as man can love a brother, friend or son"; and it is a touching feature of the loves of Brandimarte and Fiordiligi that she is so

willing to acknowledge the claims of this devotion. Since it is
his destiny to follow Orlando she is happy to make it hers to
accompany him in his adventures. As so often in Renaissance
literature, the claims of friendship are put very high. When
Orlando goes off distracted in search of Angelica (VIII. 87)
Brandimarte must follow him at once, without even finding time
to say good-bye to Fiordiligi first. The most celebrated example
of comradeship and feudal devotion in the *Furioso* is the episode
of Cloridano and Medoro (XVIII. 165–XIX. 7). Partly inspired
by the Nisus and Euryalus episode in Aeneid IX, Ariosto makes
it into one of his most beautiful and original creations. At the
end of the great battle before Paris Dardinello, one of the
Saracen leaders, has been killed. Two young Moors, his followers, cannot endure the thought of leaving him unburied.
Night has fallen and they return to the battlefield to try to find
the corpse. Since it is dark and they are unobserved they cannot
forbear to penetrate the enemy camp, where they make a great
slaughter of the sleeping Christians. Then in response to the
prayers of Medoro the moon shows her face, and by its light
they find the body of their king. They take it up on their
shoulders and are making their way back when they are sup-
prised by Zerbino with a Christian patrol. Cloridano says they
must drop the body, and makes off; but Medoro will not
abandon his dead leader and struggles on alone with the
burden. Cloridano soon finds that Medoro has not followed,
goes back to look for him, and finds him fighting in the middle
of the Christian troop. Zerbino, moved by his youth and beauty
is about to spare him, but he falls wounded in the mêlée.
Cloridano believes him killed, rushes alone against the enemy,
and is cut down dead beside his friend.

This bald summary can give little idea of the romantic and
exalted beauty in which the episode is bathed—the devotion of
the pair to each other and to their lord; the atmosphere of
stealthy midnight adventure; the sudden effulgence of the moon;
escape, and safety almost reached; and the tragic peripeteia by
which Cloridano deliberately seeks death thinking his companion
already killed. I will quote only the two stanzas where the moon
comes out and Medoro finds the body of Dardinello on the field.

La Luna a quel pregar la nube aperse
(o fosse caso o pur la tanta fede),
bella come fu allor ch'ella s'offerse,
e nuda in braccia a Endimion si diede.
Con Parigi a quel lume si scoperse
l'un campo e l'altro; e 'l monte e 'l pian si vede:
si videro i duo colli di lontano,
Martire a destra, e Leri all' altra mano.

Rifulse lo splendor molto più chiaro
ove d'Almonte giacea morto il figlio.
Medoro andò, piangendo, al signor caro;
che conobbe il quartier bianco e vermiglio:
e tutto 'l viso gli bagnò d'amaro
pianto, che n'avea un rio sotto ogni ciglio,
in sì dolci atti, in sì dolci lamenti,
che potea ad ascoltar fermare i venti.

(XVIII. 185, 186)

At this prayer the moon shone out (whether by chance or by cause of such great faith) fair as when she offered herself to Endymion and lay naked in his arms. By this light Paris was revealed, the one camp and the other; the mountains and the plain were seen in the distance, Montmartre on the right and Montlhery on the left.

Its splendour shone more brightly where Almonte's son lay dead. Medoro went weeping to his dear lord, for he recognized the white and vermilion quarterings, and bathed all his face in bitter tears—for he had a stream of tears under each eyelid—with such gentle gestures, so sweet a lament, that the winds might have stopped to listen.

I cite the Cloridano and Medoro episode for two reasons—one that it is inspired by a heroic and romantic feeling, and that this side of Ariosto has been understated. Most English and some Italian critics have so emphasized the irony and mockery in Ariosto (which is of course really present) that it has become hard to understand how Spenser can have put him among "the antique Poets Historical"; and it is therefore useful that we should see him in a Virgilian mood. Secondly, this passage is a particularly clear example of what Spenser may well have admired, but cannot do himself. The atmosphere and setting is entirely within Spenser's power, and Ariosto's exquisite scene-painting of this kind must have been a powerful influence. But the narrative and dramatic development goes outside Spenser's range. I think there is no single sequence in *The Faerie Queene* developed with this sort of rapidity, economy and closeness to the facts of the case. And this points to a difference between Spenser's and Ariosto's purposes that we shall notice throughout.

As it happens, the story also affords an excellent example of Ariosto's versatility of tone. This heroic-pathetic episode modulates rapidly into a sensuous idyll. Angelica happens to pass by, sees the wounded Medoro near to death, takes pity on him, cures him by her *arte di chirurgia*, and falls in love with him in the process. She takes him to a shepherd's hut, makes him her lover, and bestows on him, a boy and a simple soldier, the prize that she has denied to Orlando and so many of the great princes of the earth. We can see here the delicacy of Ariosto's transitions. This one is effected by a trope on the word *piaga*, wound.

> Quivi a Medoro fu per la donzella
> la piaga in breve a sanità ritratta:
> ma in minor tempo si sentì maggiore
> piaga di questa avere ella nel core.

(XIX. 27)

Here the damsel soon healed Medoro's wound; but in an even shorter time she found that she had an even greater wound in her own heart.

And as an instance of the way the various incidents are linked together in this astonishing tapestry we may recall that Angelica carelessly rewards their shepherd-host with a gold bracelet that Orlando had given her; that when Orlando happens to pass that way (XXIII) he finds it and so uncovers the story of the love-affair with Medoro; and this is the beginning of the madness that gives the whole poem its title.

So far we have said nothing of the marvellous and the fantastic. This was the side of Ariosto that most enchanted his admirers in the Romantic age, Scott and Hazlitt. Threads of it run through the whole poem and are continually affecting the action —Angelica's ring which reveals truth and confers invisibility, Astolpho's book and magic horn, Bradamante's enchanted lance, the Hippogriff and Roland's horse Baiardo, endowed with almost human intelligence. Space and time present no obstacles; everybody makes supernaturally rapid journeys. And there are the two principal magicians—Atlante the bad one who provided suggestions for Archimago and Busirane, and Melissa who acts as a beneficent *dea ex machina*. But there is something surprisingly material about these characters and their operations. They are marvellous, but they are not mysterious or haunting. Spirited and inventive to the last degree, Ariosto works his marvels in daylight. His world, for all its fantastic freedom, is very like the natural one. When Astolfo makes a magic flight on the Hippogriff it is nevertheless a geographically orderly affair—

> e secondando il Nilo a lato a lato
> tosto i Nubi apparir si vide inante
>
> (XXXVIII. 26)

And following the course of the Nile on either hand he soon saw Nubia appear before him.

Even when miracles occur they tend to be like rather spectacular scientific experiments. In the next canto Astolfo has need of a fleet and miraculously creates one:

> et avendosi piene ambe le palme,
> quanto potean capir, di varie fronde
> a lauri, a cedri tolte, a olive, a palme,
> venne sul mare, e le gittò ne l' onde.
> Oh felici, e dal ciel ben dilette alme!
> Grazia che Dio raro a' mortali infonde!
> Oh stupendo miracolo che nacque
> di quelle frondi, come fur ne l' acque.
>
> Crebbero in quantità fuor d' ogni stima;
> si feron curve e grosse e lunghe e gravi;
> le vene ch'attraverso aveano prima,
> mutaro in dure spranghe e in grosse travi:
> e rimanendo acute inver la cima,
> tutte in un tratto diventaro navi
> di differenti qualitadi, e tante,
> quante raccolte fur da varie piante.
>
> (XXXIX. 26, 27.)

And having filled his hands as full as he could with various leaves, plucked from laurels, cedars, olive-trees and palms, he went to the sea and threw them on the waves. O happy ones, O souls blessed by Heaven! O grace that God rarely grants to men! O stupendous miracle born of the leaves upon the waters.

They grew in size out of all measure; they became curved and large and long and heavy; the veins which formerly ran across them turned into firm ribs and great beams; and becoming sharp at the points, all in a trice were transformed into ships, of as many different types as they were picked from different trees.

An Italian commentator speaks of the *stupenda facilità* of this operation; it seems the right phrase for most of Ariosto's supernatural machinery. It is at the opposite extreme to Spenser's, where the invention and facility is so much less, and the suggested sense of moral and metaphysical power so much greater.

Two concentrated supernatural areas are the Alcina episode and Astolfo's visits to the Earthly Paradise and the moon. I want to leave the first for the moment, as it contains an element of allegory. The second is a peculiarly Ariostan blend of mockery, fantasy and wisdom. This supernatural adventure (Canto XXXIV) begins with Astolfo led through Hell by the Harpies. In fact we are shown very little of Hell but the smoke and the darkness and some open parody of Dante. Those who are tormented in this region are not like Paolo and Francesca, those who loved too kindly, but those who were cruel to their lovers on earth. One of these shades is greeted by Astolfo and replies. It is a patent skit on the Dantesque manner.

> e dice all'ombra: se Dio tronchi ogni ala
> al fumo, sì ch'a te più non ascenda,
> non ti dispaccia che'i tuo stato intenda.

(XXXIV. 9)

And he said to the shade: May God clip the wings of this smoke so that it no longer flies up to thee, and let it not displease thee that I should hear of thy condition.

> L'ombra rispose: Alla luce alma e bella
> tornar per fama ancor sì mi par buono,
> che le parole e forza che mi svella
> il gran desir c'ho d' aver poi tal dono.

(ibid. 10)

# A PREFACE TO *THE FAERIE QUEENE*

> The shade replied: It seems so sweet to me to return in fame
> to the fair light of day, that the great desire I have for such a
> boon becomes a power to pluck the words from me.

And the rest of the Hell scene is filled with her long and
rather tedious tale; and Ariosto escapes with his knight as soon
as may be to his purely idyllic Paradiso Terrestre. When in
Spenser we visit the underworld (*F.Q.* I. v. 27 seq.) the scene is
sombrely splendid and traditional, the model Aeneid VI. Ariosto
has recourse to the more terrible Dante, but in a spirit of pure
levity reverses the Dantesque values, and copies Dante's exordia
not in reverent imitation but in ironic pastiche. The Earthly
Paradise into which Astolfo emerges has lost all theological and
mystical significance; it is a smiling and idyllic scene, quite like
Alcina's or Armida's island. Astolfo is received there by a
venerable old man who turns out to be St. John the Evangelist.
He describes how he was taken up to Paradise, at the special
request of our Lord, without completing his earthly days. This,
like the Dantesque parody, is done in a style in which the
mockery is never over-apparent; with perfect tact Ariosto finds
a form of words that remains entirely dignified, yet deprives the
situation of all the expected moral and spiritual unction. And
when in the next stanza Astolfo tastes the paradisal fruit and
finds it

> di tal sapor, ch'a suo giudicio, sanza
> scusa non sono i duo primi parenti,
> se per quei fur sì poco ubbidienti.
>
> (XXXIV. 60)

> of such sweet taste that our first parents were not without
> excuse if they were so disobedient on this account.

—then the cloven hoof of Ariosto the ironist peeps out pretty
plainly. After that we are not surprised to find that in the
Earthly Paradise there is a practical economy in transport—that
the chariot which takes Astolfo to the moon is the same one as
was used to convey the prophet Elias into heaven; or that St.
John wishes well to the poets since he was a writer himself when
on earth.

Yet it is always a mistake to turn Ariosto into a merely comic poet in any limiting sense. When Astolfo goes to the sphere of the moon it is by divine appointment, to recover Orlando's lost wits, that he may again become the champion of Christendom. And certainly we are not to take this *au grand sérieux*. Yet when he arrives there, and finds the moon the repository of all the things that are lost or disregarded on earth, they are described in a long passage of disillusioned ironic fancy that is one of the finest things in Ariosto, with a more authentic philosophic and imaginative power, perhaps, than the rhetorical scenes of heroism or pathos.[1]

> Molta fama è là su, che, come tarlo,
> il tempo al lungo andar qua giù divora:
> La su infiniti prieghi e voti stanno,
> che da noi peccatori a Dio si fanno.
>
> Le lagrime e i sospiri degli amanti,
> l'inutil tempo che si perde a giuoco,
> e l'ozio lungo d'uomini ignoranti,
> vani disegni che non han mai loco,
> i vani desideri sono tanti,
> che la più parte ingombran di quel loco:
> ciò che in somma qua giù perdesti mai,
> là su salendo ritrovar potrai.
>
> (XXXIV. 74, 75)

Much fame is there on high, that time like a moth devours down here with its slow pace; up there are infinite prayers and vows made to God by us sinners.

The lover's tears and sighs, the time wasted uselessly in play, the long idleness of ignorant men, vain projects that never find their goal—there are so many vain desires that the better part of that world is cumbered with them: in short, whatever has been lost down here you may find again by ascending to that height.

I do not want to use Ariosto only as an object of comparison with Spenser, and there is no need to exhibit at length how far this is from Spenser's genius. This delicate control of the

[1] An incidental evidence of this is that Milton thought highly enough of this passage to imitate it for his Limbo of Vanity in *P.L.*, III, 440–480.

negative and critical emotions, the intelligence of the invention, the mingling of all with his own kind of bitter-sweet poetry, is something that belongs to Ariosto alone.

It is sometimes suggested that Spenser misread Ariosto, that his moral prepossessions and his lack of humour led him to see allegory in the *Orlando Furioso* that is not there. The general practice of *allegorizing* Ariosto, in which Spenser shared, is discussed later on; but it is often forgotten how much obvious, unabashed allegory there is in the *Furioso*, of much the same kind as Spenser himself was to employ. The most important allegorical sequence is the Alcina-Logistilla story in Cantos VI, VII, VIII and X. Ruggiero is carried off by the Hippogriff (VI. 18 seq.) to the island of the sorceress Alcina; and the description of her abode, both in its delights and its terrors, contributed to the Spenserian descriptions of the House of Pride and the Bower of Bliss. When Ruggiero arrives on this enchanted island he tethers his horse to a laurel-tree. The animal tugs roughly at the branches, and the injured tree begins to speak in a thin wailing voice. Concealed in this shape is Astolfo, an English knight, formerly one of Alcina's lovers, now abandoned and cruelly transformed. We begin to see Alcina as Circe; and when we learn from Astolfo's narrative (VI. 43, 44) that she has a sister Logistilla, virtuous and chaste, whose territory she has almost entirely usurped, a plainer allegorical significance begins to become apparent. Alcina is Luxury or Lust, Logistilla as her name implies is Reason. Ruggiero leaves Astolfo and approaches Alcina's palace (VI. 59). A crowd of monstrous figures riding symbolic beasts try to drive him into the palace, and we can recognize in the terse vivid descriptions the semblance of incontinence, violence, boastfulness, pride and the rest of the tale of vices. The leader is a figure who closely resembles Spenser's Gluttony (*F.Q.*, I. iv. 21–23).

> Di questi il capitano si vedea
> aver gonfiato il ventre, e'l viso grasso;
> il qual su una testuggine sedea,
> che con gran tardità mutava il passo.
> Avea di qua e di là chi lo reggea,
> perchè egli era ebro, e tenea il ciglio basso;

altri la fronte asciugava e il mento,
altri i panni scuotea per fargli vento.

(VI. 63)

The captain of this crew appeared, with swollen belly and bloated face; he sat upon a tortoise that sluggishly moved its steps. Some held him up on each side, for he was drunk and kept his eyes cast down; some wiped his brow and his chin, others fanned him with the skirts of their garments.

He is Sloth, parent of all the vices. But Ruggiero, as a brave and vigorous knight, is equal to this trial and puts them all to flight. It is by gentler means that he is conquered. As soon as the monsters have been vanquished two maidens mounted on a unicorn emerge from the palace. They are allegorically identified without being quite labelled as abstractions—

e tal saria
Beltà, s'avesse corpo, e Leggiadria.

(VI. 69)

such would Grace and Beauty be, if they had corporeal shape.

And they succeed in leading the hero into the palace where the monsters had failed. There is no need to trace in detail Ruggiero's meeting with Alcina and the delights he enjoyed in her society (VII. 1–44). They are so great that he would never have left them if it were not that the power of true love, represented by Bradamante, comes to liberate him from the enchantments of lust with the magic ring, and to show him Alcina as she really is, hideous and deformed. But Ruggiero is not yet in a state to enjoy the fruits of true love. He must first be instructed by Logistilla, Reason, and he flies towards her domain. Canto VIII begins with an open explanation of the allegory.

Oh quante sono incantatrice, oh quanti
incantator tra noi, che non si sanno!
che con lor arti uomini e donne amanti
di sè, cangiando i visi lor, fatto hanno.
Non con spiriti constretti tali incanti,
nè con osservazion di stelle fanno;
ma con simulazion, menzogne e frodi
legano i cor d'indissolubil nodi.

Chi l'annello d'Angelica, o più tosto
chi avesse quel de la ragion, potria
veder a tutti il viso, che nascosto
da finzione e d' arte non saria.
Tal ci par bello e buono, che, deposto
il liscio, brutto e rio forse parria.
Fu gran ventura quella di Ruggiero,
ch'ebbe l'annel che gli scoperse il vero.

(VIII. 1, 2)

How many enchantresses there are among us, how many enchanters, though unknown, who have by their arts made men and women their lovers, changing them from their own aspect. They do not do this through conjured spirits or observation of the stars, but by dissimulation, lies and fraud they bind the heart with indissoluble knots.

Whoever had Angelica's ring, or rather the ring of reason, could see any face so that it could not be disguised by fiction or by art. This now seems fair and good to us that would seem foul and evil were the veil removed. Ruggiero was indeed in luck that he had the ring that revealed the truth to him.

Ruggiero's pilgrimage is continued in Canto X. On his way to Logistilla he resists the seductions of a second bevy of damsels (X. 38). We discover what it is he will learn from Logistilla's teaching:

Il suo amore ha dagli altri differenza;
speme o timor negli altri il cor ti lima;
in questo il desiderio più non chiede
e contento riman come la vede.

Ella t'insegnerà studii più grati,
che suoni, danze, odori, bagni e cibi;
ma come i pensier tuoi meglio formati
poggin più ad alto che per l'aria i nibi,
e come de la gloria de' beati
nel mortal corpo parte si delibi.

(X. 46, 47)

Her love is different from that of others; with others fear and hope gnaw at the heart; with her desire seeks no more, but rests contented as it sees her.

She will instruct you in worthier studies than music, dance, odours, baths and rich meats; she will teach you how your thoughts new-formed may rise higher than hawks in the air, and how you may share the glory of the blest here in your mortal body.

On his arrival in Logistilla's island he is received by four maidens very different from the earlier ones, symbolizing the four cardinal virtues. And they conduct him to Logistilla herself.

So far this is entirely in the spirit that we later find in Spenser's allegory. The sequence of images, the romance-incidents, are vigorously conceived and live with a life of their own; but the thematic intention is primary and directs the course of the narrative. And this is not an isolated patch of detachable allegory; it concerns some of the principal characters in their most important relations. It is easy to see how Spenser, meeting this episode quite early in his reading of the *Orlando Furioso*, could have taken it as a poem essentially in accordance with his own purpose. Without any wresting of Ariosto's intention Alcina can become an ancestor of both Duessa and Acrasia, Bradamante play the same rôle as Britomart, Ruggiero go to Logistilla for spiritual healing as the Red Cross knight goes to the House of Holiness. Yet there is a difference in the end. In fiction vice is always more fertile of incident and imagery than virtue. We know more about it, and it is more various in its forms. But within those limits Spenser delights to expatiate on virtue as much as on imperfection; the shades and varieties of right living are for him almost as rich a subject as the picturesque conflicts that lead to them. For Ariosto this is not so. His interest is in the combats and the adventures, in "the foul rag-and-bone shop of the heart". Virtue achieved and passions conquered, though he sees them quite seriously as desirable absolutes, are not *interesting*. In spite of the promise of the stanzas last quoted we do not actually see anything of Logistilla's work of monition and regeneration. We hear none of her godly counsels. In fact after a day or two's rest, passed over in a couple of lines, Ruggiero and Astolfo hastily take their leave and go off to the West in search of new adventures—most of which are seen as allegorical only by the ingenuity of commentators. The promise of an organically allegorical romance

which is held out by the first quarter of the poem is not sustained
by the rest.

The remaining allegorical passages are a good deal less
important. In XIV and XV Silence and Discord are summoned
to the aid of Charlemagne—Silence to bring Rinaldo and his
force to the Christian camp unobserved by the enemy, Discord
to sow dissension among the Saracens. These are devices that
would be in no way out of place if we met them in *The Faerie
Queene*. And in the first part of Canto XXXV, a passage filled
with Platonic and Pythagorean ideas about pre-existence and the
world of forms, there is an elaborate allegory of Time and the
Poets. This is an isolated patch of allegory and has no connection
with the main narrative threads.

But as with Spenser there is a smooth transition from the
specifically allegorical to the romance of types. We shall see
later that the commentators found no difficulty and considerable
justification in uncovering quasi-allegorical significances where
the uninquiring reader would find only simple romance.
Ariosto's range is in fact the same as Spenser's—from pure
allegory to romance with the slenderest thematic intention. It is
only the proportions that are different. Ariosto's poem is *mainly*
controlled by the needs of pure romance, of incident and adventure; Spenser's is *mainly* controlled by allegorical intention. But
it is a difference of emphasis, not a difference of *genre*.

It is of course in his moral temper that Spenser is farthest
divided from Ariosto; yet there is the paradox that he found so
much in Ariosto that he could make his own. I suggest that the
source of the paradox is in the *Furioso* itself, rather in Spenser's
reading of it. We have seen that he could find there, besides a
vast storehouse of sheer narrative invention, images of love in all
its aspects, from the faithful and tender to the frivolous and
bawdy; chivalry and devoted friendship; war, and the defence of
Christendom against the infidel; magic and enchantment, sometimes pure fantasy, sometimes infused with allegorical significance. It would be impossible for Spenser to read this as a light
or a frivolous poem. To take even the most unpromising
example, the treatment of the religious theme—what would
Spenser find? He would find a poem whose very structural

centre is the struggle between the true faith and the false. Charlemagne besieged in Paris with the infidel hordes around is the historical focus of the whole work. The central romantic theme is the love of Ruggiero for Bradamante. Ruggiero is an infidel, and his conversion is therefore necessary as a prelude to the happy consummation. We can regard this as a mere necessity of the plot if we will, but the terms in which it is presented (XLI. 47–59) suggest a good deal more than a mere piece of rhetorical-romantic machinery. Ruggiero has been shipwrecked, and as he is near drowning, within sight of the shore, he remembers the promises he has made and has not kept—promises to turn Christian made to Rinaldo and to Bradamante herself. And he vows that he will fulfil them if he reaches the shore alive:

> e mai più non pigliar spada nè lancia
> contra ai fedeli in aiuto de' Mori;
> ma che ritorneria subito in Francia
> e a Carlo renderia debito onori;
> nè Bradamante più terrebbe a ciancia,
> e verria a fine onesto dei suo' amori.

(XLI. 49)

and never again take up sword or lance on the side of the Moors against the faithful; but that he would return at once to France and give due honour to Charlemagne; nor babble idly to Bradamante any more, but bring his love to an honest end.

He does reach the shore, and as he climbs the hill he meets a hermit, who reproaches him in the words that Christ addressed to Paul on the road to Damascus.

> Seguitò l'eremita riprendendo
> primo Ruggiero; e al fin poi confortollo.
> Lo riprendea ch'era ito differendo
> sotto il soave giogo a porre il collo;
> e quel che dovea far, libero essendo,
> mentre Christo pregando a sè chiamollo,
> fatto avea poi con poca grazia, quando
> venir con sferza il vide minacciando.

(XLI. 55)

The hermit follows Ruggiero and reproves him; in the end

comforts him; reproves him because he had delayed to place his neck beneath the gentle yoke, and what he should have done freely when prayed and called by Christ, he had done with little grace when he saw himself threatened with the lash.

It is not surprising that Harington chooses to quote this place in the preface to his translation, as "contayning in effect a full instruction against presumption and dispaire".

Later in the same canto Brandimarte, himself a converted Saracen, attempts to convert Agramante the Saracen king. Agramante remains unshaken; they fight, and Brandimarte is killed. In the lines which follow as epitaph (not spoken dramatically, lines for which the poet and the poem take the responsibility) it is made plain that he dies a martyr for his faith:

> Padre del ciel, dà fra gli eletti tuoi
> spiriti luogo al martir tuo fedele,
> che giunto al fin de' tempestosi suoi
> viaggi, in porto ormai lega le velle.
>
> (XLI. 100)

Father of heaven, grant a place among thy elected spirits to thy faithful martyr, who arrived at the end of his tempestuous voyage now furls his sails in port.

Spenser would take all this seriously, as he would take the high ideals of love and friendship seriously. Harington does so too, as we can see by reading his preface. And it would surely be a strange reading of the poem that refused to do so. Yet later criticism has tended to concentrate on the irony and the humour of Ariosto, or to deny that his poem has any serious content at all. De Sanctis has written of "this world which is utterly lacking in seriousness of inner life, empty of religion, fatherland, family, feeling for nature, and even of honour and love".[1] Croce, the great champion of Ariostan irony, speaks of the tone as "light, airy, transmutable into a thousand forms".[2] And it is easy enough to see the rationale of this too. The ideal love and friendship in the poem is found side by side with pure

[1] F. de Sanctis, Storia della Letteratura Italiana, ed. Croce, Bari, 1912, vol. II, p. 40.
[2] B. Croce, *Ariosto, Shakespeare e Covneille*, Bari, 1920, p. 46.

caprice and delighted hedonism, what Harington calls "the infinit places full of Christen exhortation, doctrine and example" side by side with indifference and scepticism. Such phenomena are not unknown elsewhere in Ariosto's age—in Rabelais, for example, or a little later, in Montaigne. Spenser took his good where he found it, and without any sign of revulsion tacitly ignored what was incompatible with his own "grave and morall" temper. Occasionally (not often) we find him transcribing in all seriousness a passage where the ironical slant is quite evident in the original. Doubtless the subtle shadings of Ariosto's attitude were not apparent to him; they were indeed outside the conceptual range of the criticism of his time, and are far more in accord with a later critical attitude. But much criticism from the nineteenth century on has tended to the opposite extreme; fascinated by Ariosto's tone it fails to do justice to the manifest content of his work. And here is the paradox of Ariosto—that a poem which indubitably contains the elements I have cited should so generally be treated as a prolonged *jeu d'esprit*. Croce points to the difficulty himself when he speaks of "la tante volte notata e denominata e non mai bene determinata ironia ariostesca"[1]—Ariosto's irony, so often observed and mentioned but never adequately defined. The Italian critics offer us the key. De Sanctis goes on to describe this Ariostan world that lacks all seriousness as "questo mondo della pura arte".[2] And this tells us something, but not enough. A world of pure art indeed—but this cannot be properly identified with a world where religion, patriotism, love, honour and the feeling for nature have no place. What the world of pure art does is to enclose all these things within its own framework, so that they exist virtually, not actually, and may co-exist with other elements that in the real world would be felt incompatible with them. Any artist's world is in principle thus enclosed and isolated, but the world of many artists continually stretches out feelers and tentacles, and attempts to establish a hold on the real world of history and moral action. Spenser does so; his aim is "to fashion a gentleman or noble person in vertuous and gentle discipline". And this

[1] Croce, op. cit., p. 46.
[2] De Sanctis, op. cit., p. 40.

means not merely to present the image of such a person, but to form the character of his readers in the same mould. Ariosto is totally without any such intention. He presents the images alone. But if they were only images of trivial and ludicrous action they could not have the hold on us that they do, and the poem could not claim greatness.

And of course the *Furioso* is a great poem; it is not trivial and ludicrous. But it is, as it were, intransitive. It exhibits with exceptional clarity the sign that, as some would say, all poetry ought in principle to exhibit—"No road through to action". This world of pure art is not what De Sanctis says it is, a world in which religion and patriotism, love and honour are absent; they are there, but they are deprived of their effect, they are present merely as items in a complex harmony. And the true definition of Ariosto's irony is that it is the means by which this distance and isolation is achieved.

It would be absurd if the talk of Ariosto's irony were to lead us to look for a sly smile beneath every incident, to suppose that we are to shrug off or devalue the emotions presented. We are not, for example, asked to feel a lurking scepticism about the martyr's death of Brandimarte or the fidelity of Cloridano and Medoro. There are of course passages of scepticism and mockery, besides much pure comedy; but the full sense of Ariosto's irony is something more general and embracing than any of these special instances of it. As Croce points out in a fine passage,[1] it is not directed to specific targets, it is an atmosphere that bathes everything in the poem. It is not something directed, say, at religion from which history is exempt, or aimed at chivalry while omitting love. There is a sense in which nothing in the poem is 'real'; it is all a world of artifice. But enter into this world and all its elements are equally real. To allow an authenticity to the 'merry tale' of Ricciardetto and Fiordispina that we deny to the moral apologue of Ruggiero's adventures with Alcina and Logistilla is a wanton deformation of the poem's economy. Both have their meaning and their place in the intricate harmony of the poem— a harmony which is not that of the 'real' world, but has its own kind of self-created reality.

[1] op. cit., p. 40 seq.

I am aware that this is a sophisticated view of the poem, and perhaps none the better for that. I think it is the right one for the modern sensibility. And needless to say, Spenser did not take it; he could hardly have done so, given the critical outlook of his time. He could, like Cardinal Ippolito d'Este, have called it a 'corbelleria', a piece of foolery; but this would have been to do it a gross injustice. Instead he does what every reader does when he actually steps inside the poem: he simply lays aside all questions about its relation to other poems and other worlds; he accepts its range, its richness and variety on their own terms. Love is love, faith is faith, valour is valour and magic is magic. In turning the material to his own ends Spenser rejects some parts entirely, and employs others for purposes far removed from Ariosto's. It would be hard to overrate his debt, but it would be wrong to underrate his originality. It is a debt paid by trans-formation and re-creation.

One ought not to leave this 'mondo della pura arte' without saying something of the art, in the more specific technical sense, by which it is all brought about. After Boiardo's agreeable simplicity Ariosto's language and versification are of infinite accomplishment and subtlety. The range is from Virgilian grandeur and pathos to the malicious and bawdy fun of the novella; and every part of it is handled with equal ease. There is an unparalleled lightness and tact in managing the transitions from one mood to another, and an exquisite adaptation of the movement and sound of the verse to the emotional tone. Just as Pope's sensibility finds its perfect expression in his heroic couplet, so does Ariosto's in the octave stanza. First impressions are of the invention and the story; greater familiarity brings a sheer delight in the skill of handling. But it would not be profitable for an English critic, who is supposed anyway to be writing mainly of an English poet, to pursue this very far. It is enough simply to record the sense, felt almost in every stanza, of Ariosto's joyous and easy mastery.

## Chapter III

# A NOTE ON EPIC THEORY

Between the *Orlando Furioso* in 1530 and the *Gerusalemme Liberata* in 1581 there was a flood of learned controversy about heroic poetry, and it is impossible to understand the later developments of the romantic epic without taking some notice of it. It has been dealt with in English before, by Spingarn and by Renwick, and most pertinently by Tillyard in his *English Epic*,[1] so I can be brief with it. I have little that is new to say, but without some mention of epic theory the story would be incomplete. We do not know what Spenser had read of this Italian criticism, but it seems clear from the structure of *The Faerie Queene* itself, and even clearer from the arguments used in the Letter to Raleigh, that he was aware of the general direction of ideas. Here I shall simply offer illustration of the most important and most relevant points of view, without any attempt at a systematic account.

From the time of Vida's Horatian *Ars Poetica* in 1527 epic or heroic poetry had come to occupy the highest place in critical esteem, in spite of Aristotle's preference for drama; and Virgil became the prime model among heroic poets. About the same time Aristotle's *Poetics* began to be applied to the epic—often by transferring bodily what he said of dramatic to heroic poetry. So a conflation of Horatian precepts, vaguely Aristotelian structural theory and Virgilian practice, grew up. Heroic poetry must deal with the illustrious deeds of kings and men great in arms; its purpose is exemplary, its business is to arouse admiration for great heroes; and it ought at least to worry about unity of action, however that is to be interpreted. Much of this

[1] J. E. Spingarn, *Literary Criticism in the Renaissance*, New York, 1899; W. L. Renwick, *Edmund Spenser*, 1925; Tillyard, op. cit.

# A NOTE ON EPIC THEORY

Renaissance criticism is of the dreariest type that gives precepts divorced from any actual poetical practice. It begins to assume a certain life when it refers to what the poets were really doing. There is a parallel here with later English neo-classical criticism which similarly comes to life when it has to find means of accommodating the work of Shakespeare. So in Italy, just as a classical theory of the epic begins to get under way, the *Orlando Furioso* makes its appearance. Its pre-eminence could hardly be denied, yet neither its material nor its structure conforms to the hardening principles of mid-sixteenth-century neo-classicism. I shall record very briefly some of the attempts to come to terms with it.

An outright denial of the validity of Ariosto's methods and an attempt to establish the epic on a firmly neo-classic base comes from Trissino. An energetic nobleman-landowner who had his finger in many pies, he staked his literary reputation on a heroic poem *L'Italia Liberata dai Goti* (1548) which is clearly meant to counteract all the faults of Ariosto. It has a historical, not a fantastic theme—the liberation of Italy from the Goths by the Emperor Justinian. Instead of the romantic supernatural apparatus of magicians, enchantresses and magic rings we have a strictly Christian supernatural—God and his angels and the opposing devils; instead of Ariostan multiplicity we have unity of action. The verses are *versi sciolti* (blank verse) instead of the seductive and semi-popular *ottava rima*; and the dedication to the Emperor Charles V, which expounds the intentions of the poem, makes much parade of going back to original Greek models. *Nel construire la favola da una azione sola, e grande, e che abbia principio, mezzo e fine, mi sono sforzato servare i regoli d'Aristotele, il quale elessi per maestro, si come tolsi Omero per Duce, e per idea*—"In constructing the plot of one single great action, which has a beginning, a middle and an end, I have endeavoured to observe the rules of Aristotle, whom I have chosen as preceptor, just as I have chosen Homer for guide and model." Trissino congratulates himself on being the first to observe these principles in the Italian language. In his critical work *La Poetica* (or rather *Pwetica*, for Trissino was the inventor of a system of spelling reform which involved the use

49

of a number of Greek letters) he rarely mentions Ariosto, and then only to reprehend the licence of his form and of his morals. Unluckily, for all its erudition and sound principles, *L'Italia Liberata* was universally found to be a failure, in the eyes of its contemporaries no less than in those of later readers. Like so many censors of extravagance, Trissino succeeds chiefly in expelling charm. All the delightful fantasy of the old romantic poems disappears, the blank verse is tame and dull, and in the parts that I have read (which is not much) there is an intolerable repetitiousness—instruction given at length to messengers repeated at equally great length and in almost the same words to the recipients, etc. One dubious legacy Trissino does transmit as far as Tasso—the Christian supernatural—the unintended but still tasteless impiety which represents the Almighty as busying himself intermittently and not very competently with the details of human history, and sending his angels off on errands which can be suitably enough carried out by the partisan and anthropomorphic deities of paganism, but can only inflict ludicrous injuries on the idea of unity, omnipotence and omniscience.

However, champions of Ariosto and his methods were not wanting, and the most notable of them is Giraldi Cinthio, author of the *Ecatommithi*, a collection of novelle which provided the source for two of Shakespeare's plays. He wrote a *Discorso intorno al comporre dei Romanzi* in 1549,[1] in which he proposes to inquire what the word Romance means, what this kind of composition is, and what relation it has to the poetry of Greece and Rome. Cinthio is a lively and independent writer with plenty of common sense and good judgement sharply expressed. The essence of his argument is that the Romances, the works of Boiardo and Ariosto, are a new kind, unknown to the ancients, and not coming under their rules. Every language has its own peculiar genius, and poetry in the Tuscan language is composed on different principles from that in Greek and Latin, yet with equal success. Tuscan poets should not be confined within the Greek and Latin limits, but should follow the ways of the best poets in their own tongue, whose authority should be equal to

[1] I have used the edition published in Venice in 1554.

that of the ancients. "And that," he says, "is the reason that I
have often laughed at those who summon the writers of
Romances under the laws given us by Aristotle and Horace,
without considering that neither Aristotle nor Horace knew our
language or our manner of composition."[1]

This is succeeded by an extremely intelligent attempt, by
means of comparison and description, to define the nature of the
Romance. The Romance is more akin to the Ovid of the Meta-
morphoses than to Virgil and Homer,[2] and it admits much longer
digressions—especially in passages of jousting, tournaments,
love adventures, descriptions of buildings, and such matters. If
we must compare it to the ancient epic it is more like the
*Odyssey* than the *Iliad*, and this looser and more episodic form
can properly admit a greater variety of characters.[3] Above all
the Romances have a different method of connecting their
actions from that of Greek and Latin poetry: and here Cinthio
gives an excellent account of the 'interwoven' plan, and a justification for it. The formal convention of the Romance is that of
oral narration, and the relatively short cantos and the breaks in
the narrative line are devices to sustain interest and whet the
appetite of the audience. Trissino was wrong to blame the
methods of Ariosto. Homer and Virgil chose a single action of a
single man for their subject, Boiardo and Ariosto take many
actions of many men and their example should have equal
authority with the moderns as that of Homer and Virgil among
the ancients. A poem may have one action or many, of one man
or many, but the subject must be rightly chosen for the kind of
treatment employed.

Parenthetically we might refer to another topic which formed
part of the epic controversy—the question of supernatural
machinery. Cinthio insists that the Romances have their own
kind of decorum, no less than the ancient epics, and this is
infringed by the introduction of the Christian supernatural.[4]
Cinthio is quite unequivocal about this, and in an excellent
passage he says that it is quite in order for the Greek and Latin

[1] p. 45.
[2] p. 60.
[3] p. 65.
[4] p. 69.

poets to show their gods inciting to battle, stirring up anger, and taking sides in mortal strife. This is proper for the nature of their religious conceptions, but it is wholly improper to ours. It is not permissible for the writer of romances on Christian themes to use the intervention of the Deity in this way. "For the Majesty of our God and of his ministers does not allow that we should call them down, and mingle them with our anger and our wars, and cause them to favour this one, and lead that other to death." And he goes on to a sharp and mocking criticism of Trissino's trick of disguising Christian angels under classical names.

Cinthio is an example of that kind of criticism, in the minority during the Italian Renaissance, which takes its rise from the actual facts of literary creation: and since that is what we think criticism ought to do it wins a natural sympathy from the modern reader. Tasso's case is more complicated. His admirable critical writing is the considered prelude to his own great work. And Tasso had grown up in a world already different from that in which the *Orlando Furioso* was born. The supreme felicity of Ariosto's poem in its own style defied imitation: and to the increasingly critical spirit of the mid-sixteenth century Ariosto's divine carelessness was impossible.

> Il mondo invecchia
> E invecchiando intristisce

This motto from Tasso's *Aminta* was aptly chosen by John Addington Symonds for his volumes on the Counter-Reformation period to which Tasso belongs. Leaving theology and religious controversy apart, even in literary matters it was a time of anxious consideration, of theoretical foundation-building and the establishment of principles. Minturno, for example, in *L'Arte Poetica* of 1563, considers the whole question of Romances again, and while praising Ariosto's genius is quite sure that he has taken the wrong road, and wonders that men of learning can still be found to defend him. There is nothing wrong with his subjects: but his chivalric themes could and should have been guided by the rules of Aristotle and Horace, and have followed the example of Homer and Virgil in matter of structure.

Tasso himself had written his first heroic poem, the *Rinaldo*, at the early age of eighteen. But even this has a theoretical preface in which the juvenile author explains that he has endeavoured to construct his poem with unity of interest and action, yet without being bound strictly by Aristotle's rules. "I have only followed such of his precepts as do not limit your delight," he says—with that antithesis between Aristotle and pleasure which is such a frequent and depressing feature of neo-classical criticism. In fact the atmosphere and subject matter of the romantic epic, the amorous and chivalric material are completely retained: only the plot becomes more orderly and more restricted. In the mid-sixties Tasso was preparing for his major heroic poem *Gerusalemme Liberata* and wrote a series of discourses on heroic poetry to establish his principles and to clear his own mind. We can see from the preface to *Rinaldo* that he was inclined to compromise—to a *via media* between the champions of Ariosto and the strict classicists. The *vaghezza*, the lyric and idyllic fantasy of the romantic epic, is ineradicably dear to Tasso; but a strong feeling for unity and order is equally a part of his mind—quite apart from any timid or superstitious reverence for authority. He is in fact a critic like Corneille or Dryden a century later, trying to find an accommodation between native creative freedoms and a set of largely imaginary classical 'rules'. I should myself say that he is a better critic than either of these successors; the whole subject of the relation of modern literature to the classics, so wearisomely stale by the time it reaches seventeenth-century France and England, can be written of with passion in sixteenth-century Italy, and Tasso's *Discorsi*, besides being very closely argued, are filled with the creative fervour of a man who really wants to get his own work right.

His final series of discourses *Discorsi del Poema Eroico*,[1] in six books, is highly abstract and theoretical, beginning from first principles with definitions of poetry, elaborate school distinctions, references to authority and all the rest of it. The common aim of all poetry is to instruct by delighting (*giovare dilettando*); the epic or heroic poem, then, must have its own

[1] Tasso, *Opere*, Venice, 1735, vol. V, p. 345 seq.

special aim, and this is to inspire *maraviglia*—admiration as our own neo-classic critics render it. This is Tasso's most notable individual contribution—the rest being mainly an able and closely-reasoned application of the usual Aristotelian-Horatian amalgam. An earlier set of discourses *Discorsi dell' Arte Poetica e in particolare sopra il poema eroico*[1] is livelier and more direct. Tasso is writing less as a theorist and more as an artist anxious to solve his own technical problems.

The first discourse is concerned mainly with the choice of material. History is the best subject for epic. Fictitious subjects are unworthy of the highest poetry. But this sets a problem. We need the marvellous in the epic, but the marvels of the Gentiles are false. "That species of the marvellous (if indeed it deserves the name) which brings in Jove and Apollo and the other deities of the Gentiles, is not only far from all verisimilitude, but is frigid, insipid, and of no value."[2] Therefore, we must choose a Christian theme, where we know the miracles are true. Tasso thus comes to precisely the opposite conclusion from Cinthio's; and if we may intervene in a long-dead controversy, it is hard to believe that the reasons he gives are the real ones. Cinthio's outspoken objections seem to reveal a far juster appreciation of the nature of the Christian supernatural than Tasso's obsequious genuflexion to Christian truth. Yet for all the strong Counter-Reformation odour of Tasso's remarks it must be admitted that his position is ultimately the more in line with that of the earliest Christian epics. *Chrétiens ont dreit mais cist gloton ont tort.* It is a modern sensibility that shrinks from involving the majesty of God in human conflicts. Tasso in going back to the historical conflict between Christendom and the infidel for his theme preserves the link with the earliest Carolingian lays.

A historical theme, then, and a Christian one. It remains to consider suitable periods. Tasso decides that the right period is one that is neither too close to us nor too remote.[3] The remoter ages labour under the disadvantage of barbarism and unpleasing

[1] ibid, p. 489 seq.
[2] p. 491.
[3] p. 494.

customs: those who have a taste for *gentilezza* and courtesy will always find them distasteful; yet to attribute to a distant antiquity modern refinement of manners would be an absurdity. Periods close to us in time have many advantages, but they have one fatal disadvantage—that their history is too well attested, and this deprives us of all licence to invent our own fictions. This *licenza di fingere* is of great importance to Tasso. Filled as he may be with the idea of the great historical theme he is still in love with the romantic material of the Ariostan epic; and his own kind of tender sensuality demands opportunities that the heroic-historical material does not afford. Therefore his poem must be set in an age that allows for these fabulous accretions. Nobody would allow us to mingle fictions and enchantments with a history of the Emperor Charles V: the right times are those for instance of Charlemagne or Arthur. A similar principle applies to sacred history: we should choose a subject drawn from the history of the true religion, but not from those parts of it that are so sacred as to be unalterable, as the central Biblical narration or the life of Our Lord must be. Tasso sums up the epic requirements in a sentence: "The authority of history, truth of religion, the licence of fiction, suitability of period, and grandeur and mobility in the incidents".[1]

The second discourse is concerned with epic structure. There is a right size for the epic; it should be of such a length that the reader does not become lost in it, that it can all be contained in a single memory.[2] Considering the *Innamorato* and the *Furioso* as one entity, they are far too long for this; they cannot be held in the memory as a whole. With this Tasso enters into the general controversy about the Romances. Although the rule just enunciated is the right one many people in our day have thought that a vast range and multiplicity of actions is suitable for the epic. The witness to this is the immense universal success of Ariosto and the flat failure of Trissino. And, Tasso admits, there is a good deal of reason in this; like Minturno he praises Ariosto with generosity and enthusiasm. Yet he is not to be imitated. His multiplicity of actions is a fault; it causes confusion. In the

[1] p. 497.
[2] p. 502.

end we are driven to say that the *Innamorato* and the *Furioso* are not one poem but many, because of their many actions. Tasso then takes up the question of whether the Romances are, as some have alleged, a different kind of poem from the epic, and so exempt from the rules.[1] And this argument, he decides, is specious. None of the differences brought forward is *essential*. Manner and subject matter may indeed differ from age to age, but the law of unity is in the nature of things; it cannot change with time, and there can be no exemption from it. And he comes to a conclusion very like Minturno's—Ariosto's real qualities, for which he is rightly praised and enjoyed by everyone, are his wealth of knowledge and the brilliance of his invention, and these are in principle entirely compatible with the unity that is demanded not only by Aristotle but by the very nature of art.

It is noticeable that even while arguing against Ariosto Tasso is still very conscious of belonging to his imaginative world. He speaks again and again of the delightfulness of the chivalric adventures, the gracefulness and courtesy of chivalric manners as against those of the ancients. He admits that the *Furioso* not only brings us more delight than *L'Italia Liberata*, but even than the *Iliad* and the *Odyssey*. And he concludes this discourse with a magnificent passage on the unity-in-variety of the epic, in which the variety, the wealth of romantic material, and the *licenza del fingere* appear to get quite as good a showing as the unity which is their bound and circumference:

> For myself I consider unity in the heroic poem both necessary and possible to obtain, for, as in this wonderful masterpiece of God called the world the sky appears scattered over and divided by so great a variety of stars and, to descend then step by step, the air and the sea appear full of birds and fishes and the earth harbours so many beasts wild and tame, the earth where are found brooks and springs and lakes and meadows and plains and woods and mountains, here fruits and flowers, there ice and snow, here dwellings and tillage, there wildernesses and terrors, yet for all this the world is one though folding into its bosom so many different things, its form and essence are one, and one the fashion in which its parts are joined and knit together with a kind of discordant harmony; and though nothing is lacking to it,

[1] pp. 504–6.

nothing is there either superfluous or not necessary. So likewise I assert that the sublime poet (called divine for no other reason than that he models himself in his works on the supreme artificer and arrives at sharing thus his divinity) can indeed shape a poem in which as in a microcosm there are brought together here the marshalling of armies, battles by land and sea, captures of cities, skirmishes and duels, tourneys, descriptions of hunger and thirst, tempests, fires, prodigies. Let there be found there heavenly and infernal councils, revolutions, strifes, errors, misfortunes, enchantments, deeds of cruelty of daring of courtesy of generosity, love-adventures prosperous and unfortunate, happy or pitiful but only so that the poem which shall include such a variety of substance should nevertheless be one; the form and the fable one; and that all things should be put together so that one thing refers to another, one corresponds to another, one either by necessity or probability depends on another, so that the removal of a single part or its transference should ruin the whole.[1]

The third discourse is concerned with 'elocution'—matters of style and rhetoric. It contains some admirable practical criticism, but much of it is not our particular concern. One point, however, is worth noting. Tasso makes the conventional distinction between the high, middle and low styles—*magnifica, mediocre ed umile*. Of these the first, the *magnifica*, is proper to the heroic poem. But the heroic or epic has its own particular kind of magnificence. The proper quality of tragedy is a *semplice gravità*, the proper quality of lyric a *fiorita vaghezza*. And between this simple gravity on the one hand and flowery sweetness on the other lies the proper style for the epic.[2] In dealing with moral matters, and when the heroic characters themselves are speaking, the heroic poet should approximate to tragic simplicity: when speaking in his own person, or dealing with those intervals of ease which occur even in an epic, he should come nearer to the lyric sweetness. But he should push neither the one nor the other to such extremes that the true epic magnificence is lost.

Both here and in his consideration of structure we seem to see Tasso writing with a genuine and strongly felt conviction of the dignity of the epic, and of the unity and grandeur that it

[1] p. 512. This passage is quoted by Tillyard in *The English Epic* and I have used his translation.
[2] p. 516.

demands—yet at the same time leaving plenty of room for his own tastes and temperamental affinities. Romantic chivalry, a tender eroticism, the *fiorita vaghezza* of the lyric, all come more easily to Tasso than heroic simplicity, and he is anxious to show that this highest and noblest form of poetry can accommodate them without departing from its own nature. It is here that Tasso's affinity with Spenser begins to seem obvious. Spenser's gesture towards unity is ineffectual and incomplete: though, as we shall see, he makes it. In his conviction that he is writing a heroic poem and that this can properly include the lyrical, the sensuous and the idyllic, he is very close to Tasso. We do not know whether he ever read these discourses. If he did he would have found much that was highly sympathetic to him; whether he did or not, the matters discussed in them are part of the background of ideas against which *The Faerie Queene* was written.

*Chapter IV*

# TASSO

The discipleship of Spenser to Ariosto is so obvious that it has never been necessary to argue it. The influence of Tasso is less marked, and it has often been played down, in spite of the fact that Spenser mentions him as one of his four exemplars. It is said that Tasso's work came too late to have much effect on *The Faerie Queene*; and as this seems to me demonstrably untrue it is as well to establish the dates at the beginning. Tasso won fame in Italy at the age of eighteen when he published his first heroic poem *Rinaldo*, in 1562. His lovely pastoral drama *Aminta*, produced at Ferrara in 1573, became equally celebrated. During the sixties he was deeply occupied with criticism and epic theory. It was in these years that he composed most of the discourses on poetry, though they were not published till 1587. These studies were the prelude to his great heroic poem the *Gerusalemme Liberata*. It was finished in 1574, badly printed in a pirated edition in 1580, and authoritatively published at Parma in 1581.

We recall that the composition of *The Faerie Queene* goes back to 1580. So the great work of Tasso, a poet already celebrated for many years, appeared almost contemporaneously with the beginning of *The Faerie Queene*; and this suggests that it came, not too late, but just in time to be an effective influence. Spenser was acquainted with *Rinaldo*, to judge by certain verbal echoes; similar reminiscences from *Gerusalemme Liberata* occur throughout *The Faerie Queene*, especially in descriptive passages, and there are, as is well known, considerable and important motifs taken from it in the first, second and sixth books.[1] The *Discorsi*

---

[1] For Spenser's borrowings from Tasso see E. Koeppel, "Die Englischen Tasso-Uebersetzungen des 16 Jahrhunderts", Anglia XI, 1889; and H. H. Blanchard "Imitations of Tasso in The Faerie Queene", SP xxii, 1925.

occupy much the same place in Tasso's work as the letter to Raleigh in Spenser's, except that Tasso cautiously completed his theoretical and structural researches before beginning his poem, while Spenser's seem to have been partly an afterthought. It is clear that the discourses cannot have affected the beginnings of *The Faerie Queene*, since they were not published till 1587. But it seems equally clear to me that they affected the *Letter*, which adopts some similar points of view, and is dated 1589, just two years after the publication of Tasso's critical writings.

Since the appearance of the final version of the *Furioso* in 1530 two profound influences had been at work on serious poetry in sixteenth-century Italy. One was the Counter-Reformation, bringing with it a spirit of moral and doctrinal rigour and even an actual machinery of censorship and condemnation controlled by the Inquisition. The other was the hardening of neo-classicism into a doctrinaire code, with much emphasis on structure and decorum. We have seen something of this in the last chapter, and of how it made the charming irresponsibility of Ariosto henceforth impossible. Tasso's nature, scrupulous and intellectually timid to the point of mania, rendered him particularly open to both these pressures. As soon as he finished the *Gerusalemme* he submitted it to censorship, and in the years from 1574 to 1576 suffered agonies of doubt and apprehension about the result, both on literary and doctrinal grounds. There is nothing in England quite like this atmosphere of constraint that surrounds Tasso's mature work; but it may be observed that similar though milder forces were not altogether absent. The Counter-Reformation, being the Catholic reaction to nascent Protestantism, partakes of the nature of that which it opposed. The scrupulousness, the elevated moral feeling of Spenser's serious Protestant circle is doubtless a more inward matter than Tasso's circumspection, which seems often enough to have been mere terror of the Inquisition. But Tasso's Italy and Spenser's England have this in common—that the conscientious heroic poet is charged, by religious influences of whatever kind, with a far graver sense of his function and obligations than any that could have been felt in Ariosto's time. I have tried to rescue *Orlando Furioso* from the imputation of being merely a comic

poem; but it was equally necessary to make clear that it is
entirely without any sense of a didactic mission. Its morality
arises accidentally out of the story, and as the story is wayward
and various, so is the morality. Neither we nor the poet know
quite what will come next. For Tasso, as for Spenser after him,
the morality is predetermined. Determined doubtless in different ways, of which Tasso's is the more sophisticated. For
Tasso the end of poetry is to delight, but it must also profit
(*giovare*, his translation of the Horatian *prodesse*). That is to say,
poetry has its own internal rightness, but is under the negative
and external control of a morality predetermined by religion
and the laws of the church. Spenser takes a simpler view and is
often content to make his fictions merely *exempla*, to illustrate a
moral idea. But in both cases the morality is something existing
outside the fiction and in some way controlling it. And for this
the gravity of religious conflict is largely responsible. As for
the pressure of classicism, there is not of course in England the
voluminous, formal and concentrated literary debate that there
was in Italy. But England soon felt its effects none the less.
Sidney's *Apology* is largely a compilation from the Italian critics.
Spenser's whole literary career from his early days in the Pem-
broke College circle was passed in an Italianate atmosphere; and
at least his second thoughts about *The Faerie Queene*, as they
appear in the letter to Raleigh, show a care to conform with
classical precept that, however unfulfilled, is not dissimilar to
Tasso's. These then are the positive grounds for considering
the *Gerusalemme Liberata* an important part of the background of
*The Faerie Queene*. Others, more a matter of temperament and
feeling, will appear as we examine Tasso's work more closely.

The *Gerusalemme Liberata* is a romantic treatment of the First
Crusade. Incited by the preaching of Peter the Hermit, the
Crusaders set out in 1096, won victories under the leadership of
Godfrey of Bouillon at Constantinople, Antioch and Tarsus,
reached Jerusalem in 1099, and captured it after a five weeks'
siege. Tasso thus had a genuinely historical subject, and he made
a careful study of chronicles and books of geography to give his
work the greatest possible authority. The choice in itself was a

good one. Deprived by the circumstances of his time of any possibility of a national theme, Tasso yet succeeded in finding one with a real relevance to the spirit of his age. After five hundred years Christendom was still at war with the Saracen; the exploits of the Emperor Charles V against the Moors in Tunis were still fresh in the memory. And on the spiritual plane the Jesuits were conducting a new crusade against heresy and infidelity. Tasso is writing the epic of the Counter-Reformation as Spenser writes the epic of Protestantism, and their common share in the post-Tridentine spirit is almost more important than the fact that they were on opposite sides. But Tasso has, as Spenser has not, a subject that can be treated on regular epic lines. His single expedition has a single purpose. He begins, as Homer did and Horace advised, near the end of his story. The Crusaders are already approaching Jerusalem in the first book, and the poem ends with the capture of the city. Goffredo is a divinely-appointed leader like Aeneas, and he has around him a compact and manageable number of warriors whose names and adventures can easily be followed and borne in mind. The poem is divided into twenty cantos; cantos which are more like 'books'; that is to say, divisions that have some integrity and structural meaning, not merely arbitrary slices controlled by the supposed endurance of imaginary listeners. And the style is grave and elevated throughout, ranging from the heroic to the pathetic. The Ariostan irony, the free-speaking and the bawdry, have entirely disappeared.

Yet no sooner is this said than we realize how much the poem still owes to the Ariostan romance. The theme is only a more authentic historical version of the struggle between Christendom and the Saracens that Boiardo and Ariosto had inherited from the Carolingian lays. And as soon as we plunge into the poem we find the typical episodes and characters of the romances all turning up again. Rinaldo in the *Gerusalemme* is not Rinaldo of Montalban, son of Aymon and one of Charlemagne's peers; but he might almost as well be, and after a time we begin to forget the difference. There can hardly have been a very strong love interest in the First Crusade; yet here it is the love-adventures that we remember—the loves of Tancredi and Clorinda, the love

of Erminia for Tancredi, above all, Rinaldo and Armida, an
episode that is more than an episode as it has a decisive bearing
on the main plot. Clorinda is a softened version of Ariosto's
Marfisa, Erminia recalls Fiordiligi, and Armida is the lineal
descendant both of Alcina and Angelica. Yet this still-enchanting
material drawn from Ariosto's world is kept well under control.
The magic and the love-affairs are all by one means or another
connected with the main design, and even in Armida's garden
the siege of Jerusalem is never forgotten for long. Tasso has
made good his claim that the delights of romance and chivalry
could be perfectly well combined with an orderly classical
structure.

Let us begin however by taking the poem at its face value as a
historical-religious epic, and see how Tasso treats his heroic
material. The obvious contrast with Ariosto is in the sustained
nobility of the tone; there are no intervals of mockery or even of
light-heartedness. Goffredo is a Virgilian hero, ideally brave,
pious and wise; he is Aeneas translated into Christian terms. The
episode with Dido, the one diversion of purpose that Aeneas is
allowed, is here transferred to Rinaldo, and Goffredo is left
unmoved in monumental perfection. There is no doubt that he is
the formal hero of the poem; yet we remember little of him.
Like Arthur in *The Faerie Queene* he represents the complete and
rounded virtue to which the other heroes more or less imper-
fectly aspire; and he is capable of repairing their faults and
supplying their deficiencies. Yet he never touches the reader's
feelings. The single story told of the historic Godfrey—that as
King of Jerusalem he refused to be crowned with gold where his
Saviour had been crowned with thorns—is moving in a way that
is never achieved by Goffredo's frigid perfections.

Noble he is, and Tasso has the power to convey nobility; for it
is a part of his own nature. Yet, it is sometimes said, Goffredo
fails and remains a purely formal hero because this power never
moves freely, never takes fire, till some element of sentiment or
tenderness is added to the situation. But this is to put Tasso's
genius too low. It is a view that has been encouraged by the
weighty influence of De Sanctis.[1] But Croce has argued against

[1] op. cit. II, chap. XVII.

this that it is at least as plausible to see Tasso as the great tragic writer of his age; it is fated love and doomed valour that inspires him as much as luxuriant tenderness.[1] Goffredo fails to move us, and his author, because he is such a success. God is on his side, he is tortured by no dangerous passions, so he cannot help winning. The great imaginative passages in the heroic part of the story tend to go to the doomed Saracens, who humanly speaking are as noble as the Christians but must lose because they are on the wrong side. Argante, that huge ferocious warrior, like the Rodomonte of the earlier romances, has his moment of tragic nobility just before Tancredi kills him in a final duel beneath the falling walls of Jerusalem. He turns away from his enemy and looks towards the city. Tancredi notices that he has no shield, and throws his own away; then asks Argante what has made him pause:

> Penso, risponde, a la città del regno
> di Giudea antichissima regina,
> che vinta or cade: e indarno esser sostegno
> io procurai de la fatal ruina:
> e ch'è poca vendetta al mio disegno
> il capo tuo, che'l Ciel or mi destina.
> Tacque: e in contra si van con gran risguardo;
> che ben conosce l'un l'altro gagliardo.
>
> (XIX. 10)

—I was thinking, he said, of the city, ancient queen of the realm of Judea, that now falls vanquished: and that I have been but a poor defence gainst its final ruin: and that your life, now granted to me by Heaven, will be but a poor vengeance.—He fell silent; and they go forward cautiously, for each knows how formidable the other is.

Solimano too dies nobly, refusing to defend himself after the death of his comrades:

> non fugge i colpi, e gemito non spande,
> nè atto fa, se non se altero e grande.
>
> (XX. 107)

He neither fled the blows, nor uttered a groan, nor made any movement that was not lofty and grand.

[1] Quoted by L. Russo in the preface to his edition of **G.L.**, Milan, 1959, p. iii.

The duels and single combats in Tasso may be literary, with images copied from Virgil and Lucan; but they are also real in one way that Ariosto's are not—real in the sense that Tasso identifies himself with the passions of his combatants, with their furies and their fears, while Ariosto remains the interested spectator, recording with lively detachment the points of technical or narrative interest. Forget the list of sources in Ferrari's commentary, and we find a fire and passion in Tasso's battle scenes that Ariosto does not attempt, and that was quite outside the range of Spenser's interests.

So it will not do to depreciate the heroic elements in Tasso's poem. It remains true, however, that almost as soon as the story opens they are fused with the erotic and the romantic. A muster of the Crusaders in the first canto introduces us to the principal champions, and Tancredi is brought before us, already in love. A short time before, chasing the flying Persians after a battle, he had sat down beside a spring to rest. (The fountain and the shade—a setting more out of pastoral than epic.) There a maiden appeared before him, a pagan, all in arms except for her head. He gazed on her, was enchanted by her, burned for her, and—

> Oh maraviglia! Amor, ch'a pena è nato
> già grande vola, e già trionfa armato
>
> (I. 47)

> Oh, miracle! Love that is hardly born already flies strongly, already triumphs in arms.

She is Clorinda, and from that moment Tancredi becomes, as well as the Christian warrior, the Petrarchan lover; gentle, devoted, unhappy and unsatisfied; for Clorinda, unlike Bradamante or Britomart, cares nothing for love, only for honour, war and hunting. So far, the nymph of Diana and the hopeless lover; and we have met them before. But Tasso has another turn to the screw. There is a mystery about Clorinda's birth, and when it is revealed to her by an old servant it turns out that though brought up as a pagan she comes from a family originally Christian (XII. 20–41). She has been taken out of her true tradition; as for Christianity, *forse è la vera fede*; the shadow of a doubt about the cause for which she is fighting crosses her mind; but she subdues it and determines to go on fighting all the same. And thus is prepared the most celebrated peripeteia and recognition-scene of the poem. When Tancredi and Clorinda next meet she is in plain arms and he does not know her. They meet alone, for the main battle is over; they fight a single combat and Clorinda is mortally wounded. And even as she falls she is transformed from the fierce warrior to the dying girl, and a new voice speaks through her lips:

> parole ch'a lei novo un spirito ditta,
> spirito di fè, di carità, di speme;
> virtù ch'or Dio le infonde, e se rubella
> in vita fu, la vuole in morte ancella.
>
> —Amico, hai vinto: io ti perdon . . . perdona
> tu ancora, al corpo no, che nulla pave,
> a l'alma sì: deh! per lei prega, e dona
> battesmo a me ch'ogni mia colpa lave.—
>
> (XII. 65)

words that a new spirit dictated to her, a spirit of faith, of charity, of hope; a virtue infused into her by God; and if she was a rebel against him in life, in death he wishes for her as his handmaid.
'Friend, you have conquered: I forgive you . . . forgive me too; not my body, which is afraid of nothing, but my soul: ah! pray for my soul, and give me baptism that washes away all my sins.'

These languid accents so different from the fierce defiance she has uttered hitherto, touch Tancredi's heart and drive out all his rage, though he is still ignorant of who his opponent is, or even that she is a woman. He goes off to fetch water in his helmet from a spring, and unlacing her helmet discovers the truth. He baptizes her; she can no longer speak, but stretches out her hand in farewell—the only contact Tancredi has had with her except at the sword's point; and then she dies.

How many elements have been brought together in this scene! Clorinda's fierce virginity, her devotion to the ideal of honour and war; her lapse into pathos and womanhood when she is wounded to death; her dramatic conversion, prepared for perhaps by what we have heard of her story, but due to no will of her own, only to the free and unexpected action of grace; the pathetic and comradely frankness of her request; the first and last service Tancredi is able to perform for her; his grief and despair. Tasso never attains the simplicity of the ancient epic. It is by complex, warring emotions and a style of the greatest flexibility and sweetness that he is able to attain his special kind of moving grandeur. It has been said that he deals only with doomed and fated love; that a happy and fulfilled love is not within his imaginative range. And it is true that there is an element of trouble, perturbation and anxiety in all Tasso's love-situations; neither the open sensuality of Ariosto nor the candid straightforward licit affection of Spenser is possible to him. But there is also a tenderness in Tasso's nature that makes him at least want to suggest a ray of happiness at the end. When Tancredi is prostrated by his grief Clorinda appears to him in a dream, radiant and in starry garments, tells him that she is among the blest, that she awaits his coming too, and that she loves him as much as it is permitted to love a creature. And though this hardly suits Clorinda's character in life, and may be seen (it has been by Croce) as a stuck-on Dantesque and Petrarchan reminiscence, perhaps with a touch of *Controriforma* pious formalism as well, it certainly indicates the direction in which Tasso's sensibility is apt to move—from tragedy to pathos, and from pathos to idyll, or to the suggestion of idyll, if it is in any way possible.

It is youth, femininity and the tender affections that most naturally stir Tasso's imagination, and his heroic poem in consequence is always passing over into romantic idyll. This seems to have been felt by his illustrators. In those seventeenth-century editions of the *Gerusalemme* adorned with engravings the crusading warriors all have faces like Fragonard shepherds. Stylistically there is something of the same relation between Tasso's early pastoral play *Aminta* and the *Gerusalemme Liberata* as there is between Milton's *Comus* and *Paradise Lost*; but in abandoning the natural utterance and the pastoral freshness of his earlier style for a Latinate heroic manner Milton also left behind for ever many of his earlier sentiments and emotional dispositions. Tasso did not, and he contrived, with what propriety I will not attempt to say, a kind of epic in which the element of idyll, of *fiorita vaghezza*, is exceptionally strong. I think we can hardly doubt that his example in this direction was powerful with Spenser. His emotional tendency was in some ways very different from Spenser's, as I shall later try to show; but they have in common an intellectual and moral devotion to the heroic-historical theme combined with an instinctive tendency to lyrical romance. And this is not achieved by Tasso without a certain element of conflict. (We shall have to speak later about conflicting tendencies in Spenser.) Goffredo, the unmoved image of heroic virtue, fills his place in the plot, but he does no more. The heroes who engage our interest are Rinaldo and Tancredi, and they engage our interest most when they are in love. What is more, their loves are all on the wrong side; Armida, Clorinda and Erminia are all Saracen maidens. Yet a fundamental tenderness of spirit allows them all their final conversion. I am sure that this represents an unconscious tendency in Tasso's emotional constitution; and what it means is that the erotic element is both cherished and feared. It has to be redeemed before it can be finally admitted, however much it may have been indulged in the meantime. Spenser's view was simpler. No enchantress is redeemed in *The Faerie Queene*; his Duessas and Acrasias are bad all through; and no one experiences an honourable love for a pagan maid.

Tasso's love for complex situations appears in Tancredi's other relationships. While he is cherishing a hopeless love for Clorinda another Saracen girl, Erminia, has fallen in love with him. Daughter of the king of Antioch, she had earlier become his captive, and had been chivalrously released; but not before he had won her heart by his courtesy and generosity. She took refuge in Jerusalem, and when Tancredi appears before the walls her love revives. She is no descendant of the Amazons but a timid shrinking girl. She is a skilful healer, and after the first duel between Tancredi and Argante there is a vivid picture of her conflicting emotions when she is employed to heal her beloved's ferocious opponent. She is tempted to put poison in his wounds, but dismisses the unworthy thought and does her best for him

(VI. 68). Then she stifles her fears and goes out to the battle-field in an attempt to succour the wounded Tancredi. Driven off by a patrol, she takes to flight, loses her way, and is received by a family of shepherds. There follows the celebrated pastoral episode (VII. 1–22) which Spenser made good use of in the Pastorella scenes of Book VI of *The Faerie Queene*. Tasso was blamed for this passage by some of his sixteenth-century critics. They complained that this Arcadian element was out of place, that its ideal of happiness is timid and bourgeois, at odds with the ardours of a heroic poem. But all generations of Tasso's readers have loved it. The old shepherd who with his family receives Erminia so kindly is something of a philosopher, and he tells (in a passage translated directly by Spenser) his tale of the virtues of his quiet life, how he had known the court in youth, *lusingato da speranza ardita*, but as youth went by began to sigh for his lost peace and returned to his native woods. Erminia in her grief for Tancredi is charmed by the kindness and the beauty of the quiet place, away from war and the world. She becomes a shepherdess herself and enjoys a time of sad tranquillity before returning to the city.

Later Erminia succeeds in her aim, finds Tancredi wounded and becomes his healer. But by this time the situation is different. Tancredi has fought a second duel against Argante and has killed him; but now his wounds are not merely the wounds of battle. He still bears about him the prostration of Clorinda's death, and Erminia has not only to heal him and win him by her tenderness, but to overcome or transmute his allegiance to the dead and sainted warrior who watches over him in heaven. We are left with the feeling that she will probably succeed; but it is characteristic of Tasso to have deserted the emotional simplicity of ancient epic, the shrewd external observation of Ariostan romance, for these melancholy and ambiguous situations. There is nothing in Tasso, and it is hard to imagine a place for it, like the happy and untrammelled reunion of Scudamour and Amoret in *The Faerie Queene*.

The theme of doubtful and frustrated love occupies so large a part of Tasso's imagination that the great episode of this nature, the story of Rinaldo and Armida, grows into something more than the traditional episode and becomes a major factor in the plot. Armida the enchantress is the Saracens' secret weapon. She steals away Rinaldo, the principal champion of the Christian host, holds him in her bower of sensual delights, and the war cannot be brought to a successful conclusion until he is restored. She appears in eight of the twenty books; one of them is entirely devoted to her, and in four others she is the controlling influence on affairs. We find her first coming into Goffredo's camp with a lying tale of woe, and drawing off a large company of the best knights to her assistance (IV). She keeps Tancredi prisoner for a time (VII. 23–49). Then we learn in Canto XIV that she has managed to entrap Rinaldo, first as his enemy, meaning to revenge herself for the frustration he has brought to some of her former designs, but in process of seducing him she has herself fallen in love, and she in his power almost as much as he in hers, has carried him off to a distant magic island where they can enjoy their love in solitude. Canto XVI brings us to the island, and to one of the most luxuriant sensuous idylls in all literature. The description of Armida's garden and palace derives in part from many another *locus amoenus* in ancient and romantic poetry, but Tasso adds a sensual richness, a sweetness and profusion that is unmatched elsewhere. It is entirely appropriate; for the whole enchanted place is not the work of nature; it is made by magic out of the substance of Armida's desires, and Armida is not a tender and serviceable lover like Erminia, she is the exploiter, and ultimately the victim, of passion.

Spenser imitated much of this description for his Bower of Bliss—in parts simply translating it. The effect is ultimately different, for Spenser's sequel is so unlike Tasso's, but the initial setting is the same; the song sung by Spenser's nymph was originally sung by a bird in Armida's garden:

> Deh mira, egli cantò, spuntar la rosa
> dal verde suo modesta e verginella,
> che mezzo aperta ancòra, e mezzo ascosa
> quanto si mostra men, tanto è più bella.
> Ecco poi nudo il sen gia baldanzosa
> dispiega: ecco poi langue, e non par quella;
> quella non par, che desiata inanti
> fu da mille donzelle e mille amanti.

Così trapassa al trapassar d'un giorno
De la vita mortale il fiore e 'l verde;
nè, perchè faccia in dietro april ritorno,
si rinfiora ella mai, nè si rinverde.
Cogliam la rosa in su 'l mattino adorno
di questa dì, che tosto il seren perde;
cogliam d'amor la rosa: amiamo or quando
esser si puote riamato amando.

(XVI. 14–15)

There is no need to offer a translation of this, as we have
Spenser's exquisite one in *F.Q.*, II. xii. 74–75. And Tasso's
groves, breezes, birdsong and nymphs bathing can all be found
in Spenser too by the English reader. What we cannot find in
Spenser's Bower of Bliss is any real counterpart to the lovingly
developed scene of dalliance between Rinaldo and Armida.
Spenser's purpose was of course different; his scene of luxury is
briefly delineated because it is equally briefly to be destroyed by
Guyon. Tasso is preparing a *coup de théâtre*, or more than one,
and for this reason, apart from any subjective and temperamental
needs, he has to establish fully the atmosphere of overwhelming
languid sweetness and complete sensual abandonment. This is
all the more seductive because it is seen through the eyes of
Carlo and Ubaldo, the two stern and soldierly messengers who
have been sent by Goffredo to recall Rinaldo to his duty.

Ella dinanzi al petto ha il vel diviso
e 'l crin sparge incomposto al vento estivo:
langue per vezzo, e 'l suo infiammato viso
fan biancheggiando i bei sudor più vivo:
qual raggio in onda, le scintilla un riso
ne gli umidi occhi tremulo e lascivo.
Sovra lui pende: ed ei nel grembo molle
le posa il capo, e 'l volto al volto attolle;

e i famelici sguardi avidamente
in lei pascendo, si consuma e strugge.
S'inchina, e i dolci baci ella sovente
liba or da gli occhi, e de la labra or sugge;
ed in quel punto ei sospirar si sente
profondo sì, che pensi: Or l'alma fugge
e 'ne lei passa peregrina.—Ascosi
mirano i duo guerrier gli atti amorosi.

(XVI. 18–19)

Her veil is open at the breast, her hair floats waywardly in the summer breeze: she languishes in joy, and drops of sweat make brighter the colour of her flushed cheeks; like sunlight through a wave a tremulous and wanton smile shines through her liquid eyes. She hangs over him: he rests his head in her soft lap and raises his face to hers;
and greedily feeding his hungry looks on hers he is wasted and consumed with desire. She bends down, and now pours sweet kisses from her eyes, now drinks them from his lips; and in that moment he heaves so deep a sigh that he thinks—Now my soul flies and passes over into her.—Hidden still the two warriors watch these deeds of love.

The weight of the poem is on their side. Rinaldo is disgracing his elected mission. Yet no shadow of disapproval is allowed to colour the voluptuous indolence of the scene while it is still there to be enjoyed. Even the material out of which Armida weaves her spells is turned to favour and to prettiness:

> Teneri sdegni, e placide e tranquille
> repulse, e cari vezzi, e liete paci,
> sorrise parolette, e dolci stille
> di pianto, e sospir tronchi, e molli baci:
> fuse tai cose tutte . . .
>
> (XVI. 25)

> Tender scorns, mild and tranquil denials, dear caresses and happy peace, smiling and tender words, sweet tear-drops, broken sighs and gentle kisses: all these she mixed together . . .

There is always an element of conflict, as we have suggested, in Tasso's love-passages; but here he can abandon himself to a sensuous idyll because it is so powerfully balanced by masculine strenuousness and duty outside—Carlo and Ubaldo hidden in the bushes; and because he has several other moves in view, at this stage unforeseeable. Armida goes off to attend to her duties in the palace, and at once Carlo and Ubaldo reveal themselves. They utter their reproaches. Rinaldo has made himself the plaything of a girl; he is dressed like a girl, perfumed, and his sword is hung with flowers. They are in armour; and Rinaldo feels ashamed. The recall to duty is soon heard, and Rinaldo tries to steal away with his companions unobserved. But Armida

surprises him and a confrontation is inevitable. The latter half of
this canto is occupied by a terrible debate, in which Rinaldo, in
spite of having God, Goffredo and *raison d'état* all on his side,
cannot but come out badly. He hopes to placate Armida and to
convince her where his duty lies, but he discovers, like others
before and since, that there is no way of dealing gracefully with
this situation. Tasso has given to Armida's invective such fury
and such pathos that anything Rinaldo can find to say is over-
whelmed. He leaves, all the same. And Armida in a final access
of grief and rage destroys the palace and the garden. It was the
projection of her love, and now—

> come sogno sen va, ch'egro figura;
> così sparver gli alberghi: e restar sole
> l'alpe e l'orror che fece ivi natura.
>
> (XVI. 70)

> as a sick man's dream fades away, so these dwellings disappeared,
> leaving only the alps and the natural horror of the place.

Something has happened to Armida during these last scenes.
Up to now she has been of the line of Angelica, Alcina and the
Fata Morgana—ultimately of the line of Circe; sinister enchantresses who for their pleasure of their own designs seduce men
from their duty and their destiny. But now she has become
Dido, the princess deserted by the man to whom she has given
her love: and whatever the necessities of the war demand, it is
Rinaldo's ingratitude that we feel. A great part of her invective
is taken from Dido's in the Aeneid, and we are to see Rinaldo
like Aeneas as one whom a higher command has obliged to be
impervious to personal obligations. And there the classical
temper would leave it; Dido has no recourse but her funeral
pyre. But Tasso is not content to leave it there. Armida is on the
wrong side and has employed dubious methods, but she is not
inherently evil, because she has really loved. Tasso is not concerned like Spenser to distinguish healthy from unhealthy
sensuality. Armida's crime as we see it in the poem was not
*luxuria* (to this Tasso shows some complacency), but that she
stopped Rinaldo getting on with the First Crusade. So, when the
object is in any case attained, there is no reason why she should

not be forgiven, and all Tasso's gentle spirit is eager that she should be. Accordingly in Canto XX, when Jerusalem is taken, Aladino and Solimano killed and the Christians triumphant, Armida meets Rinaldo again. She tries to kill herself for grief and rage; but Rinaldo speaks gently to her, and prays that Heaven will dissolve *il velo del paganesmo* and bring her to the true light. Whereupon Armida submits, and in words audaciously borrowed from the Scriptures—*Ecco l'ancella tua*—bids her law be his. Circe at last has turned into something like the Magdalen; but her words are those of the Virgin at the Annunciation.

This strange mixture of romantic enchantment, epic severity, voluptuousness and religion is peculiarly Tasso's own. There is perhaps nothing quite like it in literature, though parallels from painting would not be hard to find. If Tasso in the shadowy softness and delicacy, prettiness almost, of some of his scenes reminds us of Correggio, in other places he looks forward to the mixed motives, the strained pieties of the baroque painters of the seicento. More than with Spenser, and less reconciled, there is a tension between the sensuous and the moral tenor of his poem. In later years, ill, oppressed with morbid anxieties about the orthodoxy of his work, terrified of the Inquisition and his critics, Tasso recast the whole *Liberata* as *Gerusalemme Conquistata*, cut out the magic and erotic episodes, and destroyed all the charm of the poem in the process. But if we must think of *Gerusalemme Liberata* coming under the severities and pruderies of *controriforma* clerical censorship, it is easy to see that the Armida episode, both in its central scenes and in its conclusion, was sailing pretty near the wind.

The strictly supernatural passages, the heavenly and infernal councils, the operations of angelic and diabolical emissaries, need less attention for our particular purpose. They are relevant to Milton, but hardly at all to Spenser. Attempting to make a rational epic with a Christian supernatural, Tasso involves himself in all the notorious difficulties of such an enterprise— difficulties that even Milton, with a far more inward and less formal religious sense than Tasso's, could not escape. The Christian supernatural was to be chosen because it was true. Therefore a far higher level of conviction is required than in merely making plausible a fanciful mythology. And it is just this that is not possible when presenting the dealings of eternity and omnipotence with human and temporal affairs. The difficulty is not stylistic; in that respect Tasso is equal to the task.

> Sedea colà, dond'egli e buono e giusto
> dà legge al tutto, e 'l tutto orna e produce
> sovra i bassi confin del mondo angusto,
> ove senso o ragion non si conduce;
> e de la eternità nel trono augusto
> risplendea con tre lumi in una luce.
> Ha sotto i piedi il Fato e la Natura,
> ministri umili, e il Moto e chi 'l misura
>
> e 'l Loco, e Quella che, qual fumo o polve
> la gloria di qua giuso e l'oro e i regni,
> come piace là su, disperde e volve,
> ne, diva, cura i nostri umani sdegni.
> Quivi ei cosi nel suo splendor s'involve,
> che v'abbaglian la vista anco i più degni:
> d'intorno ha innumerabili immortali,
> disegualmente in lor letizia eguali.

(IX. 56–57)

There he sits, whence, good and just, he gives laws to everything, adorns and produces everything, above the low confines of this narrow world, where sense and reason cannot lead; and from all eternity on his lofty throne he shines with three lights in one light. Beneath his feet he has Fate and Nature, his humble ministers, and Motion, and Time that measures motion, and Place, and Fortune, she who scatters and rolls away, like smoke or dust, the glory of this world, and the gold and the kingdoms; nor, being a goddess, cares for our human wrath. Here he so wraps himself in his own light that even the worthiest sight is dazzled: around him are innumerable immortal spirits, unequally equal in their joy.

But the Dantesque elevation of these verses cannot overcome such absurdities as the passage where the Padre Eterno, omniscient and omnipotent, suddenly notices (I. 8–9) that the war is not progressing very well, or (IX. 58) that the devils have got out of hell and are attacking the Christians; or, for that matter, the Archangel Michael's last minute intervention on the Christian side. If he was to come at all, as Boileau pertinently remarked, why not come rather earlier? Spenser's allegorical method, whether by luck or wisdom, has immense advantages over this. Where all is myth, contradictions of this kind cannot arise. Since substantial truth is not predicated even of his human characters like Arthur, substantial truth need not attach to his spiritual agents either. All equally inhabit the realm of imagination. "The poet nothing affirms, and therefore never lyeth." And doubtless Sidney's dictum is in principle as true for Tasso as for Spenser. But Tasso makes the mistake of appearing to affirm; and not all his affirmations live happily in the same world.

The council in Hell (IV. 1–19) is more amenable to his treatment. The Devil has always occupied an ambiguous, quasi-mythical position in Christian story, and if Tasso cares to call him Pluto his status is not too gravely impaired. The whole passage is brilliantly and learnedly compounded from reminiscences of Virgil, Claudian, Dante and Vida's *Christiad*; and for the English reader it is almost impossible not to read it backwards through its descendant, Book II of *Paradise Lost*. The elements of grandeur, defiance and sad fallen majesty are too familiar to need description. Nor is this the place to discuss the stylistic links between Milton and Tasso. For the devils themselves Tasso has relied on a mass of classical lumber about Gorgons, Hydras and Chimeras dire, and plays every conceivable variation on bellowing, roaring, hissing and howling. He succeeds in creating a rich effect of grotesque violence and terror, but never comes within sight of the metaphysical horror of hell. Nor perhaps should he. If the Christian supernatural in either its celestial or infernal aspects were to be given its full value the autonomy of the human agents would be entirely swamped. The funtion of these angelic and diabolic beings is to provide the machinery for a heroic poem whose real sphere of operation is middle-earth.

As an afterthought Tasso provided an allegorical interpretation of his poem; and this we shall discuss in a later chapter. It is a question, however, whether there is a real element of allegory in the poem itself. In a sense of course there is. The angels and devils can easily be seen as a mere exteriorization of purely human forces, Armida as an embodiment of the seductions of the flesh. But this way of looking at the poem hardly forces itself upon us. There are no isolated patches of transparent allegory, like the Alcina-Logistilla episode in *Orlando Furioso*. If we compare Armida with her predecessor Alcina we find her a far more rounded and human character. All in all, it is her passion as a woman, not her function as an instrument of temptation that is felt most strongly, and it is probably true to say that there is no more of the allegorical element in *Gerusalemme Liberata* than in most literary epics. There is another point too. Professor Lewis has remarked that the Protestant mind tends to see the ritual and sacramental side of religion as itself allegorical; while to the Catholic it is part of the literal sense. And Tasso belongs both to an age and to a personal type of Catholic Christianity for whom the literal is in the foreground. Much that in Spenser is allegorical is for Tasso part of the normal furniture of life. Confession and ghostly admonition in Spenser for example tends to be an allegory of inward regeneration. For Tasso it is normal devotional exercise. And this explains, I think, how Spenser can read Tasso, receive quite whole-heartedly much that he finds there, and transpose it to his own different plane.

I had meant to go on to a separate discussion of the moral and religious temper of *Gerusalemme Liberata*, but much of what is to be said has been said already in speaking of its other aspects. It is not a poem with an inside and an outside. The criticism that tends to depreciate Tasso (and there is some in his own country) might take into account the remarkable completeness with which its spirit informs its matter. When the main narrative strands have been followed with understanding Tasso's moral orientation has also been implicitly understood. The very fabric of the poem shows the dual devotion which seems deeply rooted in its author's nature—to a rational and comprehensible order on the one hand, on the other to the vagaries and indulgences of romance. There is a similar duality in the moral sphere. In religion and ethics Tasso shows on the surface a formal scholastic rigidity. Reason is paramount, until it falls under the law of revelation; then it submits. Goffredo, for example, represents at all times considered wisdom and rational judgement. Yet it is not a free personal judgement. Even when his heart is most inflamed with ardour to finish the war, the cautionary note is appended:

> ma il suo voler più nel voler s'infiamma
> del suo Signor, come favilla in fiamma.
>
> (I. 18)

> But his will grows bright in the will of his Lord, like a spark within a flame.

And we do not feel in reading this the profound weight of willing sacrifice, as in Dante's *In la sua voluntade è nostra pace*. It is far more a formal and programmatic obedience. "Tasso is a good Christian of the Counter-Reformation. His hero must think of nothing that has the quality of spiritual autonomy," as Luigi Russo acidly remarks. But perhaps too much has been made of Tasso the poet of the Counter-Reformation: first he is a poet; and the instinct for submission to an ordered scheme, devotionally, morally and artistically, is very much part of his nature—as we can see from many of the events of his life.

But only a part of his nature. On the other side he is instinctively drawn to the pre-lapsarian idyll, the *bella età del'oro* where the only law is "If it pleases you, you may", celebrated in the most famous chorus of his *Aminta*. And the tension between these two elements leads him continually to the ambiguous situation, to the doubtful meeting-place of sensuality and devotion, to loves that are forbidden, and only legitimated by conversion at the last moment. In Canto II of the *Gerusalemme* (II. 19–55) Sofronia offers herself to the stake out of faith and piety; Olindo offers himself in her place for love; and they are condemned to suffer together. Tasso seems to delight in this conjunction, the sensuous-ideal passion of the Petrarchan lover bound back to back with the cold exaltation of the martyr who is beyond all human attachments. The principal love-objects are all pagans; all, that is, on the wrong side: all these loves have to be redeemed. A heroine like Una or Britomart whose love is in itself a redeeming force, is not to be found in *Gerusalemme Liberata*. Tasso is not without this feeling—that love, even human *amour-passion*, has a smack of salvation in it; but it can only find a side-

long and surreptitious expression. Clorinda is converted at the
last by the free action of grace, as we are explicitly told. Yet in
the imaginative economy of the poem surely she is saved, and
must be saved, because she is the worthy object of Tancredi's
love. When we see Armida, who has shown little sign of grace
throughout her story, at Rinaldo's feet, offering herself as his
handmaid, we seem to see a secular parallel to the figure of the
Magdalen, so much delighted in by the painting of the coming
century. She is forgiven, in fact, because she has loved much.
And Erminia, pagan though she is, is turned by her love into a
singularly attractive example of the Christian virtues, humble,
devoted, charitable—towards her enemies as well as those to
whom natural affection draws her.

These complexities of sentiment in the poem are the complexities of Tasso's own mind. They point to a radically subjective element in his art. In theory the heroic poem should not be
dependent on the personal sensibility of its author. Its style and
feeling are dictated by its kind, its theme, its material. But
whatever his theoretical allegiance Tasso is always the creature
of his own temperament, as his life again bears witness. This
shows in the poem as a pervading lyricism, the pressure of
vague, incompletely objectified emotions, which cast a light veil
over the outlines of the heroic narrative and give it its peculiarly
seductive charm—or, if you dislike Tasso, are an element in its
weakness. Symonds, with other critics, has remarked on Tasso's
addiction to the phrase *un non so chè*, "an I-know-not-what", in
describing indefinable emotions—emotions which he then does
not attempt to particularize further, but presents, by modulating
from the plastic into the melodic. In key passages much of the
weight, far more than we should consider normal in a heroic
poem, is carried by the lyrical sweetness of the verse. This is
why even in vigorous battle-scenes it is perhaps the moments of
pathos that are most memorable—the death of Latino and his
five sons (IX. 27–39), Solimano avenging the death of his
beautiful young page (IX. 74–88). We then remember that in
his criticism Tasso had made a *fiorita vaghezza* one of the requirements of the epic style. There is nothing in his tradition to
authorize this demand. It is a response to the need of his own

nature—a need and a response to which Spenser, with his different temperament, was not a stranger, for which he more than once found precedent and example in Tasso's work.

But this must not be dwelt on to the exclusion of other considerations. We must not forget the learning, the fundamental artistic research that has gone into Tasso's style. To balance the subjective emotional indulgence there is a prodigious amount of hard intellectual labour, careful study of the best and most difficult models, both in the classics and the literature of his own tongue. The list of Tasso's sources is very wide, ranging from Homer and Virgil, through Lucan and Claudian, to Dante, Petrarch and Ariosto. This in itself means little; but they have in most cases been put to admirable and appropriate use. Tasso is in the best sense a learned poet, and his style is a learned style. The Latinate involutions he imposed on the Italian language need not concern us here, for though they affected Milton they left Spenser untouched. Tasso shows little intellectual power in the thought, the dianoia of his poem: in its verbal organization he shows a great deal. There are weak lines, especially final couplets, and frigid passages; but as a whole the *Gerusalemme* excites just that *maraviglia* that its author hoped for at the controlled strength with which it rises to the very various occasions that the story presents.

Tasso I believe is very little read in England today. For the last generation of his English admirers, the Victorian readers of whom we spoke in an earlier chapter, it was probably the *non so chè di flebile e soave* that was his principal attraction. I am the last to want to depreciate this pathetic power; but if he is to be read again we should think also of other qualities. We should think particularly of the many and diverse elements that have been united and fused together to make this complex and superbly accomplished art. Let us enumerate some of them: the resuscitation of the Christian theme as the effective inspirer of a heroic action; the erudite energy with which the historic and warlike parts are handled; the ingenuity with which the old material of romance and enchantment has been combined with the central subject; above all, the fluidity, the multiform power of identification by which Tasso can enter into the various, almost discordant parts of his poem—the construction of an assault-tower no less than the coming of a rose and pearly dawn, the tumultuous howling of demons no less than the calm sacrifice of Sofronia, Rinaldo's luxurious sojourn in the arms of Armida no less than his morning of purgation and illumination on the slopes of Mount Olivet.

*Chapter V*

## STRUCTURE OF *THE FAERIE QUEENE*

I

To inquire into the structure of *The Faerie Queene* is not a merely formal inquiry; or at least it should not be. It is to ask what kind of poem *The Faerie Queene* really is, and with what expectations we are to read it. Are we to be content with pathless wandering through an enchanted forest? Is this all that is really felt and living in the poem? If so we are deluding ourselves or wasting our time in perusing the letter to Raleigh and trying to make it square with the poem as it stands. We shall be looking for a formal plan where none is really achieved and the actual merits of the poem survive quite independently. Or are we to do what on the face of it is not unreasonable—take Spenser's announced intention as his real directing scheme and suppose that apparent inconsistencies would have disappeared or been reconciled in the completed version? We shall read the poem very differently if we do. And there is a third possibility: that *The Faerie Queene* has a constitutive formal principle, that it is not merely a congerie of romantic tales and motives; but this principle is different from that which Spenser explicitly professed. After all, this state of affairs is not unfamiliar. If authors invariably did just what they supposed themselves to be doing literary study would be a simpler and less interesting matter than it is. It is easy to get bogged down in speculative quagmires and tangled in irrelevant learned briar patches: and it is no disrespect to the great Spenser scholarship to say that this has often happened in the structural study of *The Faerie Queene*. But there is after all a criterion of relevance—how is the poem actually to be taken; not how many ingenious explanations can be found; but what sort of shape can we expect to see really emerging from our reading.

It is right to speak of expectation rather than fulfilment, for the poem is incomplete. How much its incompleteness matters will depend on what kind of design we expect it to have. Professor Lewis wishes to emphasize the incompleteness at the start, and with this we may well agree. He goes on to say that ideally we should speak of Books I, II and III as Fragment A, and IV, V and VI as Fragment B.[1] And here surely we ought not to agree. It is true that Books I to III appeared in 1590 and the remaining three books not until 1596. But we have no idea whether this accident of publication represents the order of composition, or anything in the real plan of the poem. It seems unlikely. If *The Faerie Queene* does divide into fragments it is certainly not between Books III and IV that the division can be made. These two books form the most clearly continuous block in the whole work; and W. J. B. Owen has argued plausibly that they are its oldest layer.[2] Janet Spens has suggested the existence of an earlier scheme, based on the seven deadly sins rather than twelve virtues, and consisting of eight books.[3] But this is the merest speculation. The fact is that we do not *know* anything about the order of composition, or the possible existence of an earlier scheme, and there is no means by which we can know. There is no real alternative to taking *The Faerie Queene* as it stands, six books of an unfinished poem, with the two Mutability cantos as an unplaced appendix. At the other extreme stands Professor Arthos who as far as I understand him seems to suggest that we can take the six books and the two cantos as a whole unified poem: a genial view for which I have the greatest sympathy and which I shall later try to defend; but plainly not defensible on the level of simple fact.[4]

Incomplete as it is, *The Faerie Queene* has been judged very harshly from the structural point of view. De Selincourt writes, "The plot as originally designed was loose enough, and in the process of development it became looser still."[5] Church had said earlier, "In the first two books he proceeds from point to

---

[1] *English Literature in the Sixteenth Century*, Oxford, 1954, p. 379.
[2] "The Structure of The Faerie Queene", PMLA, LXVIII (1953).
[3] *Spenser's Faerie Queene: an interpretation*, 1934, p. 27.
[4] John Arthos, *On the Poetry of Spenser and the Form of Romances*, 1956.
[5] Introduction to the Oxford Spenser, 1912.

point with fair coherence and consecutiveness. After them, the attempt to hold the scheme together, except in the loosest and most general way, is given up as too general or too confined. . . . Still the complexity, or rather the uncared-for and clumsy arrangement of the poem is a matter which disturbs a reader's satisfaction, till he gets used to the poet's way and resigns himself to it."[1] We might be tempted to think, on reading these and similar judgements, that *The Faerie Queene* was a very artless production. But if there is one thing we can fairly deduce from the letter to Raleigh it is that this is not so. The letter shows Spenser as very much aware of epic decorum, of traditional structural principles, of great models, both classical and modern. And we have already seen enough of the elaborate care bestowed on epic theory in the sixteenth century to make us suspect that he must have been acutely aware of the formal problem.

The formal debate in Italy was mainly between Virgilian unity and Ariostan multiplicity. We do not know what Spenser had read or how precisely he was conscious of this; but there is much in the letter to suggest that he was acquainted with Tasso's writings on heroic poetry. The Arthurian theme is in accord with Tasso's precepts, and justified in the letter in Tasso's terms. So is the concern in the letter with securing both unity and variety of design. As we have seen, Tasso was essentially an eclectic; he wished to enrich the unity and severity of the ancient epic with the graces of modern romance—the single great and serious subject combined with episodes, variety of incident and picturesque description. It seems likely that Spenser's purpose was very much the same.

A letter from Gabriel Harvey to Spenser in 1580 cites Spenser as hoping "to overgo Ariosto"; and some writers, notably Courthope among the older ones, would make Ariosto responsible for all the major structural and material features of *The Faerie Queene*. But this is not quite true as far as structure is concerned. The Ariostan plan of interwoven stories is only partial in *The Faerie Queene*. Book I is complete and almost entirely self-contained. It is, as has been said, a whole miniature epic in itself. The Red Cross Knight makes only brief and

[1] R. W. Church, *Spenser*, 1888, pp. 162, 168.

unimportant appearances in later parts of the poem. Duessa and Archimago appear again, but in contexts quite unconnected with the story of Book I. Una never reappears at all. Book II is again a complete unified quest with a single hero whose adventure is brought to a conclusion within the limits of the book. But Books III and IV are constructed on quite a different plan. The main narrative threads of the poem as a whole are concentrated here— the stories of Britomart and Artegall, Amoret and Scudamour, Florimell and Marinell, with the subsidiary adventures of Belphoebe and Timias, the false Florimell, and a number of self-contained interpolated novelle. These are put together on the 'interwoven' plan of Ariosto. Spenser even revises the conclusion of the story of Amoret and Scudamour in order to keep the end in suspense. And all these long narrative threads are kept going throughout Books III and IV, and some even continued into Book V. Book V on the whole, however, is a return to the earlier design, in that it has a single hero whose adventures we follow fairly consistently. With Book VI we return to a medley of romantic motifs, again put together mainly on the 'interwoven' principle. Church and de Selincourt and in general those who are disturbed by the structural inconsistency of *The Faerie Queene* tend to suppose that the unified self-contained plan of Book I represents the vigour of Spenser's original design, accidentally relaxed by the time he got to Book III and had forgotten what he was doing. But it at least is probable, as W. J. B. Owen's valuable article suggests,[1] that the purpose of overgoing Ariosto belongs to Books III and IV, that they represent the earliest layer of the poem, and that Books I and II were antechambers to this main edifice, constructed later. Since we can never know, to spend too much time on this speculation must be vain.

A minor feature of the Italian controversy was a debate about the merits of cantos against 'books' as subdivisions of the poem. It seems a singularly arid and futile discussion; but it is not quite pointless. Cantos are merely slices of convenient length, broken off wherever the narrator or the audience is in need of a rest; often, indeed most commonly, in the middle of a story.

---

[1] W. J. B. Owen, "The Structure of The Faerie Queene", PMLA, LXVIII (1953). See also J. W. Bennett, *The Evolution of The Faerie Queene*, 1948.

*Quel che segui ne l'altro canto e scritto,* as Ariosto is constantly saying. Whereas a book (though not originally so) was by this time conceived as an integral section of the plot—a member of the whole, but a member with some provisional completeness and unity of its own. *The Faerie Queene,* we notice, has both cantos and books. It looks like an attempt to combine the features of the formal and the informal methods of construction.

Perhaps what we have then is an attempt to combine the form of the classical with that of the romantic epic. We turn for confirmation to the letter to Sir Walter Raleigh, dated January 1589, and published with the first three books in 1590. Now the composition of *The Faerie Queene* goes back to 1580 at least. We first hear of it in a letter from Spenser to Harvey in that year, and Harvey's reply, already referred to, is pretty frankly contemptuous of the 'Elvish Queen'. "If so be the Faerye Queene be fairer in your eyes than the Nine Muses, and Hobgoblin runne away with the garland from Apollo . . . fare you well, till God or some good aungell putt you in better mind." This hardly sounds as though Harvey had heard of Spenser's imposing plan, with its decorous citing of epic principle and authority. It is possible that the plan outlined in the letter to Raleigh was not the original design, but rather a later attempt to superimpose some sort of classic order on the original romance.

The letter tells us that "the generall end of all the book is to fashion a gentleman or noble person in vertuous and gentle discipline", and that this was most plausibly and pleasingly to be done under the guise of a historical fiction. That is to say Spenser emphasizes the general Renaissance conception of the exemplary nature of the epic, that the soul of it is in the nobility and virtue of the hero, exhibited as a model for its readers. And he has chosen the history of King Arthur, he tells us, "as most fitte for the excellency of his person, being made famous by many men's former works, and also furthest from the daunger of envy, and suspition of present time"—reasons which sound like an abbreviated version of Tasso's. In choosing an exemplary history of this sort Spenser conceives himself to be following the practice of his great epic predecessors, ancient and modern: Homer, who has exhibited political virtue in

Agamemnon, private in Ulysses; Virgil, who combined both in the person of Aeneas; Ariosto, who did the same in Orlando; followed by Tasso, who again separated them, showing the private virtue in Rinaldo, the public in Goffredo. This is a strange way of reducing four different narrative poets, belonging to different ages and civilizations, each with his own distinct ethos and moral colouring, to a common purpose; but in this Spenser is in accord with much of the cultivated opinion of his time. His Arthur, treated before he became king, is similarly to be an example of the private moral virtues, the public ones perhaps to be pursued in another poem, or another part, showing Arthur after he had assumed the crown.

The actual phrase used is "the image of a brave knight perfected in the twelve private morall vertues as Aristotle hath devised". Arthur himself represents "magnificence in particular . . . for that (according to Aristotle and the rest) it is the perfection of all the rest, and conteineth them all". Arthur then is to be Aristotle's *megalopsychos* the great-souled man, and Spenser translates *megalopsychia* as Magnificence. Having established his single hero and his unitary theme in this way Spenser (again in a spirit that recalls some of Tasso's precepts) "for the more variety of the history" makes twelve other knights to be the patrons of the twelve separate virtues that have contributed to Arthur's total magnificence. The chronological beginning of his story is the annual feast of the Faerie Queene, held for twelve days, on which the quests of the twelve several knights were begun. Had Spenser been writing history, he says, this would have come at the beginning: but "the Method of a Poet historicall is not such as of an Historiographer". The historian tells things in their order; but epic decorum requires that "a Poet thrusteth into the middest" of the action and tells other parts by reminiscence or prophecy. This is not of course a caprice on Spenser's part; it is simply a rather naïve interpretation of the Horatian precept that a heroic poet is to begin *in medias res*. Throughout the letter the desire to follow the best models and observe the established principles is almost painfully evident.

Such is Spenser's account of his procedure. It is admirably lucid, attentive to authority and precedent, and ingenious in combining unity of theme with variety of adventures. In fact if we had the scheme without the poem everything would be entirely satisfactory. As soon as we start to bring the two together, however, we are beset with difficulties. The first difficulty is about the virtues. Spenser speaks as though Aristotle's twelve private moral virtues were an established tally like the ten commandments or the seven deadly sins; as though a reader turning to the Nicomachean Ethics would find them duly listed. But this is not so.[1] Aristotle does discuss separate moral virtues by name, but his enumeration is not very distinct. Some overlap with others or are only subdivisions of the main ones. Perturbed commentators on Spenser have succeeded in adding them up to nine, or ten, or eleven, or even thirteen; the one number that seems difficult to arrive at is twelve. We need not perhaps be surprised at this; Aristotle's three unities have also been a stumbling-block, and it is easier to count three than twelve. There was, it appears, a persistent tradition from the time of Aquinas that Aristotle had twelve moral virtues,[2] and some scholars, by a good deal of manœuvring and special pleading, have contrived to adjust Spenser to Aristotelian ethics. But they do not really fit. The difficulty is not only numerical; Spenser's virtues are not the same as the Aristotelian ones, and some could not possibly be; Holiness and Chastity could find no place in Aristotle's ethical system.

Turning to the poem itself, we find that the relation of the virtues to the books is extremely variable. I, II and V are very much what we should expect from the account given in the letter —developed *exempla* of Holiness, Temperance and Justice respectively, each virtue being embodied in a single knight. But however the word Chastity may be interpreted—and Spenser's interpretation of it is a highly idiosyncratic one—the Britomart of Book III is something more than and different from the mere embodiment of it. There is no single knight for Book IV; the two titular heroes play a very small part; and the virtue of

[1] See J. J. Jusserand, 'Spenser's "twelve private morall vertues as Aristotle hath devised" ', MP 3 (1906); (Works I, p. 327).

[2] See Viola B. Hulbert, 'Spenser's Twelve Moral Virtues "According to Aristotle and the rest" ', Univ. of Chicago Abstracts of Theses, Humanistic Series 5, (1926); (Works I, p. 353).

friendship is only intermittently exhibited in the intertwining narratives. In fact IV continues the main narrative lines of III, and it is plausible to take these two books together, and to see them, whatever their formal titles, as a large central block concerned with love, its varieties, its perversions and its right course. And Book VI, though it has a single courteous hero, is not consistently about Courtesy; it is made up of a variety of romance and pastoral motives.

Prince Arthur is clearly an attempt to impose unity of hero on the multiple scheme. Spenser makes much of him in the letter and he does appear at critical points (Canto viii in each case) of every book except III. But he never occupies a commanding position. The student, concerned to interpret the allegory and find the rationale of Spenser's plan, may contrive to make something of Arthur, but I think it is safe to say that the ordinary reader hardly notices his alleged central importance. His personal quest is to love and seek the Faerie Queene—

> To seek her out with labour, and long tyne,
> And never vow to rest, till her I find,
>
> (I. ix. 15)

But although he never rests he never appears to take any definite steps to discover her, or to inquire of her from those like the Red Cross Knight who have just come from her court.[1] He merely wanders about at random, accepting whatever adventures may befall. In fact his position in the scheme is never more than half-heartedly worked out. As a unifying factor he is of no effect whatever on the poem as we have it, though he might have acquired a retrospective importance by the time we arrived at the Faerie Queene's court at the end, where doubtless he would have been finally united to her. At best this is no more than a single strand in the whole intricate web. It is not the backbone of a structure. Most of the time we forget about Arthur and his love for the Faerie Queene far more easily than we forget about the love of Ruggiero for Bradamante which occupies a similar position in the *Orlando Furioso*.

[1] This is not quite right; he does ask Guyon in II. ix. 5, but never follows the matter up.

# A PREFACE TO *THE FAERIE QUEENE*

The Faerie Queene's feast itself presents difficulties. It is the chronological antecedent of all the quests and they are supposed to start there—though this is not borne out in the books themselves. The letter, for example, tells that Guyon's quest begins with the arrival of the Palmer at the Faerie Queene's court, bearing an infant with bloody hands. But in II. ii itself Guyon finds the slain Mordaunt and Amavia and the babe with bloody hands in the ordinary course of his errantry, and there is no mention of a quest formally inaugurated at court. The initial feast at the Faerie Queene's court is postponed for structural reasons, but we can hardly suppose it to be the actual conclusion of the poem. Surely the quests must end, their success be reported, the knights return to their royal mistress, and she be united to Arthur. And this would seem to require another feast, or at least a formal reunion at the Faerie Queene's court. If we consider the amplitude with which Spenser is apt to treat such scenes we seem to have matter here for something like another book, as Janet Spens has argued.[1] Twelve books are required for the quests of the individual knights. We can hardly suppose that, besides the displaced beginning, the grand finale of the whole, the fate of Arthur and the long-delayed epiphany of the Faerie Queene herself could be huddled up at the end of a book mainly devoted to something else. So we need thirteen books, not the twelve that have been announced. One begins to suspect that the twelve books were chosen because that was a respectable Virgilian number rather than for the exigencies of the twelve virtues.

In fact we are driven to conclude that the letter to Raleigh simply does not account for the poem as it stands, and it is almost as hard to see how any plausible revision could have brought about a correspondence. It is not however quite good enough to dismiss the letter with "I don't believe a word of it". We are in a region where all is conjecture; but if we are to refuse the letter, as I think we must, it is at least decent to offer some conjecture about why it was written, and how far its correlation with the poem can be supposed to go, for a partial correlation there certainly is. I should suppose that *The Faerie*

[1] op. cit., p. 28.

*Queene*, like so many other poems, began as a kind of vision—a vague, all-embracing vision of its atmosphere, its colour, its moral temper and its type of incident. Such visions are intoxicating; and part of the poem was probably not only conceived but written under its spell. Then came the realization that *The Faerie Queene*, like other poems, could not be completed in vision; for a work on this scale an architectonic, a rational order is required. The letter I take it belongs to this second phase. It is not completely in accord with what has been written, and it is not yet clear how matters are to be adjusted and worked out. Above all, the letter was a second thought, not the shaping spirit that gave rise to the poem in the first place. We can then continue our conjecture on either of two lines. We can suppose that if Spenser had lived to complete his plan he would have eliminated the inconsistencies and found a way of working out the design, which after all is not impossible. The vision would have been adjusted to the plan, and the plan, secondary in order of time, would have grown into the vision and become its authentic structure. This is a possibility, and we must in that case allow the letter to Raleigh to return, as an ideal scheme towards which the poem is moving; what is inconsistent with it would be only an accidental incompleteness. Or we can look at the plan of the letter in another light, and suppose that it would never have become the real structural principle of *The Faerie Queene*. It might indeed have become part of the pattern, threaded some continuous lines through the whole intricate tapestry, as the stories of the siege of Paris, of Orlando and Angelica, Ruggiero and Bradamante do in the *Orlando Furioso*. But the real formal principle would be of another kind; it would be something inherent in the original vision, that had never reached the level of conscious formal exposition at all. When Hurd and the eighteenth-century critics said that *The Faerie Queene* "must be considered under the idea of a Gothic poem" it was something of this sort that they had in mind. It is this second conjecture that commends itself to me, and this is the line of inquiry I wish to pursue.

# A PREFACE TO *THE FAERIE QUEENE*

"Never trust the author, trust the tale." What does the tale itself tell us? In the first place, in spite of Spenser's obvious worry in the letter, the actual bow in the direction of formal epic is very slight. Spenser in the manner of his time modelled his career on Virgil's, beginning with pastorals and proceeding to heroic poetry. He duly opens *The Faerie Queene* with an imitation of the cancelled opening of the Aeneid:

> Lo I the man, whose Muse whilome did maske,
> As time her taught in lowly Shepheards weeds,
> Am now enforst a far unfitter taske,
> For trumpets sterne to chaunge mine Oaten reeds.

There are numerous scattered Virgilian similes, echoes and allusions—

> Now when the rosy-fingered Morning fair
> Weary of aged Tithones saffron bed—

and passages of that kind. Avernus in II. iv. 34 seq. is imitated as we should expect from Aeneid VI. But these are separable, not organic. There is much less classical colouring in the style and management of *The Faerie Queene* than there is in Ariosto. Indeed in a certain antique gentlemanly simplicity Spenser is nearer to Boiardo, and far enough from the cultivated grand manner of the literary epic. Above all, Spenser is really working in a different mode from epic altogether. We have discussed *The Faerie Queene* as an example of the romantic epic; the term is traditional and is not worth quarrelling over. But in fact Spenser's whole way of dealing with his material is not only remote from epic in the classical sense, but different even from Ariosto. And this is something intimate and intrinsic, far more than a matter of external structure. It is not an accident that Aristotle finds epic to contain the same elements as tragedy, except for melody and spectacle; for epic depends on full dramatic realization of character and situation. It is narrative in which parts, and many of the most important parts, are presented in highly dramatic fashion. Great weight falls on the speeches and on the exchange of dialogue. Spenser does not dramatize; the speeches of his characters are not as a rule very fully realized or individualized; they are for the most part in the same tone as the narrative. The 'dreamy beauty' theory of Spenser's poetry is an absurd sentimentalization; there is great variety in his descriptions and incidents; but it remains true that his characteristic gait is an equable, even-paced narration, contemplative and set at a little distance, as if we were watching a pageant move by. Character is not completely developed and individualized. At one extreme we have the mere notation of a quality, Furor or Occasion: at the other we have Britomart—whatever she represents allegorically she is also a girl in love, and is capable of jealousy, suspicion and anguish. But even she remains to some degree typical and impersonal; the principal knights, Artegall, Scudamour and Guyon still more so. It is not that another kind of characterization is attempted and fails; it is simply not attempted. Scenes of a single emotional stress are sometimes powerfully realized; but the conflict of character and motive is undeveloped; in a word, Spenser's mode of presentation is pictorial rather than dramatic. However successful he had been in beginning in the middle, imposing a single hero and a unified theme and all the rest of it, the pageant-like movement of most of *The Faerie Queene* would always have distinguished it sharply from the true epic mode.

This means that much of the concern over construction that is evident in the letter to Raleigh is not fundamentally relevant. It is relevant formally and externally to the kind that Spenser believes himself to be practising, but not to the real nature of his work. In fact most of the critical questions about the structure of *The Faerie Queene* become idle or simply disappear when it is actually read; for in fact it is all of a piece; we are always aware of being in a varied but consistent world. This unity of atmosphere (it has been particularly remarked by Professor Lewis) is far more of a present reality than any discontinuities in the plot. The very multiplicity of incidents is a help in this direction; the effect is that of an all-over pattern rather than that of a picture composed on a few broad structural lines. *The Faerie Queene* is composed of many relatively small parts, each commanding our appreciation by itself and all harmonious with each other; and this is its structural principle. Its essence is immanent in these multitudinous local effects, not in an over-riding plan which could be abstracted and schematically displayed. We can compare the regular epic to a High Renaissance painting, learnedly composed on a pyramidal or circular plan. We can compare *The Faerie Queene* to a page of medieval illumination, which exhibits a harmonious texture, bright and delicate detail everywhere, many individual miniatures which must be looked at separately—but no very striking general design, and what there is contributes little to the effect of the whole. The unfinished state of the poem therefore matters less than it might. It is a misfortune that half of this richly patterned page is missing; but what is left retains its full vitality. That the parts are parts of a whole need not be doubted; but they have their own life and their own kind of mutual coherence without reference to the total design.

Forget all we have heard about the intended plan, and we can say of *The Faerie Queene* pretty nearly what John Addington Symonds says of the *Orlando Furioso*:

> It [has] the unity of a vast piece of tapestry rather than of architecture. There is nothing massive in its structure, no simple yet colossal design like that which forms the strength of the Iliad or the Divine Comedy. The delicacy of its connecting links, the perpetual shifting of its scene, distinguish it as a romantic poem from the true epic . . . the principal figures are confounded with a multitude of subordinate characters; the interest is divided between a succession of episodical narratives.[1]

The material, characters and properties of this huge tapestry picture are those that are usual in romances of chivalry: knights, ladies in distress, lovers false and true, single combats, tournaments, magicians male and female, giants, enchanted lances, magically impregnable armour, magic potions, magic islands. The main scene is a forest, rather thinly interspersed with castle and hermits' huts and caves. There are pastoral areas, shepherds and foresters, satyrs and savage men. And there are other beings too, of a less expected kind; the figures of the classical

[1] *Renaissance in Italy*, vol. 5, p. 13.

pantheon, Neptune, Venus, Cupid and the Graces; personified natural objects, like Thames and Medway; above all, personified moral objects, Faith, Hope, Charity, Despair, Strife and the seven deadly sins. It is like opening a contemporary manual of iconography such as Ripa's *Iconologia*, where Abundance, Filial Piety, Purity of the Atmosphere, Nine o'clock and Calabria are all presented on the same level and illustrated in the same way. Dramatic conflict, the play of motive and character, could not steadily subsist among creatures drawn from so many different planes of being.

But does not all this put us back with Hazlitt and critics of his kind who see only an enchanting fairy-tale, and as for meaning—well, we are not to expect too much? I do not think so; nor do I think that if even the most undemanding reader cares to question his experience, this accurately describes his feeling as he goes through *The Faerie Queene*. Where have we met this sensation before—the variety and multiplicity of incident, the characters drawn from a dozen different realms, the unpredictability of narrative development; suffused at the same time with a feeling of harmony, that all belongs in the same world, that with all the solutions of narrative logic, changes of direction and temper, there is yet a purpose, if not a purpose that lends itself easily to conceptual explanation? For we do feel that we have met it before. Neither *The Faerie Queene* nor its literary ancestors are much read today, the organization of the whole is puzzling, the ramifications of the plot hard to follow. Yet our feeling on encountering the poem is one of familiarity. These stories that begin inexplicably, do not end, are interrupted and resumed, fade into each other and go on in an order apparently emancipated from time and space—they only "disturb a reader's satisfaction", in Church's phrase, when he begins to stand outside them and subject them to external criticism. In the actual experience of reading he feels quite undisturbed and quite at home. This is because we have all met such experiences before—in dreams. The organization of *The Faerie Queene* is like that of a dream. I do not use the word with the mere connotations of vagueness or enchantment, or in the sense in which it could be used of any romance. Something of the dream quality intended here is implicit in Symbolist conceptions of 'le rêve'; but more is to be found, quite explicitly, in Chapter VI of Freud's *Interpretation of Dreams*.

We are not at the moment concerned with symbolism or interpretation, but with the mere mechanics of the way the story is put together. This is far more dream-like in Spenser than in his Italian originals. There is to begin with the free, undetermined unlocalized setting. It would seem at first sight that no one could make more free with space and time than Ariosto. But this is not entirely so. His characters perform miraculously rapid journeys, but many of them are exactly located. Charles is fixed with his army at Paris; Rinaldo goes to Scotland for aid (VI). Astolfo leaves Logistilla's island, which is apparently somewhere near Japan, follows the coast of Cathay, seeing the various islands of the Indian Ocean and the China Sea on the way, turns round India and arrives in the Persian Gulf. There he leaves his ship and travels overland across Arabia to Suez (XV. 10 seq.). Tasso with his historical theme is naturally more strictly tied to geography; and even when he might be expected to escape from it, in the voyage to Armida's magic island (XV) Carlo and Ubaldo go on a geographically detailed journey from Palestine along the north coast of Africa and out through the Straits of Gibraltar. But Spenser's scene is Fairyland; its physical appearance has already been mentioned; it apparently has no cities, except Cleopolis which we never see, and as far as the poem tells us, no determinate physical features. Strictly the events take place *nowhere*; a castle or a cave or a lake appears when it is required by the narrative situation; but we never feel that it has been arrived at by a geographical journey. As in dreams, the situation simply calls up its appropriate setting, which becomes vividly present for a time and then disappears.

The personages exhibit a corresponding mobility. Duessa, stripped and revealed in her true nature at the end of I. viii goes off "to wander wayes unknowne", to reappear in her old state in IV; and again in V, the same in name, but with quite a different set of qualities—and curiously transformed almost into a figure of pathos in V. ix. It is only in dreams that characters have this strange quality of being the same yet not the same. Arthur's wanderings are quite undetailed: he simply appears when he is required, and it would be vain to ask where he had been or what he had been doing in the meantime. Britomart, though we see more of her and follow her more closely, has the same quality of ubiquity when wanted and total disappearance otherwise. In the quest books (I, II and V) we do indeed follow the titular hero's travels fairly continuously; but other characters simply emerge from the obscurity of the forest and vanish again into it. It is noticeable that this tendency affects characters who are important for their intrinsic worth or significance, like Arthur and Britomart. The interpolated novelle (Paridell and Hellenore, Mirabell) and long episodes of a less central kind, more dependent on pure romantic charm (the stories of Flori-mell and Serena, for example) preserve more of an ordinary narrative continuity. We seem to see Florimell only in fleeting glimpses between mysterious absences, but in fact she can always be accounted for.

To illustrate further the dream-like structure of the poem and to display more clearly its likeness to the findings of the dream-psychologists would take us beyond the limits of pure narrative structure into allegory, and that is to be discussed later. We shall try to see how condensed *The Faerie Queene* is, in spite of its length; how a single character represents a number of latent realities; how composite characters are formed, or alternatively how a single character is split up among several embodiments; how narrative sequence is used to present logical relations. These are all well-known elements of the dream-process, and *The Faerie Queene* is full of them. As it is the latent meaning that gives its purposiveness to the apparently illogical dream, so it is the latent purpose that controls the apparent planlessness of *The Faerie Queene*—though this latent meaning need not always be the straightforward Christian moral allegory that is so often proposed. We have a dream-poem; and the dream is often interpreted by Spenser himself in moral terms, because they are the only terms of conceptual analysis that he really knows or consciously attends to. But in poetry the analytic power is nearly always in arrear of the imagination; the poet-critic's explanation is of something less than the poet-creator's achievement. This is so with Spenser. At this point it is enough to notice the outward and obvious likeness to dream-organization: the emancipation from time and space, the solutions of narrative continuity, the neglect to explain what is actually presented. We read the poem as we experience a dream, with the same slight bewilderment yet sense of latent purpose; and Spenser's second thoughts about formal structure, twelve virtues and the Faerie Queene's feast occupy only a shadowy place on the fringes of consciousness. We cannot neglect them altogether (there is no law that confines a poet to his first thoughts); but they are not central. It is the animating spirit of the poem that conditions its shape; and that has very little to do with the formal scheme.

But if it is a dream, what is the dream about? We know other dream-poems, and they often tell us what they are dreaming of —*A Dream of the Rood*, *A Dream of Fair Women*. We could give no such title to Spenser's poem. It is not like *The Romance of the Rose* or even *Piers Plowman*, confined in intention to certain areas of human life and leaving others deliberately aside. It is not simply about love, or war, or religion, or morals, or history: it tries to be about them all. We have already entertained the supposition that Spenser may have read some of Tasso's Discourses; if he had he would have found there the magnificent passage on the unity-in-variety of the epic which we quoted earlier on. With a slight change of emphasis this might serve as an admirable summary of the spirit of *The Faerie Queene*.

It describes the epic as an image of the world, something encyclopaedic, including a panorama of all experience. This is the romantic epic as the sixteenth century saw it. It is different in principle from comedy, tragedy or pastoral, each of which by definition includes only a certain area of human experience. All that Tasso says can be said of *The Faerie Queene*, with one important qualification. It is an image of the world—but an image of the interior world. The conflicts, enterprises, deeds of valour and love are not there as a mimesis of the outer world in which these events physically occur. They are an image of the inner world—a huge panorama of man's inner experience, political, military, social, erotic, moral and religious. The forest is the *selva oscura* of man's life; the characters do not need to be dramatized and individualized. Primarily they are not individuals, but aspects of our experience, as in dreams. Here we pass from the outer organization of the poem to the inner, from structure to allegory.

## Chapter VI

# ALLEGORY IN *THE FAERIE QUEENE*

## I

The Last Judgement is not Fable or Allegory, but Vision.
Fable or Allegory are a totally distinct and inferior kind of
Poetry. Vision or Imagination is a Representation of what
Eternally Exists, Really and Unchangeably. Fable or Allegory
is formed by the Daughters of Memory . . . Note here that Fable
is seldom without some Vision. Pilgrim's Progress is full of it,
the Greek poets the same; but Allegory and Vision ought to be
known as two distinct things, and so called for the Sake of
Eternal Life.[1]

So Blake wrote in reference to one of his own paintings. And
what Blake wished to distinguish for the sake of eternal life
has since been distinguished in the name of literary criticism.
The distinction between allegory and some other mode, usually
seen as more authentic and more reputable, has attained the
status of a dogma from the Romantic age on. The term opposed
to allegory is not always Blake's 'vision'; symbol or symbolism
is the opposite most employed by later criticism. Coleridge in
*The Statesman's Manual* draws the contrast in this way:

Now an allegory is but a translation of abstract notions into
a picture-language which is in itself nothing but an abstraction
from objects of the senses; the principal being even more worthless than its phantom proxy. . . . On the other hand a symbol . . .
is characterized by a translucence of the special in the individual,
or of the general in the special, or of the universal in the general,
above all, by the translucence of the eternal through and in the
temporal. It always partakes of the reality which it renders
intelligible; and while it enunciates the whole, abides itself as a
living part in that unity of which it is the representative.[2]

[1] *Poetry and Prose of William Blake*, ed. Geoffrey Keynes, 1927, p. 810.
[2] Appendix B to *The Statesman's Manual*, 1816.

Yeats quotes the Blake passage, and then identifies Blake's vision with the symbolic imagination; and uses symbol as his opposite to allegory thereafter:

> A symbol is indeed the only possible expression of some invisible essence, a transparent lamp without a spiritual flame; while allegory is one of many possible representations of an embodied thing, or familiar principle, and belongs to fancy and not to imagination: the one is a revelation, the other an amusement.[1]

And C. S. Lewis in *The Allegory of Love* draws a similar contrast between allegory on the one hand, and symbolism or sacramentalism on the other:

> On the one hand you can start with an immaterial fact, such as the passions you actually experience, and can then invent *visibilia* to express them . . . this is allegory. . . . But there is another way of using the equivalence, which is almost the opposite of allegory, and which I would call symbolism or sacramentalism. If our passions, being immaterial, can be copied by material inventions, then it is possible that our material world in its turn is the copy of an invisible world. . . . The attempt to read that something else through its sensible imitations, to see the archetype in the copy, is what I mean by symbolism or sacramentalism.[2]

Blake's 'vision' is not quite the same thing as the 'symbol' of Coleridge, and Professor Lewis's 'symbolism' is slightly different again: vision for Blake is an intuitive and immediate view of super-sensible reality, symbolism for Professor Lewis is an attempt at spelling this out; and Coleridge's symbol seems to embrace Professor Lewis's, with a number of more commonplace operations as well, including even synecdoche—"the translucence of the general in the special". But in all cases the root of the antithesis is the same—it is the contrast between allegory as a kind of picture-writing, a translation into visible form of concepts that were formulated in advance, and some other process in which an object perceived is taken as a revelation of some super-sensible reality not previously apprehended.

---

[1] *Essays*, 1924, p. 142.
[2] *The Allegory of Love*, 1936, p. 44.

Yet different as they appear to be in value and direction, Blake says that there is seldom allegory without some vision, and Professor Lewis adds that symbolism and allegory are closely entwined.

Setting aside the depreciation of allegory in Blake, Coleridge and Yeats (to depreciate allegory is not Professor Lewis's business) the distinction seems to be mainly one of priority and direction. If the concept comes first and is then translated into a visible equivalent, this is allegory. If the visible object comes first and an immaterial reality is seen behind it or through it, this is symbolism. Clear enough; but it hardly seems weighty enough to account for the strong emotional colouring of the language in which the distinction is generally made. Literary distinctions do not commonly arouse much passion unless there is some other factor at work. Perhaps there is one here. It is plain, I think, that allegory, on our present definitions, does not require any particular view of the world; it is a rhetorical device, quite compatible with the blankest positivism. One could write an allegory of Dialectical Materialism (probably somebody has), or the Business Cycle. But with symbolism the case is different. If we start with the material world and see in it "the copy of an invisible world" (Lewis), if what we perceive in symbol is "the translucence of the eternal through and in the temporal" (Coleridge) it is implied that the invisible and the eternal really exist. We are not adopting a manner of speech, we are seeing something that we believe to be really there. For the Jewish people and for the Christian middle ages history was the sensible embodiment of the actual intentions of God. For Baudelaire nature is the partial evidence of a mysterious system of correspondences that actually pervades the universe. Ultimately, symbolism as generally described is compatible only with some kind of belief in the supernatural, or at least some kind of idealism. For the materialist there is no invisible or eternal world that the object could be a symbol of.

In fact a metaphysical spectre has been lurking behind the allegory-symbolism distinction. Allegory is an inferior mode because it is a pragmatic device, compatible with a purely empirical cast of mind. It abstracts certain qualities from experience, and then looks for sensible images, mere conventions of presentation, to bring them vividly tó the mind of the reader. Symbolism at least sets our foot on the platonic ladder that leads from sense experience to the ideal world, at best takes us up to the top rung in one instantaneous leap. (The social superiority of idealists to other forms of life has long been acknowledged in literary circles.) Or if we employ Coleridgean terms, allegory is a product of the mechanical fancy, symbolism of the intuitive imagination. And even if, as with Professor Lewis, there is no animus against allegory, it yet turns out to be a mere rhetorical device as against a whole mode of apprehension.

But ideally the literary critic should have no metaphysical or epistemological axes to grind. He is concerned with images used in literature, and certain ways of using them. Whether the images represent what eternally exists is not a matter on which he can form any opinion, as long as he confines himself to criticism. (As a man, of course, he is entitled to any opinion he likes.) Dante's hell was for Dante a representation of what eternally exists; for most of his modern readers it is not. But the literary phenomena remain the same. The questions the critic should ask are how the allegory-symbolism opposition works out for literature; whether it is valid, if he can decide this point; how far it is useful, if he cannot. At once he meets a peculiar feature in this case. Allegory and symbolism are irrevocably opposed, yet we are told there is seldom allegory without some symbolism (or vision), the two are closely intertwined. If this is so it is natural to ask how far it is going to prove possible to distinguish them. What principle have we for deciding whether the image or the concept came first? Nevill Coghill has recently argued that as far as *Piers Plowman* is concerned we cannot decide, unless we happen to have some quite fortuitous external evidence.[1]

And surely the opposition between the two has been made too absolute? There is a third possibility. The poet may present an

---

[1] *Some Figures in Langland's Vision.* Paper given at the Conference of the International Association of University Professors of English, Lausanne, 1959. I have seen only an abstract of this.

object or an event or a series of events in the material world, and without predicating or supposing anything about an invisible world beyond them, he can see a pattern in them—a pattern which he can recognize as having occurred before in other objects and events, and as likely to occur again. In fact he sees it as typical. Any Rake's Progress or tale of virtue rewarded will afford an example. The moral extracted from it is irrelevant; the point is that the individual tale is seen as a type; and it is often impossible to say which is primary, the pattern or the events in which it is embodied. Here we seem to have something intermediate between allegory and symbolism as defined up to now. Perhaps if the matter were pursued further we should find that there was not one intermediate but an indefinite number of gradations.

As it happens this suggestion, or something very like it, has been made by Northrop Frye, in the "Theory of Symbols" essay of his *Anatomy of Criticism*:

> Within the boundaries of literature we find a kind of sliding scale, ranging from the most explicitly allegorical, consistent with being literature at all, at one extreme, to the most elusive, anti-explicit and anti-allegorical at the other. First we meet the continuous allegories, like *The Pilgrim's Progress* and *The Faerie Queene*, and then the free-style allegories just mentioned (works of Ariosto, Goethe, Ibsen). Next come the poetic structures with a large and insistent doctrinal interest, in which the internal fictions are exempla, like the epics of Milton. Then we have, in the exact centre, works in which the structure of imagery, however suggestive, has an implicit relation only to events and ideas, and which includes the bulk of Shakespeare. Below this, poetic imagery begins to recede from example and precept and become increasingly ironical and paradoxical.[1]

Here we have a graduated scale, whose earlier gradations at any rate seem on the face of it accurately descriptive. But what has happened to symbolism? It seems to have dropped out altogether, unless it is included under "ironical and paradoxical" imagery—terms which, I confess, in this contest I do not fully understand.

In all these formulations there is one conspicuous lack. There

[1] Northrop Frye, *The Anatomy of Criticism*, Princeton, 1957, p. 91.

is no mention of plain, straightforward, univocal mimesis, innocent as far as may be of conceptual or typical suggestion altogether. Surely if allegory has a polar opposite, this must be it. I shall call it realism, not because I like the term, but because I cannot find any other. At one extreme, then, the simplest kind of allegory in which the interest of the objects and events is entirely subordinate to that of the concepts; at the other, realism, in which the interest of the concepts is entirely subordinate to that of the objects and events. It will be evident by now that I have my own formula to propose. Deprecation and persuasive rhetoric are omitted to save time; but what is said dogmatically should be read simply as suggestion towards the solution of an obviously large and complex question.

Allegory in its broadest possible sense is a pervasive element in all literature. Unlike scientific or discursive writing, literature hardly finds it possible to present actions, events, objects or characters without at least an implied reference to some wider pattern of human experience. (This is said purely empirically, not as a deduction from the nature of literature, but as an observation of the way works of literature actually behave.) Sometimes this reference is explicit and dominant, and at the extreme of this kind of literature we are aware of allegory as a formal constituent of the work. Sometimes this reference is obscured and recessive, and we shall not be inclined to use the term allegory at all, though quasi-allegorical implications are always likely to make their appearance in commentary and criticism. Allegory is naturally most at home in fictional literature (works in which there are internal characters besides the author); but it is not impossible elsewhere. The description of a landscape, for example, can be allegorical. At this point we need some technical terms. I shall use 'theme' for the moral or metaphysical 'abstract' element in allegory, and 'image' for the 'concrete' characters, actions or objects in which it is embodied.

We have then two extremes, literature in which theme is dominant, and literature in which image is dominant; and a number, perhaps a large number, of gradations in between. It is probable that the relations between theme and image vary in other ways too, besides this simple quantitative way. We have two kinds of literature, for example, in which theme and image seem equally balanced; first, that represented by Shakespeare in which the two seem completely fused and can only be separated by an act of critical violence; and second what we have vaguely called symbolism, where theme and image are separable, but where image, to use Coleridge's phrasing, "always partakes of the reality which it renders intelligible, and while it enunciates the whole, abides itself as a living part in that unity of which it is the living representative". This suggests that we might look not for a linear arrangement, but for a circular one, in which through one half of the circle we recede from simple allegory to the opposite extreme of realism, while in the other half we return towards simple allegory again, by another route.

I believe that such a circular arrangement represents the nature of the case better than any other. It can be represented diagrammatically; and since we need some means of notation for the various phases I will use the familiar figures of the clock-face for this purpose. The four key points are at twelve, three, six and nine. I shall proceed clockwise round the circle, and for each quarter I shall isolate the key point first, and then fill in the intermediate stages.

At twelve o'clock we have naïve allegory. (I borrow this term, and much of the description through the first quarter of the circle, from Northrop Frye. Indeed this whole essay is in the nature of a footnote to his treatment of the subject, to which anyone who thinks at all on these matters must be deeply indebted.) In naïve allegory theme is completely dominant, image merely a rhetorical convenience with no life of its own. In its pure form it is, as Frye puts it, "a disguised form of discursive writing, and belongs chiefly to educational literature on an elementary level: schoolroom moralities, devotional exempla, local pageants and the like." It is properly described in the terms which anti-allegorical critics use of allegory in general—a picture-writing to transcribe preconceived ideas. Where theme is so completely dominant, image tends to become incoherent, insipid or characterless; and we are on the verge of passing out of literature altogether, into moral suasion, political propaganda or what not. Naïve allegory appears in literature proper mainly in the form of small patches in long and complex works conceived on other lines; and they cannot sustain more than a very limited amount of it.

At three o'clock we have the kind of literature best represented by the work of Shakespeare, in which theme and image

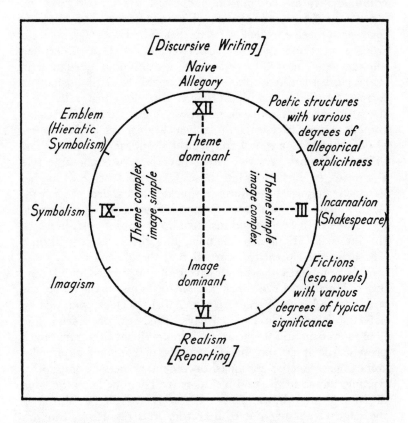

are completely fused and the relation between them is only implicit, never open or enforced. We have not yet found a name for this. For want of a better I shall call it incarnation (without any theological implication). Incarnational literature is that in which any 'abstract' content is completely absorbed in character and action and completely expressed by them. Between twelve

107

and three lie various forms of literature in which the relation
between theme and image is of varying degrees of explicitness.
At about one o'clock we have allegory proper. This differs from
naïve allegory in that, though theme is still dominant, image
now assumes a vitality and interest of its own. Here we find the
continuous formal allegories, like *The Pilgrim's Progress* and
Book I of *The Faerie Queene*. (I cannot agree with Frye, or
Spenser himself for that matter, that *The Faerie Queene* as a
whole is continuous allegory.) Between one and three, between
allegory and incarnation, there is a continuous gradation in
which close scrutiny would doubtless be able to distinguish many
forms. Briefly, at half past one we could situate 'humour'
literature and the romance of types. A good deal of Jonson's
comedy comes here, and the romance episodes in *The Faerie
Queene* that have a moral and typical significance but fall short
of pure allegory. At two are what Frye calls the freestyle
allegories, poetic fictions like those of Ariosto, Ibsen and Goethe,
in which allegorical significance is picked up and dropped at will.
At half past two we have (I quote Frye again) "the poetic
structures with a large and insistent doctrinal interest, in which
the internal fictions are exempla, like the epics of Milton."
These are the closest to incarnation at three o'clock.

This completes the first quarter of our circle, and I now
desert Northrop Frye's formulation to follow up the rest of the
circumference in different terms. At six o'clock, opposed to
naïve allegory, we find what I have called realism. Here image
is predominant and theme at a minimum. That literature which
presents itself as the direct mimesis of common experience
comes here—realist and quasi-documentary fiction, descriptive
writing and so forth. And just as naïve allegory is on the edge
of passing out of literature into discursive writing, so this is on
the edge of passing out of literature into reporting. Literary
realism is in fact a highly unstable compound. As soon as it
ceases to be mere factual reporting, that is as soon as it becomes
literature at all, the element of theme tends to grow unconsciously and turn it into something else. Zola, the great naturalist,
has had a come-back in this century as a sort of symbolist; and
no doubt this critical vagary corresponds to a tendency really

present in his work. In the quarter between three and six we have again a densely populated gradation of forms with a gradually increasing dominance of image over theme. This is pre-eminently the territory of the novel, a kind which can only live by the vitality and integrity of the image, but can accommodate very various proportions of theme. Nearest to Shakespeare we should find Tolstoy, both hedgehog and fox, moralist and observer, in still undissolved alliance. In the middle of the quarter, at half past four, is Fielding, in whom thematic interest is still strong, but beginning to come apart from his structure of images, and decidedly overshadowed by their interest and variety. With him I suppose would go most of the traditional English novelists—Dickens and Thackeray and a number of lesser Victorians. At five o'clock we pass to the professed 'realists', Flaubert and his disciples; and from there to six, 'pure' realism, the last hundred years will provide innumerable examples. But this is a crowded and complex area, although so much of it seems plain sailing. The decorum of the novel, the relation of theme and image within it, still requires a long discussion to itself.

The next quarter, from six to nine, is a difficult one, for it includes forms that, though much discussed in recent years, have not had the prolonged and familiar attention that has been given to those of the first quarter. Realism is a *ne plus ultra*; any farther in that direction takes us outside literature altogether. So now the literary circle begins to return towards allegory. At nine o'clock we find symbolism, like incarnation a form in which theme and image have equal weight, but opposed to incarnation because the relation between the two elements is different. In symbolism there is none of the harmonious wholeness of incarnational literature. Theme and image are equally present, they assert their unity, but the unity is never achieved, or if it is, it is only a unity of tension. The archetype for incarnational literature is the union of soul and body in the human person, but symbolism resists this human and accessible integrity. It seeks for the union of theme and image not through the representation of living, acting and suffering human beings, but through words as talismans, *alchimie du verbe,* or through direct visionary experience. It seems to divide itself into two realms, one a realm of stratagems and devices, *dérèglement de tous les sens*, things seen as the equivalent of concepts, fragments that mysteriously contain wholes; the other an attempt like that of Blake to *see* the invisible with all the concreteness of sense-experience.

We can understand this more clearly if we look at an intermediate phase. Between realism at six o'clock and symbolism at nine stands imagism. Realism attaches value to the thing itself rather than to the verbal image of it; it is often associated with coarseness of style and a relative indifference to verbal art. In a period when realist influence is strong an empirical, material, brass-tacks attitude is hard to escape from—we see it in Pound's early criticism. When this attitude prevails in writers whose verbal, 'poetic' interests are also strong the natural response is imagism. Here the image itself begins to acquire special value, rather than the thing that it is the image of. At the same time theme is still depreciated; it is regarded as something vague and 'abstract'. There is a growing belief that all the work of literature is done by images, not by syntax or dianoia. Poetry is 'thinking in images'. (We recognize the clichés of yesterday's criticism.) There is a tendency to regard images atomically and disjunctively, and the longer poetic units try to make their effect by the juxtaposition of images—like *The Waste Land* or Pound's *Cantos*—theme is only allowed to make its appearance surreptitiously. We are presented simply with petals on wet black boughs and must make what we can of them.

This is the intermediate stage, somewhere about half past seven, between realism and symbolism. (I am aware that this is not the historical sequence.) But imagism, like realism itself, is an unstable compound. When brooded over to this degree images tend to acquire magical properties. They engage in mysterious correspondences and enter into occult relations with vision. When this happens imagism passes over into symbolism. And with symbolism we enter the last quarter and are already well on our way back to naïve allegory again.

But as before there is an intermediate stage. Half-way between symbolism and naïve allegory we have what I will call emblem or hieratic symbolism. It exists largely outside literature—its special field is iconography and religious imagery. There is a tendency for symbolism to become fixed; the image shrinks and becomes stereotyped, and theme expands. We think of emblems like the cross or the marriage ring, heraldic devices or of various sacramental objects—baptismal water, oil of consecration. There is perhaps no literature written entirely in this mode, unless some of the more gnomic sacred scriptures, wisdom of the East, etc. But in much literature, especially of an occult kind, it is a strong element. Yeats uses imagery in this way. The scope of emblem or hieratic symbolism is both limited and inflexible. Its strong thematic interest, as far as literature is concerned, is always likely to carry it over into naïve allegory where image is more flexible and obedient. And so by a commodious vicus of recirculation we come back to our starting point.

II

With this armament at our disposal we can look more closely at the allegory of *The Faerie Queene*. We can I think determine Spenser's field of operation. It extends from eleven o'clock to two—from hieratic symbolism through naïve allegory, allegory proper and the romance of types to the freestyle allegory where thematic significance is picked up and dropped at will. Its centre is in allegory proper. There is a little hieratic symbolism, in the heraldic devices borne by the knights—the red cross, the figure of Cupid in Scudamour's shield and in some of the pictorial set-pieces such as the procession of the seven deadly sins. There are patches of naïve allegory, as in the castle of Alma and a number of minor figures. On the other hand much of Book IV is less explicit than allegory proper; it consists of romance stories with a typical significance: and in the pastoral episodes of Book VI allegory is only faintly and intermittently present and often seems to disappear altogether. But we rightly feel that these are the outlying areas of *The Faerie Queene*. Its core is in the long sustained allegorical portions—Books I and II and the central narrative threads of Books III and V. However near Spenser may come to 'humanizing' his characters (and he sometimes comes

very near) he never touches the confines of incarnational literature—he never embodies his themes in the completely rounded
and individual representation of a human person. And on the
other side, symbolism, in either the verbal or the visionary
sense, is quite alien to Spenser's mode of perception.

All this is quite unhistorical. Since Spenser is a conscious and
acknowledged allegorist it is now appropriate to inquire how he
himself conceived of allegory, or is likely to have conceived of it.
Apart from the internal evidence of *The Faerie Queene* itself we
have a little Spenserian documentation, in the letter to Raleigh,
and a great deal of documentation derived from contemporary
critical works and from Spenser's earlier models.

In the letter to Raleigh Spenser calls *The Faerie Queene* "a
continued Allegory, or darke conceit". 'Dark' in Elizabethan
literary discourse steadily means obscure; and 'conceit' in this
context means conception, idea, thought. Allegory then is an
obscure conception that needs explanation. And Spenser "knowing how doubtfully all Allegories may be construed" sets out in
the letter "to discover unto you the general intention and
meaning, which in the whole course thereof I have fashioned,
without expressing of any particular purposes or by-accidents
therein occasioned". Courthope acutely points out that in fact
he hardly does this.[1] Most of the letter is far more concerned
with plan and narrative structure than with allegorical intention
as such—that is, more concerned with the disposition of the
images than with discovering the theme hidden behind them.
Here at the beginning we get a strong though unintentional hint
that as far as the structure of *The Faerie Queene* as a whole is
concerned allegory is not so decisive a factor, theme not so
dominant over image, as we have sometimes been led to expect.
This is reinforced by the conclusion we reached in the previous
chapter—that the conventions of romantic epic, the desire to
reconcile the antique unity with modern variety, had a great
deal to do with giving the poem its general shape. And this has
nothing to do with allegory at all.

Nor is the central idea as the letter expounds it expressly
allegorical: "To fashion a gentleman or noble person in vertuous

[1] W. J. Courthope, *History of English Poetry*, vol. II, 1897, p. 248.

and gentle discipline", and to present this "coloured with an historical fiction", is the announced "generall end" of all the book; that is to portray the ideal knight in the person of Prince Arthur. This is no more allegorical than the *Aeneid*; and in what sense the *Aeneid* is allegorical we shall have to inquire in a moment. But then Spenser goes farther. Besides choosing Prince Arthur for historical and heroic (and Tassonian) reasons, "as most fitte for the excellency of his person, being made famous by many men's former workes, and also furthest from the daunger of envy, and suspition of present time", he has chosen him to represent Magnificence, that virtue which "according to Aristotle and the rest" is the sum and perfection of all the virtues. We may then be permitted to ask in what sense Arthur represents magnificence. Surely not in the same sense as Ate represents strife, Furor anger, or Despair despair. These personages carry their *significatio* in their names and have no other function but to illustrate it. Ate and Furor are figures of naïve allegory, or something not much more advanced; Despair, splendidly and sombrely dramatized, is a figure of true allegory at its richest and most expressive. All three are created out of thematic needs. But Arthur is not of this kind. His existence as a mythico-historic figure, a perfect knight, a wise leader, and a British leader at that, is logically anterior to the thematic idea of magnificence. The process by which the Arthur-Magnificence fusion is created is surely more akin to the *allegorizing* of an existing story than to allegory in its pure form. Does anyone feel when Arthur sets off in pursuit of Florimell (III. i. 18) that Magnificence is about to succour Distressed Beauty? Not in the least. A knight is going to the rescue of a lovely lady, inspired by the usual mixed chivalric motives. We can see that they are mixed because they are contrasted with those of Britomart, which are not, in the next stanza—

> The whiles faire Britomart, whose constant mind,
> Would not so lightly follow beauties chase,
> Ne reckt of Ladies Love, did stay behind.

There is nothing blatantly incompatible with Arthur's ascribed character here, but he is not really behaving like Magnificence;

he is behaving like Rinaldo in the first canto of the *Furioso*.
And even in less unguarded moments he never seems to
represent Magnificence in any explicit fashion. A brave knight,
able to succour the other knights in times of distress by his
courage and military prowess; and that is all.

Red Cross on the other hand stands for Holiness, Guyon for
Temperance, and Artegall for Justice in quite a different way.
We see each vanquishing the temptations appropriate to his
condition. Red Cross has to face the dangers that beset the
religious life—Pride and Despair; Guyon the seductions of the
flesh and the passions; Artegall battles with unjust external foes.
We never see Arthur in any distinct moral relation at all. What
we seem to find is a number of local allegories of considerable
clarity embedded in a framework that is only allegorical in a
vaguer and more general sense. This may amount to a "continued Allegory, or darke conceit"; in Spenser's estimation it
apparently did; but it certainly does not justify what is sometimes attempted—an unremitting allegorical interpretation,
conducted on the same level throughout.

A better illustration would be the figure of Britomart, since
she is far more fully drawn than Arthur and we see more of her.
She is the titular hero of a book, and with her magic lance, her
invulnerability, and her ability to rescue other lovers in distress
or failure she is a worthy representation of Chastity—chastity
in Spenser's special sense of faithful, pure and honourable love.
When she passes through the flame that guards the house of
Busirane (III. xi), the flame that Scudamour, the less perfect,
the merely erotic lover is unable to pass, she is behaving
allegorically. I shall try to avoid making too many direct
translations of image into theme, for the proper way to read
allegory is the same as the proper way to read any other
literature—to apprehend as far as may be, the living whole; but
here it is necessary to make my point. And surely the thematic
meaning here is that a wholly pure and selfless love is immune
to sensual obstacles and disturbances that can be fatal to even a
devoted love of a lesser kind. But in III. ii we see Britomart
portrayed in quite another way. She has seen the vision of
Artegall in the magic mirror, she has fallen in love with him,

she pines, and her nurse tries to comfort her. But she will not
be comforted.

> These idle words (said she) doe nought asswage
> My stubborne smart, but more annoyance breed,
> For no no usuall fire, no usuall rage
> It is, O Nurse, which on my life doth feed.

> Sithens it hath infixed faster hold
> Within my bleeding bowels, and so sore
> Now ranckleth in this same frail fleshly mould,
> That all mine entrailes flow with poysnous gore,
> And th'ulcer growth daily more and more;
> Ne can my running sore find remedie,
> Other then my hard fortune to deplore,
> And languish as the leafe falne from the tree,
> Till death make one end of my dayes and miserie.
>
> (III. ii. 27–29)

This is no representation of chastity; it is a proud girl in the
grip of what she fears is a disastrous passion. And in V. vi. 12–14,
when she hears of Artegall in the power of Radigund, she is
plainly a jealous young woman, and she is compared to a froward
child who "kicks and squals, and shriekes for fell despight".

We then remember Britomart's literary ancestry. She is a
reincarnation of Bradamante of the *Orlando Furioso*, one of a long
line of warrior maidens who love and fight through the romantic
epic—romantic heroines, not allegorical personifications; and
Britomart partakes of their nature, whatever her activities as a
type of chastity. We begin to suspect that allegory was conceived by Spenser in a more relaxed and intermittent way than
many of his modern interpreters would have us suppose.

This suspicion is confirmed when we look at the contemporary
interpretations of Ariosto. There are of course a few passages in
Ariosto that are overtly allegorical—the Alcina and Logistilla
episodes, for example, with their antithesis of passion and
reason; and the passage in XIV. 76 seq. where Silence and
Discord are summoned to bring aid to Charles besieged in Paris.
They are few, comparatively short, and quite distinct in method
from the general run of the narrative. But a very few years after
the appearance of the *Furioso* we find that the poem as a whole,

including some of the most obviously romantic and fantastic episodes, begins to be subjected to allegorical interpretation. This is simply the continuation of a very old practice, nearly as old as epic poetry itself, by which all the great epics were read as allegories. This habit of mind is foreign to us, and we must again diverge from *The Faerie Queene* itself in order to understand the tradition in which Spenser was working.

## III

The allegorizing of Homer[1] goes back as far as the pre-Socratics. As early as the sixth century B.C. protests were made against the fanciful and immoral Homeric mythology. Defenders of Homer replied by saying that the superficial sense was not the true one, there was a deeper meaning (ὑπόνοια, it was not called 'allegory' till some centuries later). Theagenes (fl. 525 B.C.) suggested a twofold allegory, moral and physical. The names of the gods express either mental faculties in man or the elements in nature—Apollo is fire, Poseidon water, Pallas wisdom, Hermes intelligence. This is perhaps little more than an attempt to exorcize the more inconveniently human aspects of the gods by identifying them with their functions. Other allegorizations were more far-fetched. Anaxagoras early in the fifth century saw an elaborate emblem of the rules of dialectic in the web of Penelope. His pupils interpreted the Homeric myths in a moral sense. Cleanthes of Assos at the end of the third century found fanciful allegories in Homer, and his is the earliest known use of the word ἀλληγορικός.[2] With Plato the moral objections to the mythology of Homer revived, and in the Republic there is no other remedy but censorship. Among the neo-Platonists, however, allegorical interpretations were proposed. The discourse of Porphyry (A.D. 233–301) *On the Cave of the Nymphs* is an elaborate commentary on *Odyssey* XIII. 102–112, in which the cave is treated as an allegory of the universe and the fate of the soul within it. In most of these cases

[1] See S. E. Sandys, *History of Classical Scholarship*, 1903, vol. I, p. 29 seq.; and E. R. Curtius, *European Literature and the Latin Middle Ages*, trans. Willard Trask, 1953, pp. 203–7.
[2] Sandys, op. cit., p. 147.

the purpose is to give an acceptable meaning to something that was on the face of it either indecorous or morally neutral. In Porphyry, as is usual with neo-Platonists on poetry, we find rather the construction of a free philosophical fantasia, using the poem as the merest pretext.

By the time commentaries on Virgil begin to make their appearance the allegorizing of heroic poetry was already well-established. Allegorical commentaries on the *Aeneid* were produced by Donatus in the fourth century, by Servius and Macrobius in the fifth. There is not the same necessity to excuse Virgil for the immorality of his tales about the gods; but for the early Christian centuries the same sort of problem appears in another form. How is the Christian to be excused for reading these false pagan fables? The answer is that they conceal a store of moral and religious truth. The most elaborate allegory is that of Fulgentius, *Virgiliana Continentia*, (*c.* 530); and the allegorical interpretation was accepted by Bernardus Silvestris, John of Salisbury, as well as by Dante. Nor was it abandoned during the Renaissance. Cristoforo Landino, a member of the famous Platonic academy of Florence, wrote the *Disputationes Camaldulenses* about 1470. In Books III and IV Alberti, a fellow-academician, is represented as producing an elaborate allegory of the first six books of the *Aeneid*.[1] It is a lengthy argument explaining the travels of Aeneas as an allegory of the soul, forsaking all earthly passions, symbolized by Troy, struggling with the perturbations of the senses and passions, and ultimately arriving in the true heavenly kingdom. There are two loves, a true and divine one, and a false and earthly one. Paris gives himself to the false love and perishes with Troy, Aeneas gives himself to the true celestial love, and *si non recta navigatione* (*id enim humanae conditioni, aut nunquam, aut raro conceditur, ut eodem tempore et stulticiam exuat, et sapiens efficiatur*) *tamen post multos errores, in Italiam ad veram sapientiam pervenit*.[2] Much is made of the antithesis between heavenly and earthly love; the authority of Plato is constantly cited, sometimes in the same breath with

---

[1] *In P. Virgilii Maronis Allegorias*, printed with Hortensius *In Virgilium*, Basel, 1577, p. 3000 seq.
[2] ibid., p. 3007.

that of St. Paul and Dionysius the Areopagite—in short this is a typical Renaissance neo-Platonic document. And yet when all is said the extravagant platonizing only extracts the archetypal pattern that actually underlies the story—the leaving of a city of destruction, the perilous voyage, the coming to a land of promise. With this plot, so naturally analogous to the story of Israel, captive, wandering and restored, or to the individual pilgrim's progress, it can never have been hard to turn Virgil into an honorary Christian poet.

About fifty years later than Landino, Ariosto was writing the *Furioso*, in the last days of Italian freedom, and in the last days of Renaissance liberty of expression. The carefree atmosphere of the court of Ferrara was not long to subsist. Within thirty years of the publication of the poem, Counter-Reformation rigidity and the fear of ecclesiastical authority had already begun to make some excuse for its irresponsibility and licence seem desirable. And of course the time-honoured remedy was applied—the poem was an allegory. There are indeed considerable areas of explicit allegory in the *Furioso*, as we have seen in an earlier chapter. What we are discussing now is something different. It is the deliberate allegorizing of that far more extensive part of the poem where the unsophisticated reader would see only simple romance. From the fifteen-forties[1] on almost every edition of the poem appears "con le allegorie", "con le nuove allegorie", "con l'allegorie a ciascun canto di Thomaso Porcacchi", and the more popular allegorical annotations were reprinted many times. In addition, separate commentaries on the poem were published. Two were available by Spenser's time—Fornari's *Spositione sopra l'Orlando Furioso* (1549) and Toscanella's *Bellezze del Furioso* (1574).[2]

Toscanella has not a great deal to say about allegory, but he provides at the beginning a list of the allegorical equivalents of the principal characters, and some allegorical suggestions in

---

[1] The first edition with 'allegories' attached was published at Venice in 1542.

[2] These allegorizers of Ariosto are discussed by S. J. McMurphy in *Spenser's Use of Ariosto for Allegory*, Seattle, 1924. Miss McMurphy was in error in supposing that Porcacchi's allegories came too late to be used by Spenser. They first appeared in 1568, and were several times reprinted. Oratio Toscanella's *Bellezze del Furioso* was printed at Venice in 1574.

the introductions to the several cantos. Fornari's[1] work is in
two parts; the first is a minute commentary, mainly mythological
and historical; in the second (1550) he undertakes the allegorical
explanation of the poem. An introduction *Agli Studiosi Lettori*
explains that all through nature the most precious things are
hidden, like jewels in the earth; so it is with the meanings of the
poets. According to Anaxagoras, the Pythagoreans and the
Platonists, things above correspond with things below, and the
poets in describing material and earthly things often signify
heavenly ones. It is right and sanctioned by ancient usage to
hide the most precious thoughts from the unworthy in this way;
besides, by this means sound doctrine is insinuated under the
delights of fiction. Coming to Ariosto in particular, as he need
give way to none of the ancient poets in ingenious and delightful inventions, so in moral fiction he surpasses and leaves behind
all others. The parts of the poem most suited for this kind of
interpretation are the stories of Ruggiero and Astolfo, which
Fornari then proceeds to expound.

It is impossible to say how much of this exegesis Spenser
used, but that he did use it, and turn it to good purpose, is quite
clear from internal evidence. Editions with allegories were also
very much more numerous than those without. Some writers
have suggested that it was a sort of British or puritan obtuseness
in Spenser that made him read the irresponsible Ariosto as
allegory. This is mere ignorance. Spenser read Ariosto in the
manner of the Italians of his time. So, it would appear, did
others. Harington, who cannot be suspected of undue rigour,
who is quite capable of producing a slyly tolerant defence of the
poem, also regards it as allegorical, on more than one level.[2]

When in the *Orlando Furioso* we meet Bradamante, with her
high spirit, her devotion and her very human jealousy, she does
not appear to be an allegorical character at all. However, for
Fornari she represents sacred or spiritual love; for Porcacchi

---

[1] Simone Fornari, *La Spositione sopra l'Orlando Furioso*, first part Florence,
1549, second part Florence, 1550.

[2] Sir John Harington, *Orlando Furioso in English heroical verse*, 1591. See the
preface "or rather a Briefe Apologie of Poetry" prefixed to the translation, and the
Allegory of the Poem appended to it. This latter is mostly from Fornari. The
preface is also reprinted in G. Gregory Smith's *Elizabethan Critical Essays*, 1904.

she is *pudicizia*; for another anonymous allegorist (Venice, 1588) she is *virtù congiunto con la ragione*; while for Toscanella she is simply a portrait of an affectionate and devoted wife. It is easy to see how these suggestions, or some of them, or others like them, could combine to produce Britomart, the brave, loving and devoted girl who is at the same time the symbol of chastity —in Spenser's special sense of honourable love. I am inclined to believe that he used Porcacchi, for with his frequent vagueness in rendering abstract terms from other languages (his temperance is Aristotle's continence, his magnificence is Aristotle's megalopsychia) *pudicizia* could easily have been translated by the not very distant chastity.[1] Similarly Atlante the enchanter, from whose castle Bradamante liberates prisoners as Britomart liberates Amoret, represents Lust for Fornari, Love for Toscanella and Porcacchi—and for Porcacchi, love described specifically as an *appetito*. Here we have clearly the origin of Busirane and his house. (Professor Lewis identifies Busirane with Courtly Love.) The suggestion must come from the commentators, for in the poem itself it is by no means plain that Atlante has anything to do with sensual appetite at all.

It is noticeable that these allegorical commentaries are extremely arbitrary and capricious. Toscanella in the "allegory of the proper names" at the beginning of the *Bellezze* equates Atlante with Love; but in the commentary to canto iv he identifies him with Time, and gives quite a different explanation of the whole canto. The choice of passages for allegorical interpretation also seems largely fortuitous, and other parts of the narrative are left unexplained. In the commentary on canto i. for example, Porcacchi concentrates on the perturbation of Rinaldo, Ferraù and Sacripante at not being able to enjoy Angelica, and says that it shows how often the heavens are contrary to the desires of men. He then goes on to explain (very feebly) the two fountains of love and disdain. Toscanella and an anonymous allegorist of 1588, on the other hand, are struck by the pride and ingratitude of Angelica in refusing worthy suitors; and say nothing about the fountains at all. Fornari confines his allegorizing to two parts of the plot—the first, Ruggiero's

---

[1] Though in fact *pudicizia* appears as Shamefastness in the House of Alma.

story, being obviously a moral allegory; the second a fantastic tale easily susceptible to recondite explanation. And he particularly deprecates the industrious extracting of allegories from unpromising places. Often the alleged allegories are mere statements of the most obvious implications of the narrative. Rinaldo is angry and in love, he therefore represents anger and the effects of love. Medoro and Cloridano are devoted to their lord and to each other; they therefore represent feudal and mutual devotion; and so on. I deduce from this that in reading Ariosto as he did Spenser must have become completely habituated to *discontinuous* allegory, which can be picked up and dropped at will; and to a conception of allegory that is often enough fulfilled by the simplest moral implications drawn from a pre-existing romantic tale.

The allegorical interpretation of Tasso followed a different course. He wrote the allegory for the *Jerusalem Delivered* himself.[1] He suffered great anxiety about the orthodoxy of his poem and constantly suspected that it was about to be condemned by the Inquisition; and the allegory is an afterthought designed to vindicate the purity of his intentions. It is far more complete and consistent than the allegorizings of Ariosto, and aims at exhibiting the whole poem as a "continued allegory or dark conceit", showing that it was all informed by a single idea. Tasso sees all earlier epic poetry as conceived in this way. The *Odyssey* and the *Comedy* of Dante are types of the life of the contemplative man; civil life is 'shadowed' in the *Iliad*; and the *Aeneid* shows a mixture of the active and the contemplative. For his own poem Tasso establishes a hierarchy of the virtues on Platonic lines. "The army compounded of divers princes, and of other Christian soldiers, signifieth Man, compounded of soul and body, and of a soul not simple, but divided into many and diverse powers." Goffredo signifies the Understanding, "lord over the other virtues of soul and body". Rinaldo stands for the Ireful Virtue, next in dignity to the virtue of reason itself; since "Rinaldo, which in Action is in the second degree of honour, ought also to be placed in the Allegory in the answerable degree". The other

---

[1] I quote from Fairfax's translation of *G.L.* 1600. The Allegory is to be found on p. 436 seq. of Henry Morley's edition of Fairfax, 1890.

Princes are in lieu of the other powers of the soul, and the body is figured by the less noble soldiers. The resemblance to the Arthur passages in the letter to Raleigh can hardly be missed; and though Tasso adheres to Plato not Aristotle it is surely here rather than in any authentic inspiration from Aristotle that we are to look for the source of the idea of Magnificence and the twelve virtues. If this is so, our suspicion that this part of the plan is a second thought finds confirmation. Spenser cannot have known Tasso till after *The Faerie Queene* had been begun.

There are other likenesses too between Spenser's allegory and Tasso's. We have in both the same sense that the romantic and sentimental episodes tend to escape from the allegory altogether, the same sense of a mind that is deeply desirous of unity of being, but still in some degree divided between the erotic and sensuous on the one hand, the moral and spiritual on the other. But Spenser is less inclined to psychologize than Tasso, and his vast varied composition is far more recalcitrant to such a process. We could at a pinch concede that the *Jerusalem* might be taken to represent the structure of the soul—the hierarchy of the Christian army typifying the hierarchy of mental powers, the external war representing the internal psychomachia. But even in the Letter Spenser hardly insists on the figures of Arthur and the knights as internal constituents of the soul. They rather seem to represent their several virtues as active in the world. This way of interpreting epic narrative as typical psychology is neo-Platonic. We find it in Porphyry and Landino. But I can see no sign that Spenser had read Landino at all. The lofty Platonic tone, lifting the true meaning of a poem above the sphere of earthly experience altogether, is not that of *The Faerie Queene*. Love in *The Faerie Queene*, however nobly and tenderly idealized, remains love that hopes for an earthly fruition; it cannot be translated into the heavenly love which *ad divinam nos pulchritudinem rapiat*; nor does Spenser suggest that it should. For this reason the comprehensive metaphysical-psychological allegory that we find in Landino and Tasso is not really his chosen method. The mazy diversity of actual moral and erotic experience is his field, and the discontinuous, capricious allegorizing of the commentators on Ariosto was more influential with him.

IV

Other forces may have been at work in the same direction. Allegory is a standard rhetorical term in Spenser's day. It is one of the tropes defined in all the rhetoric books. It is true that the definitions are not particularly illuminating; but they do give us a general sense of what the word meant to the sixteenth century. It always means something very short, and is always closely connected with metaphor. The most compendious statement I have found is in Peacham's *Garden of Eloquence*:

> Allegoria, called of Quintilian, Inversio, is a Trope of a sentence, or forme of speech which expresseth one thing in words, and another in sense. In a Metaphore there is a translation of one word only, in an Allegorie of many, and for that cause an Allegorie is called a continued Metaphore.[1]

Like the other English rhetoricians Peacham is derivative. He draws his material from Susenbrotus, Melanchthon, and Robert and Henry Etienne; so it is not surprising that the same sort of definition and the same relation to metaphor is found in the other English rhetorical writers. Angel Day in *The English Secretarie* defines allegoria as:

> . . . a kind of inverting or change of sense, as when we shew one thing in words, and signify another in meaning: a Trope most usual among us, even in our common speaking, as when we say, Bow the with while it is green, meaning to correct children whilest they be young: or, There is no fire without smoake, meaning that there is no ill conceipt without occasion: or, I smell a Rat, that is, I know your meaning.[2]

And he makes the distinction from metaphor simply that metaphor is a "Trope of words", that is, it is confined to a single word, while allegory extends through a whole sentence. And rather earlier Puttenham had written at great length in the same sense:

---

[1] Henry Peacham, *The Garden of Eloquence*, 1593, p. 25. (This is the second edition.)

[2] Angel Day, *The English Secretarie*, n.d., but actually 1595. Part II, p. 79.

123

> *Allegoria* is when we do speake in sence translative and
> wrested from his own signification, nevertheless applied to
> another not altogether contrary, but having much conveniencie
> with it as before we said of the metaphore: as for example if we
> should call the common wealth a ship; the Prince a Pilot, The
> Counsellors mariners, the stormes warres, the calm and haven
> peace, this is spoken all in allegorie: and because such inversion
> of sence in one single worde is by the figure *Metaphore*, of whom
> we spake before, and this manner of inversion extending to
> whole and large speeches, it maketh the figure *allegorie* to be
> called a long and perpetuall Metaphore.[1]

The most notable feature of these definitions is that allegory
is typically considered to be a matter of a single sentence.
Puttenham, who gives it the widest range, allows it to extend to
"whole and large speeches". But the rhetoricians' definitions
never consider allegory as the informing principle of a whole
work. They also insist that it is a common feature of our
ordinary discourse—"a trope most usual among us in our
ordinary speaking" (Day); or as Puttenham puts it, "The use of
this figure is so large, and his vertue of so great efficacie as it is
supposed no man can pleasantly utter and persuade without it."
How can we suppose Spenser to have been affected by this conception of allegory? First, apart from the idea of an allegorical
structure underlying a whole poem, there would have been
present to his mind the normal rhetorical conception of allegory
as a short form; and when he speaks of *The Faerie Queene* as a
'continued allegory' a good deal of stress should fall on 'continued'. He is aware that he is making a more extended use of
allegory than the normal. As allegory is a continued metaphor,
*The Faerie Queene* is a continued allegory. But this need not
mean continuous and uninterrupted—simply that he is using
allegory continually, in our popular sense of the word 'continually', to mean 'repeatedly' or 'pervasively'. And the
general insistence on allegory as a common feature of all discourse would allow for a great deal of only half conscious,
'natural' allegory, no more deliberate than the ordinary use of
metaphor in ordinary speech. I do not wish to make too much of

[1] G. Puttenham, *The Art of English Poesie*, 1589, Book III, chap. XVIII. The
whole chapter is relevant.

this, but I think we can derive from the rhetorical definitions a useful warning against pressing too hard on Spenser's allegorical purpose, against the relentless discovery of deliberately inserted allegorical intentions at every point. The consistency we are to expect is the kind of consistency we should expect from the metaphors in a long poem—that various in kind and material as they may be, they should all subserve a consistent tone and purpose. And as in the metaphorical content of a long poem we should expect a good many 'accidents' as well as 'intendments', so we should in the allegorical content of *The Faerie Queene*; particularly since Spenser has expressly told us to do so.

v

We have been speaking up to now of the formal principles of allegory in *The Faerie Queene* and have said little or nothing about its actual content; for this is almost co-extensive with the poem itself and is so shifting and various that it can only be discussed in direct commentary on the several books. But there is one constant preoccupation among the scholiasts on Spenser that can be discussed briefly now, both in its formal and material aspects; and some of it put out of the way for good. This is the so-called historical allegory. It has given rise to voluminous and unhelpful commentary, it is a stumbling-block to most readers of the poem, as far as they allow themselves to consider it; yet it is indubitably there, and it is necessary to realize the limits of its importance.

In the first place the poem is called *The Faerie Queene*, and by that Faerie Queene, Spenser tells us in the Letter, he means glory in general intention, "but in my particular I conceive the most excellent and glorious person of our soveraine the Queene, and her kingdom in Faery land." Queen Elizabeth, then, is the eponymous heroine, and a romantic glorification of the Queen and her England is very near to Spenser's central intention—however little she may appear in the structure as it stands. Spenser also tells us that she is otherwise 'shadowed' as Belphoebe; and though he does not tell us this, she appears

125

equally clearly as the Mercilla of Book V. Britomart is among her ancestors, and may, if we care, be supposed to bear among other attributes a foreshadowing of her qualities. Nor is this all. The announced general hero is Arthur, the legendary embodiment of the glory of Britain, in love with the Faerie Queene, and again one of the historical Queen Elizabeth's putative forebears. So, even though it is not clearly apparent in the existing narrative structure, the spirit of dynastic and national panegyric pervades the whole poem. It would be strange if it did not. Besides all that we know of the expanding national consciousness of Spenser's time, we must add that it is part of the *genre* in which he is writing. As Northrop Frye has put it, the centripetal gaze, directed to a court or a sovereign, is the typical note of the high mimetic style. To be more specific, it goes back at least as far as the *Aeneid* with its glorification of Augustus; and both Ariosto and Tasso are celebrating, in their several ways, the glories of the house of Este. Legendary genealogies, mythical history, and visionary anachronistic links between past and present are the ordinary procedure of such things.

Secondly there is, very unevenly distributed, a good deal of intermittent allusion to contemporary persons and events. Its extent and importance has been much disputed, but there are places where it is unmistakable. What is called the historical allegory therefore divides itself into two aspects, one the general encomium on England and her Queen, the other an occasional specific comment on current affairs. There can be little doubt that the first is the more important of the two.

For his general glorification of England Spenser employs what may be called the political mythology of his day. It is now well known that part of the elaborate apparatus of history and legend by which the Tudors established their dominance over the English imagination was their claim to be descendants of the ancient kings of Britain. The matter is illustrated at length in Greenlaw's *Studies in Spenser's Historical Allegory*,[1] and it is discussed by Dr. Tillyard in his book on Shakespeare's histories. Not only did Henry VII in his person unite the rival roses and

[1] Edwin Greenlaw, *Studies in Spenser's Historical Allegory*, Baltimore, 1932.

bring to an end a long period of civil strife, but he fulfilled an old prophecy. The case is summarily stated in Hall's chronicle:

> It was by a hevenly voice reveled to Cadwalader last kyng of Brytons that his stock and progeny should reigne in this land and beare dominion again: Whereupon most men were persuaded in their awne opinion that by this heavenly voice he [i.e. Hy vii] was provided and ordeined long before to enjoye and obteine this kyngdome.[1]

Henry in fact, according to this story, was the heir of Brut, grandson of Aeneas, the mythical founder of Britain; and even more important for Spenser's purpose, he was the heir of Arthur. Henry himself recognized the political value of this by giving his eldest son the name of Arthur. This Prince Arthur died young, but the legendary succession was easily transferred to his brother, Henry VIII, who was in fact hailed as Arturus Redivivus. This return of the ancient line of Arthur was an important topic for the Tudor chroniclers and antiquaries, and was frequently celebrated in pageants and royal entertainments in Queen Elizabeth's reign. The prime source for the history of the ancient British kings is Geoffrey of Monmouth, their story had been elaborated by later chroniclers, and the more striking parts of it were taken over by the poets and dramatists. The history had also been attacked, notably by Polydore Vergil in Henry VII's reign, who is scornful of Geoffrey and distinctly ironical about the story of Arthur. This un-British scepticism (Polydore was an Italian) called forth a strong response from the traditionalists—chroniclers, antiquaries and poets; and to their party Spenser naturally belonged.[2] In making Arthur the hero of his poem he was not only celebrating the legendary British hero, but the supposedly historic ancestor of the Tudor line.[3]

Had Queen Elizabeth been a king his course would have been simple; Prince Arthur would simply have been the type of his sixteenth-century successor. But a queen cannot be personally

[1] Quoted in Greenlaw, p. 9.
[2] Greenlaw, op. cit., chap. I.
[3] It is noticeable that though Malory was read, he exerted little influence in Tudor times. It is the historical British Arthur, not the hero of French romances, that the Elizabethans cared for. Hence the absence of direct debt to Malory in Spenser.

Arturus Redivivus; she must then become his destined bride.
And this introduces an additional element of romantic vagueness
into Spenser's honorific genealogies. In II. x Arthur at the house
of Alma reads the book called *Briton Moniments*, and in it
traces his own ancestry down to the time of Uther Pendragon
his father. His exclamation at the end of the recital shows the
spirit in which we are to read it:

> At last quite ravisht with delight, to heare
> The royall offspring of his native land,
> Cryde out, Dear countrey, O how dearely deare
> Ought thy remembrance, and perpetuall band
> Be to thy foster Childe, that from they hand
> Did commun breath and nouriture receave?
> How brutish is it not to understand,
> How much to her we owe, that all us gave,
> That gave unto us all, what ever good we have.
>
> (II. x. 69)

In III. iii Britomart is shown by Merlin the tale of her
descendants; a place is ingeniously found for her and Artegall in
the succession (she is inserted into the chronicle history, without
authority from the chronicles, just after Arthur) and from their
offspring the line continues down to the time of Elizabeth herself.

> Then shall a royal virgin raine, which shall
> Stretch her wide rod over the Belgicke shore,
> And the great Castle smite so sore withall,
> That it shall make him shake, and shortly learn to fall.
>
> (III. iii. 49)

On the other hand the Faerie Queene, who is also Elizabeth,
is provided with a purely fanciful genealogy. While Arthur is
reading his *Briton Moniments* in II. x Guyon is equally eagerly
devouring a book called the *Antiquitie of Faerie Land*, which
traces the forebears of Tanaquil-Gloriana from the original
Elf and Fay through such monarchs as Elfin, Elfinan and
Elfinell—all apparently creatures of Spenser's own fancy, though
clear enough glances at Henry VII (Elficleos), the young prince
Arthur (Elferon), and Henry VIII (Oberon) occur at the end of
the story (St. 75).

# ALLEGORY IN *THE FAERIE QUEENE*

So Queen Elizabeth is furnished with two genealogies, one supposedly historic, through the British kings, and one purely in the fairy line. In the face of this it is surely impossible to distinguish clearly (as Greenlaw and others try to do) between British and fairy knights, or to see any subtle significance behind the distinction between Britain and Fairy Land. The Britain of *The Faerie Queene* is England, and so is Fairy Land. British knights are symbolically English champions, and fairy knights no less. Gloriana stands for Elizabeth the historic Tudor princess, on the one hand; and on the other for Elizabeth the half-magical object of a nation's devotion. And this is hardly *allegory* at all. It is a piece of legendary and historical machinery, immensely important in most epic poetry, which links the supposed time of the story both backward to a still remoter past and forward to the present. It gives *The Faerie Queene* its extremely un-Italian, autochthonously British air, while at the same time assimilating it in spirit to the Latin and Italian poems that were its forerunners.

The second element in the historical 'allegory' (if we are to call it allegory) is the intermittent allusion to contemporary events and persons. It has been a happy hunting ground for fruitless and misguided ingenuity. Some of the allusions were naturally recognized in Spenser's own day; but the idea that all the principal knights are contemporary portraits has no Elizabethan authority; it goes back no further than Dryden. Dryden, in the *Discourse on the Original and Progress of Satire* in 1693, said that "the original of every knight was then living in the court of Queen Elizabeth; and he attributed to each of them that virtue which he thought most conspicuous in them". Dryden must have got the idea from Spenser's dedicatory sonnets to *The Faerie Queene*, in which a number of famous persons are promised immortality by the poet. But carefully read, the sonnets do not bear this interpretation. The immortality promised by the poet is guaranteed by the rehearsing of these distinguished names in the sonnets themselves, and by their association with so great a subject. However, the idea of *The Faerie Queene* as a historical and political *roman à clef* was continued by Warton, by the early editors Upton and Todd, and confirmed by Sir Walter Scott. The principal modern monument of this line of thinking is Miss Winstanley's edition of Book I, which treats the whole book as a disguised transcript of Tudor history. And there is a mass of what I suppose must be called scholarship, aimed at identifying the principal characters, of a particularly contentious and inconclusive kind.

Let us admit that an element of allusion to contemporary history is inescapable in reading the poem. The identification of Duessa with Mary Queen of Scots was made in Elizabethan times. There are prolonged and unmistakable references to events in Ireland and the Low Countries in Book V. Less certainly, but still fairly obviously, the Timias-Belphoebe story seems both to present a somewhat idealized version of the Queen's displeasure with Sir Walter Raleigh; and to suggest a happy termination. But to pursue such identifications very far is both uncertain and poetically unilluminating. Some of Artegall's enterprises clearly glance at those of Lord Grey in Ireland. Some on the other hand do not; they refer to the wars in the Low Countries in which Leicester and not Lord Grey was engaged. If we care to think that Leicester is somewhat allusively celebrated in Arthur, Sidney in Calidore, we may. But if we try to multiply and elaborate these allusions we shall find ourselves taken farther away from the poem, not closer to its heart. Those who go too far find themselves near the territory inhabited by measurers of the Great Pyramid and discoverers of cryptograms in Shakespeare.

Glorification of England and her queen through history and legend, passing allusions, sometimes more sustained, to the splendours and miseries and conflicts of the day—all this is a part of the intricate web of *The Faerie Queene*. But it is not a sustained historical allegory. If it is to be called allegory at all it is only an intermittent and occasional strain. But a better term, as Greenlaw has suggested, would be historical allusion. And the best way to deal with it is to appreciate it where it is evident, for what it is worth, as part of a crowded and complex pattern, one of the elements which helps to give such density to the whole; and to be at no great pains to look for it where it does not make its presence plain.

VI

In speaking of the structure of *The Faerie Queene* we have compared its organization to that of a dream; we must now continue this argument into the allegory. If we believe that dreams have meaning at all (as by now we surely must), there is an obvious parallel between dream and allegory. The *dream-content*, as Freud calls it (the manifest content), is used to represent in a disguised form the *dream-thoughts* (latent content).[1] Thus the dream-content corresponds to what in allegory we have called image, the dream-thoughts to what we have called theme. In much allegory however the relation between the two elements is quite unlike that found in dreams. In naïve allegory, and even in developed religious allegory like *Everyman* or *The Pilgrim's Progress*, the image is a simple translation of the theme, by a series of one-to-one correspondences: one element in the theme corresponds to one in the image. (*The Pilgrim's Progress* escapes from naïve allegory not because of any complex relation of theme to image, but because the image-sequence has so much vitality and coherence of its own.) This is not the relation in dreams. One of the principal dream-mechanisms recorded by Freud is *condensation*: one single element in the dream-content corresponds to more than one in the dream-thoughts. To transfer this to our terms for allegory one element in the image refers to more than one element in the theme. Even from the limited observations we have made already it will be apparent that Spenser often proceeds in this way. I will now try to illustrate this in more detail.

The most obvious illustration is that in so many places there is a double reference—to the moral or psychic life in general, and to particular historical events. The attempt to read Book I as a transcript of Tudor history is strained and uncertain; but clearly a strong strain of allusion to the English reformation runs through it. The Red Cross Knight is Holiness, fighting against the temptations and errors that must universally beset

[1] All the features of the dream-process referred to here are described in Chapter VI of Freud's *Interpretation of Dreams*. I have used A. A. Brill's translation (1913).

such a virtue. But he is also, more intermittently and imprecisely, English religion (why else should he bear St. George's cross?) struggling against the conspiracies and misdirections of the time, as Spenser saw them. But he is not always Holiness as an achieved state; he is often the universal *miles Christianus*, the militant Christian who must struggle and learn and seek to perfect himself in his journey through the world. Similarly, three themes (not unrelated but certainly distinct) stand behind the figure of Arthur—Magnificence, the historic might and glory of Britain, and the Earl of Leicester. Artegall's adventures are sometimes those of an abstract and general justice, sometimes those of Lord Grey in Ireland.

We have already spoken of the ambiguity of Britomart in another context—of her way of stepping beyond her allegorical rôle. But what is her allegorical rôle? She represents Chastity, in Spenser's special sense of the word, but not exclusively that. She represents also a quite complex Renaissance ideal of female *virtù* (*virtù* meaning strength and energy, not virtue) which Spenser was familiar with through the virago heroines of the Italian epic, and which has nothing to do with chastity at all.

We are of course meant to admire both equally; but there are times when this kind of dual or multiple significance can introduce a moral ambiguity as well. Duessa in Book I is the embodiment of falsehood, outwardly fair but in reality hideous and deformed. When she reappears in Book V a whole cluster of notions connected with Mary Queen of Scots has become attached to her. She is still falsehood, and still to be rejected, but she is also misguided beauty, and a decided element of sympathy for the unhappy queen as a woman has crept into the *significatio*. I do not wish to enter into the vexed question of the Bower of Bliss at this point, except to remark that it cannot represent a simple concept. The idea sometimes put forward that Spenser was secretly on Acrasia's side is obviously wrong; but it could hardly have arisen if the allegory of the bower were a totally unambiguous affair. There *is* an element of indulged and happy voluptuousness in the description of Acrasia's abode, that takes us back to Tasso's Armida, Spenser's principal source.

And Armida at the end of the *Gerusalemme Liberata* is not rejected but forgiven.

Frequently, then, more than one theme lies behind the same image, and this is one of the features of *The Faerie Queene* that assimilates it most closely to the dream. "The construction of collective and composite personages is one of the principal methods of dream-condensation," as Freud puts it. I do not believe that we should avert our eyes from this, or try to explain away any ambiguities to which it may give rise. Spenser's moral attitude as a man may have been unambiguous enough, but an element of ambiguity is an essential part of his imaginative procedure. This means in fact that there is a far greater quantity of psychic material behind Spenser's romance-figures than a simple translation of them into the obvious moral terms would suggest.

It is worth noting that Spenser's multiple significance is quite unlike the medieval four levels of meaning as applied to the interpretation of Scripture, and Spenser shows no sign of being aware of this tradition.

> Littera gesta docet,
> Quid credas allegoria,
> Moralis quid agas,
> Quo tendas anagogia.

The literal sense, that is, is concerned with historical facts, the allegorical with belief, the moral with right action, and the anagogical with man's last end. Now Spenser's literal sense is not historical; his historical allusions are always concealed. He is concerned with *quid credas* only in Book I; and even there it is *how* we should believe, and how act on our belief, rather than *what* we should believe that is his main subject. The whole book is based on the necessity of cleaving to truth, and what happens when we depart from it; but truth is never given any doctrinal content. The moral sense, *quid agas*, is of course omnipresent; the right conduct of life in this world is Spenser's real field. But anagogia, *quo tendas*, man's last end, only appears directly in the vision of the heavenly city in I. x, and in the two lovely closing stanzas at the end of the Mutability cantos. The grades of reference for Spenser's allegory are not the medieval ones, they are the romantic, the historical, the moral and the psychological. And in the simpler and less developed parts, that is in the minor characters who are mere narrative or thematic conveniences—Sansfoy, Sansjoy and Sansloy, Furor, Occasio, etc. —the underlying sense is always the moral one.

A second feature of the dream-process mentioned by Freud is the converse of condensation—it is that an individual dream-thought may be represented by several different elements in the dream-content. Or again to translate this into terms of allegory, a single theme can issue in several images. Freud is not particularly clear about this in *The Interpretation of Dreams*; but he illustrates an aspect of it more fully in the essay "Character Types in Analytic Work" in Vol. IV of the Collected Papers; and any student of recorded dreams will be familiar with the way that a single idea appears in the dream under various guises. This happens in Spenser too, and it has sometimes disquieted his commentators. Legouis remarks that Red Cross, who is Holiness, goes to the House of Holiness; that Guyon who is Temperance goes to the Castle of Temperance. Pride appears twice over in Book I, as Lucifera and Orgoglio. True we can explain this if we will; Red Cross and Guyon, besides standing for their respective virtues, are also their yet imperfect human embodiments; Lucifera and Orgoglio are two different kinds of pride. But the resemblance to the dream-mechanism can hardly be missed.

Often in the dream a single character is split up into its several components, who are exhibited in the dream-content as separate figures. There are places where Spenser seems to be working on the same lines. It is often remarked that it is not easy to give any simple allegorical interpretation of the principal woman-figures in Books III and IV. This is probably because they are dissociated parts of the total image of woman. The most obvious dissociated character of this kind is Amoret-Belphoebe. Twin sisters given totally opposite educations, one brought up by Venus, the other by Diana, they stand for two opposed aspects of womanhood—woman as the overflowing fountain of love, and woman as the virgin, the solitary, the untouchable. Their sisterly relationship makes this particularly clear; but I should be inclined to go farther and include Florimell in this group-figure—Florimell who stands for woman as the object of desire, and who herself splits into two; the true Florimell, the right object of love; and the false Florimell, its factitious and deceiving semblance. We could include Britomart too—the active virtue of womanhood; and perhaps we should; all that forbids it is that she is a so much more developed figure in her own right.

Amoret, Belphoebe and Florimell are all aspects of the idea of woman. They do not represent virtues; they cannot be translated into clear-cut moral qualities at all. They are both more and less than that; more because they represent the unconscious, unformulated psychic background, out of which morals and virtue are yet to be developed; less because they are severally incomplete. They are a composite portrait of the anima, and they have their curious, unseizable charm not because they are romance-heroines, or not mainly for that reason, but because each is a glimpse and only a glimpse of the total image of womanhood that dominated Spenser's imagination.

Lastly (for I wish to make these dream-analogies suggestive rather than exhaustive) Freud inquires how logical relations can be represented in dreams. "What representation", he asks, "do 'if', 'because', 'as though', 'although', 'either-or' and all the other conjunctions without which we cannot construct either a phrase or a sentence, receive in our dreams?" And he finds that the dream has no direct means of exhibiting these. Causal relations are expressed in dreams by mere succession; alternatives by taking both members of the alternative into the same context. In fact the ample array of logical relations is reduced to a simple parataxis; apparently discrete events simply occur one after another. This is of course characteristic of romance-literature in general. Malory's typical conjunction is 'and'. But Malory's 'and' rarely means anything more; Spenser's temporal sequences often do imply more—or to put it in a fuller form, what appears as temporal sequence in the image conceals another relation, usually causality, in the theme. Immediately after the Red Cross Knight is separated from Una or Truth (I. i) he meets with Duessa or Falsehood. This appears as mere temporal sequence in the story, but thematically it is a matter of cause and effect. It is *because* he has been separated from Truth that the knight falls into the company of Falsehood. We take the meaning without noticing the mechanism because the narrative sequence is so much the expected one; having lost one lady the romance-hero naturally meets another one. Sometimes however the sequence of images conceals a thematic meaning that is less obvious. It is on her wedding-day "before the bride was bedded" (IV. i. 3) that Amoret was stolen away from Scudamour by Busirane. Busirane has never cherished any designs on Amoret before; in the image-sequence this appears as an uncaused, inconsequential calamity. Thematically it means that *because* of the wedding she was stolen away; it is *because* their consummation is so much desired and is close that the lady is tortured and her lover frustrated by the perverse cruelty of amour-passion.[1]

Other relations similarly find expression in dream-fashion. *Although* Guyon is attracted by the loveliness of the Bower of Bliss he knows it must be destroyed and destroys it. The 'although' hardly finds expression in the narrative; there is simply an abrupt temporal transition, astonishing to most readers, from the manifest seductions of the bower (II. xii. 70–78) to its sudden hastily described overthrow (83). Alternatives likewise: woman's beauty as the object of desire can be either true beauty (the outward expression of gentleness, innocence and chastity), or its false simulacrum (the outward covering of flightiness, greed and untruth); and this is expressed by the two Florimells, absolutely indistinguishable in appearance. What appears then in *The Faerie Queene* as the simple alogical sequaciousness of naïve romance conceals a wealth of more complex thematic relations; and meaning must be sought almost as often in these relations as in the isolated signification of individual figures.

Most of these points must be taken up and illustrated more fully later on. To make an end of this general discussion we should try to sum up the special distinguishing characters of Spenser's allegory. In the first place, it *is* allegory, not symbolism

---

[1] But this is a difficult matter. Full discussion of it is postponed till later.

in either a Blakean or a Mallarmean sense; nor fully incarnate literature like Shakespeare. It is of very varying degrees of explicitness, ranging from naïve allegory to romance with only the vaguest thematic significance. It is discontinuous—the general directing allegory announced in the Letter is only faintly developed, and the greatest allegorical intensity is reached in certain of the local stories. And as we have seen there were models of this kind near to Spenser's hand in the allegorizing of Ariosto. The allegory is in the most important places multivalent; it is on the whole only the minor characters who have a single simple allegorical significance. And last, in some ways most important, and to some readers most difficult to accept, it proceeds by loosely associative, half-unconscious methods like those of the dream, rather than by the rigorous translation of clearly formulated conceptual ideas. All the thematic content of *The Pilgrim's Progress* could have been as easily formulated in a sermon. This is true of parts of *The Faerie Queene*, but in all the best parts the thematic content finds its only possible embodiment in the actual image-sequence that the poem presents. And the poem is both—theme and image in perpetually shifting relations, variously interwoven, sometimes perceived separately, often talked of separately as a matter of expository convenience; but ultimately indissoluble.

*Chapter VII*

## BOOK I: HOLINESS

The first book of *The Faerie Queene* is by far the best known, partly because there are many readers who never get beyond it, and partly because it can be read as a complete poem on its own. Book II is similarly self-contained, but it is less completely unified in spirit, and the end is curiously hasty and huddled. So, as the whole poem is often considered too long to be easily manageable, Book I has commonly stood as the typical and accessible sample. In many ways this is unfortunate. Spenser has the best of reasons for putting it where he does, but it is not in fact quite typical of the poem as a whole. It is a theological prologue to a poem whose main existence is on a different plane. It is more fully and consistently allegorical than any of the other books, and the substance of the allegory takes us into a different world. Those who approach *The Faerie Queene* entirely in the spirit of Book I will do full justice to the "sage and serious" Spenser, but will be apt to see the whole poem as a less various and surprising one than it is.

What this means can be partly made clear by a consideration of sources. The prospect sounds threatening. Source-hunting has been one of the banes of Spenser scholarship, and the tracing of isolated images and generally received ideas back to dubious originals occupies too much space in the commentaries. A poem is what it is wherever it comes from; and it is possible to sympathize with those who are only interested in what it is. But no poem exists in isolation. The thought, the rhetoric, the form of a poem all belong to a tradition as well as to an individual author. To see the work in relation to the traditions that have gone to shape it can be one of the ways to see what it is in itself. And to do this for *The Faerie Queene* has been the idea of this book. But differences are as important as resemblances. We have been attempting to place Spenser's poem in the tradition of the romantic epic to which it belongs. But it belongs in its own way, and makes its contribution by its own individual quality. *The Faerie Queene* is like the *Orlando Furioso*, but it is also different. Spenser translates and imitates from *Gerusalemme Liberata*, but he is making a poem of a different kind. And this is nowhere clearer than in Book I. Indeed it is almost too clear, as we began by saying. The rest of the poem conforms more closely to the spirit of the *genre*. For behind Book I there is another archetype that hardly forms part of the romantic epic inheritance.

Superficially the conformity to the romance tradition is plain enough. We have the familiar material, knight-errantry, chivalrous devotion to a lady, witchcraft and a fight with a monster. Parallels to the Italian epics are frequent and easily discerned. Archimago is Ariosto's enchanter Atlante, Duessa is Alcina.[1] The passage where her true foulness is revealed (*F.Q.* VIII, 46–8) is literally translated from Ariosto (*O.F.* VII. 71–3). The Red Cross Knight's fight with the dragon repeats Orlando's fight with the Orc (*O.F.* XI. 22 seq.). The episode of Fradubio transformed into a tree echoes the story of Astolfo (*F.Q.* I. 11–31 seq.; *O.F.* vi. 23) and the education of Satyrane closely resembles that of Ruggiero (*F.Q.* I. vi. 24 seq.; *O.F.* vii. 57). Minor echoes are not wanting. The dragon crest on Arthur's helmet is copied from the Soldan's (*F.Q.* I. vii. 31; *G.L.* IX. 25); Arthur's magic shield is the shield of Atlante (*F.Q.* I. vii. 32–6; *O.F.* II. 55–6); his horn is the horn that Logistilla presented to Astolfo (*F.Q.* I. viii. 3–4; *O.F.* XV. 14); and Spenser echoes Ariosto's diatribe against firearms. These are a few examples among many. There are more general similarities between the Red Cross Knight's story and that of Rinaldo in *Gerusalemme Liberata*.[2] As Rinaldo is diverted from

[1] For nearly all the parallels between Spenser and Ariosto I am indebted to the articles of R. E. Neil Dodge, "Spenser's Imitations from Ariosto" PMLA XII, 1897, and its "Addenda", PMLA XXXV, 1920; and A. H. Gilbert "Spenser's Imitations from Ariosto", Supplementary, PMLA XXXIV, 1919.

[2] Tasso parallels in E. Koeppel, "Die Englischen Tasso-Uebersetzungen des 16. Jahrhunderts", Anglia XI, 1889; H. H. Blanchard, "Imitations of Tasso in the Faerie Queene", SP XXII, 1925; A. Castelli, *La Gerusalemme Liberata nella Inghilterra di Spenser*, Milan, 1936.

his duty by Armida, so is Red Cross by Duessa, but the resemblance is not close as the enchantresses' modes of operation are quite different. But after this temptation is over Spenser follows Tasso very closely. When Rinaldo is liberated from his thraldom he does penance with a hermit; so does Red Cross. Rinaldo outside Jerusalem ascends Mount Olivet and greets the dawn with prayer and contemplation; Red Cross similarly ascends a mountain, from which he sees a vision of the heavenly Jerusalem (*G.L.* XVIII; *F.Q.* I. x); and as the Mago Naturale reveals to Rinaldo the glory of his ancestors, so the hermit Contemplation reveals to Red Cross his future and his descendants.

Yet with all these debts to the Italian epic, of motif, character and descriptive detail, we do not feel in Book I that we are moving in the same world. The story of Una and Red Cross is cast in the form of a romance, and can therefore borrow all the material we have just noted; but in fact the primary source of the plot is not anything in the romantic epic; it is the St. George legend. Spenser probably had it from the *Golden Legend*, popular and accessible in Caxton's translation, with some assistance from Mantuan's Latin *Georgius* for the dragon-fight. Apart from the general similarity of the stories, Red Cross is expressly identified with St. George (ii. 12; x. 62) and the choice of this champion as the hero of his first book is a peculiarly happy one for Spenser. St. George is a knight (so described in *The Golden Legend*) who is also a saint; and he is the patron saint of England as well. In medieval tradition he is pre-eminently the *miles Christianus*; he is also the patron saint of England, and famous as such in many popular redactions. Thus Spenser has a theme to begin with in which three of the main interests of his work, the religious, the chivalric and the national are already combined. The love-theme, on the other hand, is very little developed. In the original story of St. George it is not present at all. The king's daughter who is rescued from the dragon by the saint is not his lady; she is an entirely impersonal object of chivalry, and the tale does not conclude with their marriage. And in Spenser's treatment of Una and the Red Cross Knight there remains something abstract and impersonal, very different from the frank and human loves of Amoret and Scudamour, Britomart and Artegall.

# BOOK I: HOLINESS

Some misunderstanding of *The Faerie Queene* springs from a failure to realize sufficiently the different planes on which it moves. Those who are looking for romance find something much remoter and less warm in Book I; and those who form their expectations on Book I find in the middle books a relaxation of allegorical purpose. It should be observed at the start that the exquisitely realized beauty of Una is not the beauty of a heroine of romance, nor is the relation between her and the Red Cross Knight of the kind that is usual in romantic love-stories. When we first meet them in canto i their relation is the still relatively distant one of protector and suppliant maiden. He is "Sir Knight" to her, and she is "the chastest flower that e'er did spring". Red Cross is horrified at the amorous visions aroused by the wiles of Archimago; but in response to the advances of what he believes to be Una he makes a somewhat formal profession of love (I. i. 54). Really it has not occurred to him to see her otherwise than as the pure object of his assigned championship. Then they are parted, and do not meet again till canto viii, when Redcross is rescued by Arthur from Orgoglio. In speaking of him to Arthur Una refers to him as "My dearest lord" (viii. 28), and when he emerges from the dungeon she treats him almost as a lover (viii. 42, 43). But Red Cross is too ill to take much notice of the situation, and Una's converse is entirely with Arthur. In canto ix Red Cross falls into the power of Despair, and is only saved by Una's intervention. Here she appears far more as his mentor than his mistress, and this relation continues through canto x, where she is guide to the House of Holiness. Canto xi is devoted to the dragon-fight; and in xii. 19 we hear *for the first time*, from Una's father, of "the marriage vow betwixt you twain". The marriage in the event has to be delayed, for the Red Cross Knight has still to perform six years' service to the Faerie Queene; but there has never been the slightest suggestion up to now that he and Una are to be regarded as betrothed lovers. This may be taken simply as an example of Spenser's narrative carelessness; and it does indeed illustrate his loose grip on the mechanics of his story, compared with the brisk competence of Ariosto or Tasso's careful planning. But it will commonly be found that when Spenser is vague or careless about the detail of his story it is because he has another aim in view. What that is in the present case appears in the following stanzas.

Una appears, radiantly beautiful, "And on her now a garment she did wear/ All Lilly white, withoutten spot, or pride." As Upton was the first to point out,[1] these lines recall the passage in *Revelations* 19.7 "The marriage of the Lamb is come, and his wife hath made herself ready; and to her was granted that she should be arrayed in fine linen, clean and white, for the fine linen is the righteousness of saints". Upton's note continues "This passage plainly alludes to the mystical union of Christ and his Church, and this too is the allegorical allusion of our poet." Guided by the hint, it is then possible to see a considerable number of allusions to the Apocalypse in the latter part of Book I. In xii. 36 Archimago is bound and cast into a dungeon, but we are warned that he will escape—"Who would then think, that by his subtle trains/He could escape fowle death or deadly paine"; and in II. i. 1 we find that he actually has escaped; just as in *Revelations* 20.2–7 "the dragon, that old serpent, which is the Devil and Satan" is bound and cast into a pit, yet after a thousand years "he must be loosed a little season". The well of life and the tree of life which successively restore the Red Cross Knight at different stages of the dragon-fight are from *Revelations* 22.1, and to quote Upton again, at this point, "the reader knows that the scene of action is in Eden, and that our knight, emblematically 'the Captain of our Salvation' is come to restore lost Paradise".

Earlier in canto viii Duessa is assimilated to the Whore of Babylon of *Revelations* 17 (viii. 12, *Rev.* 17.6; viii. 14, *Rev.* 17.4; viii. 50, *Rev.* 17.16). And then we begin to understand the fundamental symbolism of the book; the dragon who is to be subdued, the evil woman whose designs are to be frustrated, the true maiden who is to be united to her saviour, owe more, at the deepest level, to the Apocalypse than to the romantic epic in

[1] *See* Works I, p. 308. The student of *F.Q.* soon learns the value of the notes of Upton's edition (1793) especially for Book I. He had, at an unlikely time, a particularly clear idea of Spenser's Biblical symbolism. Warton and Christopher North have also commented on the parallels with *Revelations* (Works I, pp. 368–372); and later J. W. Bennett, *Evolution of F.Q.*, 1948, pp. 109–14.

whose guise they appear. *Paradise Lost* shows a similar but more evident adaptation of Biblical material to the formal Renaissance epic. In both cases a translation has been made from one mode into another. Milton's complete and elaborate theological argument has proved recalcitrant to his severe epic form; and this has landed him in notorious difficulties. Spenser's theology is far more partial and fragmentary and his romance form far more flexible. As a result he has been able to make a looser, and if I may put it so, more comfortable accommodation between his scriptural and theological material and his romantic epic. But though the form is that of romance it is a visionary theology that lies at the heart of the first book of *The Faerie Queene.*

It is important to define what is being claimed here. Not that the Red Cross Knight is, or becomes at any point, Christ the Redeemer; or that Una is or becomes the Church or the Protestant faith. They are what they appear to be on the face of it, characters in a romantic story about a distressed maiden, an evil enchantress, and the delivery of a wasted land. But they are characters like those in a dream who contain within themselves a multiple significance. Redcross is a knight errant; he is also the militant but imperfect wayfaring Christian, still in need of personal sanctification and completion. When he succumbs to Orgoglio or all but falls to the temptation of Despair we cannot take him as a type of Christ—Christ who can suffer as a man but whose divine victory is assured. In canto ii when he is deceived by Archimago and Duessa, in cantos vii, viii and ix when he becomes the victim of Orgoglio and Despair, the Red Cross Knight's victory is by no means assured. His scene of operation is the world, and all the world's ordinary uncertainties and temptations are still active. After his sojourn in the House of Holiness we move, not so much to a different ground as to a different phase in the world's drama, a phase that we can know only from apocalypse, not from history or ordinary moral experience. It is still important not to take a too rapid allegorical short cut. We must still as the naïve reader does keep in the foreground of our mind the quite consistent and harmonious romance story. But what we can see through it is now a vision of a different kind—a vision of a land that was once Eden, laid waste under the depredations of a dragon, the old serpent who is Satan, of his slaying by a Champion, afterwards reunited to his bride, who is the Church, that is the whole body of the faithful, now redeemed. I do not at all suppose that the patristic four senses[1] for the interpretation of Scripture formed any part of the mental equipment with which Spenser composed *The Faerie Queene*, but if we may use them ourselves, simply as instruments of explanation, we may say that it is a view of 'quid credas' that we have been led to in cantos i and ii; 'quid agas' in vii and viii; but in xi and xii it is the anagogical vision, 'quo tendas'. We have a prospect of man's last end; in Red Cross we can see a type of the Redeemer, in Una a type of the redeemed.

Yet only a few cantos before the relationship was quite opposite. Red Cross was weak and imperfect, and it was only by Una's intervention that he was saved. If we regard the image —human characters in changing circumstances—this presents no difficulties. Thematically it is impossible, unless the theme changes and is different in different parts of the narrative. And indeed it is. How is it that these incompatible thematic contents can be subsumed under the same images? The answer in my view is that the image, the romance story, must always be given its due; it provides the continuum in which the poem moves; and its relation with the moral and spiritual theme is a close but everchanging one. If instead of living in the narrative surface we insist on breaking through too rapidly to the allegorical content we shall fail to do justice to Spenser's unique fusion of diverse elements. What is more, we shall find the allegory itself confusing and inconsistent, even here in Book I where it is most complete. Like Jusserand we shall complain the Redcross who is Holiness is brought to the House of Holiness to complete his spiritual education. Or we shall be troubled by the inconsistent relations between Redcross and Una, in which he is sometimes her saviour, she sometimes his; possible, indeed frequent enough as a relation between man and woman; but hardly possible as a

[1] See Dante's letter to Can Grande for the most generally accessible explanation of the four senses.

relation between two theological absolutes.

The classic exposition of the allegory of Book I is to be found, rather strangely, in Appendix 2 to the third volume of Ruskin's *Stones of Venice*. Since nobody reads Ruskin nowadays we can hardly do better than reprint it.

> The Redcrosse Knight is Holiness,—the "Pietas" of St. Mark's, the "Devotio" of Orcagna,—meaning, I think, in general, Reverence and Godly Fear.
>
> This Virtue, in the opening of the book, has Truth (or Una) at its side, but presently enters the Wandering Wood, and encounters the serpent Error; that is to say, Error in her universal form, the first enemy of Reverence and Holiness; and more especially Error as founded on learning; for when Holiness strangles her,
>
> > "Her vomit full of bookes and papers was,
> > With loathly frogs and toades, which eyes
> > did lacke."
>
> Having vanquished this first open and palpable form of Error, as Reverence and Religion must always vanquish it, the Knight encounters Hypocrisy, or Archimagus: Holiness cannot detect Hypocrisy, but believes him, and goes home with him; whereupon, Hypocrisy succeeds in separating Holiness from Truth; and the Knight (Holiness) and Lady (Truth) go forth separately from the house of Archimagus.
>
> Now observe; the moment Godly Fear, or Holiness, is separated from Truth, he meets Infidelity, or the Knight Sans Foy; Infidelity having Falsehood, or Duessa, riding behind him. The instant the Redcrosse Knight is aware of the attack of Infidelity, he
>
> > "Gan fairly couch his speare, and towards ride."
>
> He vanquishes and slays Infidelity; but is deceived by his companion, Falsehood, and takes her for his lady: thus showing the condition of Religion, when, after being attacked by Doubt, and remaining victorious, it is nevertheless seduced by any form of Falsehood, to pay reverence where it ought not. This, then, is the first fortune of Godly Fear separated from Truth. The poet then returns to Truth, separated from Godly Fear. She is immediately attended by a lion, or Violence, which makes her dreaded wherever she comes; and when she enters the mart of supersitition, this Lion tears Kirkrapine in pieces: showing how Truth, separated from Godliness, does indeed put an end to the abuses of superstition, but does so violently and desperately. She then meets again with Hypocrisy, whom she mistakes for her own lord, or Godly Fear, and travels a little way under his

guardianship (Hypocrisy thus not unfrequently appearing to defend the Truth), until they are both met by Lawlessness, or the Knight Sans Loy, whom Hypocrisy cannot resist. Lawlessness overthrows Hypocrisy, and seizes upon Truth, first slaying her lion attendant: showing that the first aim of licence is to destroy the force and authority of Truth. Sans Loy then takes Truth captive, and bears her away. Now this Lawlessness is the "unrighteousness", or "adikia", of St. Paul; and his bearing Truth away captive is a type of those "who hold the truth in unrighteousness",—that is to say, generally, of men who, knowing what is true, make the truth give way to their own purposes, or use it only to forward them, as is the case with so many of the popular leaders of the present day. Una is then delivered from Sans Loy by the satyrs, to show that Nature, in the end, must work out the deliverance of the truth, although, where it has been captive to Lawlessness, that deliverance can only be obtained through Savageness, and a return to barbarism. Una is then taken from among the satyrs by Satyrane, the son of a satyr and a "lady myld, fair Thyamis" (typifying the early steps of renewed civilization, and its rough and hardy character, "nousled up in life and manners wilde"), who, meeting again with Sans Loy, enters instantly into rough and prolonged combat with him: showing how the early organization of a hardy nation must be wrought out through much discouragement from Lawlessness. This contest the poet leaving for the time undecided, returns to trace the adventures of the Redcrosse Knight, or Godly Fear, who, having vanquished Infidelity, presently is led by Falsehood to the house of Pride: thus showing how religion, separated from truth, is first tempted by doubts of God, and then by the pride of life. The description of this house of Pride is one of the most elaborate and noble pieces in the poem; and here we begin to get at the proposed system of Virtues and Vices. For Pride, as Queen, has six other vices yoked in her chariot; namely, first, Idleness, then Gluttony, Lust, Avarice, Envy and Anger, all driven on by "Sathan, with a smarting whip in hand." From these lower vices and their company, Godly Fear, though lodging in the house of Pride, holds aloof; but he is challenged, and has a hard battle to fight with Sans Joy, the brother of Sans Foy; showing, that though he has conquered Infidelity, and does not give himself up to the allurements of Pride, he is yet exposed, so long as he dwells in her house, to distress of mind and loss of his accustomed rejoicing before God. He, however, having partly conquered Despondency, or Sans Joy, Falsehood goes down to Hades, in order to obtain drugs to maintain the power or life of Despondency; but, meantime, the Knight leaves the house of

# BOOK I: HOLINESS

Pride: Falsehood pursues and overtakes him, and finds him by a fountain side, of which the waters are

> "Dull and slow,
> And all that drinke thereof do faint and feeble grow."

Of which the meaning is, that Godly Fear, after passing through the house of Pride, is exposed to drowsiness and feebleness of watch; as, after Peter's boast, came Peter's sleeping, from weakness of the flesh, and then, last of all, Peter's fall. And so it follows, for the Redcrosse Knight, being overcome with faintness by drinking of the fountain, is thereupon attacked by the giant Orgoglio, overcome, and thrown by him into a dungeon. This Orgoglio is Orgueil, or Carnal Pride; not the pride of life, spiritual and subtle, but the common and vulgar pride in the power of this world: and his throwing the Redcrosse Knight into a dungeon is a type of the captivity of true religion under the temporal power of corrupt churches, more especially of the Church of Rome; and of its gradually wasting away in unknown places, while Carnal Pride has the pre-eminence over all things. That Spenser means especially the pride of the Papacy, is shown by the 16th stanza of the book; for there the giant Orgoglio is said to have taken Duessa, or Falsehood, for his "deare", and to have set upon her head a triple crown, and endowed her with royal majesty, and made her to ride upon a seven-headed beast.

In the meantime, the dwarf, the attendant of the Redcrosse Knight, takes his arms, and finding Una, tells her of the captivity of her lord. Una, in the midst of her mourning, meets Prince Arthur, in whom, as Spenser himself tells us, is set forth generally Magnificence; but who, as is shown by the choice of the hero's name, is more especially the magnificence, or literally, "great doing", of the kingdom of England. This power of England, going forth with Truth, attacks Orgoglio, or the Pride of Papacy, slays him; strips Duessa, or Falsehood, naked; and liberates the Redcrosse Knight. The magnificent and well-known description of Despair follows, by whom the Redcrosse Knight is hard bested, on account of his past errors and captivity, and is only saved by Truth, who, perceiving him to be still feeble, brings him to the house of Cœlia, called, in the argument of the canto, Holiness, but properly, Heavenly Grace, the mother of the Virtues. Her "three daughters, well upbrought", are Faith, Hope and Charity. Her porter is Humility; because Humility opens the door of Heavenly Grace. Zeal and Reverence are her chamberlains, introducing the new-comers to her presence; her groom, or servant, is Obedience; and her physician, Patience. Under the commands of Charity, the matron Mercy rules over her hospital, under whose care the Knight is healed of his sickness; and it is to be especially noticed how much importance Spenser, though never ceasing to chastise all hypocrisies and mere observances of form, attaches to true and faithful penance in effecting this cure. Having his strength restored to him, the Knight is trusted to the guidance of Mercy, who, leading him forth by a narrow and thorny way, first instructs him in the seven works of Mercy, and then leads him to the hill of Heavenly Contemplation; whence, having a sight of the New Jerusalem, as Christian of the Delectable Mountains, he goes forth to the final victory over Satan, the old serpent, with which the book closes.

Ruskin's own idea of Protestant virtue was closely akin to Spenser's, and he has a genius for the allegorical interpretation of works of art which is unfashionably explicit today, but puts him far more in tune with medieval and Renaissance tradition than any other nineteenth-century writer. As an interpretation of the moral and ecclesiastical-political significance of Book I this passage could hardly be bettered. But he dismisses the last two cantos in a sentence—"whence, having a sight of the New Jerusalem, as Christian of the Delectable Mountains, he goes forth to the final victory over Satan, the old serpent, with which the book closes".

But it is these final cantos that introduce us to Una's ravaged land and her imprisoned parents, and remind us of what we have learned about them in canto i. Una's parents are only comprehensible as our common parents, Adam and Eve, the types of human kind; their land is Eden ravaged by the Fall. And Una as their daughter cannot now be understood as Truth or Faith, but only as the Church, the whole body of the faithful, waiting to be redeemed; and the Red Cross Knight as a type of the Redeemer. We need not dwell on the ever-present historical connections with the English Reformation; in general terms they are obvious enough. In this light we shall find another *significatio* for the Red Cross Knight; he must be identified with the English Church, vanquishing error, external hostility and oppression, and ultimately united in triumph to Una, the true faith. I do not want to dwell on this because it has become crisscrossed with a multitude of personal and political identifications, whose diversity defeats the authority of any. Only one has any contemporary status—Duessa was early identified with Mary

Queen of Scots. But we can hardly doubt that there were some such specific allusions, now doubtful or wholly lost. What we may learn from all this is that even Book I, the clearest and most simply constructed part of all *The Faerie Queene*, the allegory is of a far from simple kind. The student of Spenserian exegesis soon learns to recognize interpretations that are locally plausible but inadequate to the richness and variety of the whole book.

How then should it be read? Are the multiple significances, to be studied, superimposed on each other, and kept in the foreground of the mind? Studied by all means, for any one who wishes; but not I think kept too sharply before the mind in reading. To do this as is sometimes done is to go looking for the construction lines, the indications of measurement, beneath the surface of the painting which is what we are meant to see. I must recall what was said in the last chapter about the dream-like quality of Spenser's allegory, the condensation of his figures, their plurality of meaning. But this should not take us away too soon or too far from the dream-images themselves. Above all it must be realized that Spenser's chiaroscuro, the quality by which some parts of his painting stand out sharply drawn and clearly lit while other parts retire into shadow, is not an accident or an obstacle to be got over, but an essential part of his art. The shadows are not indeed bituminous darkness; they contain exquisite though not prominent drawing. Thought and study can reveal ever greater depth in them. But it should not be the object to bring them up to a brightness and clarity that on the face of it they do not possess.

This quality by which forms and outlines appear, recede into shadow and re-appear occurs in Spenser whether we are attending to his image or to his theme—or, as we should do, to both together in a synoptic vision. The process by which Una and Redcross become betrothed lovers is, as we have seen, quite obscure as far as the story is concerned. This is one of the places where the image is concealed in shadow. In a pure romance such as Ariosto's this would have been a defect; in his kind of poem the springs of action should be, as they are, few and clearly defined. In Book I of *The Faerie Queene* the espousal of Redcross and Una is to be more like mystic marriage than any

149

earthly bond. Any suggestion of the usual romance of courtship would be utterly out of place. Moreover, their ultimate relationship, he as the deliverer, she as the delivered, reverses the moral and theological relation in which they have lately stood. It should break upon us with a kind of visionary radiance, as it does, the connection with ordinary earthly struggle being only maintained by the delayed wedding, the six years' service to the Faerie Queene that Redcross has still to perform. The general reader probably does not notice the solution of narrative continuity and therefore does not need the explanation; but if he did, this could be given. The demands of the shifting theme have affected the image and caused part of it to be placed in shadow.

A similar but rather cruder case occurs where the Red Cross Knight is reunited to Una in canto viii. 33–34. He has left her hastily and unjustly on a suspicion of her infidelity. On the straightforward romance-narrative level he still has reasons for his suspicion and she has reasons to feel sorrow and resentment. But they are reunited at once without a word of explanation. We can imagine what a field-day a Tassonian or Ariostan heroine would have had on this occasion. Again what would seem the obvious narrative line has retired into the shadow. The reason is that we are not now to see Redcross as a knight errant subject to the ordinary jealousies and suspicions. We are to see him as the pilgrim Christian whose trials and misfortunes have changed his spiritual nature, and without any circumstantial enlightment have taught him truer values: Una as constant truth cannot change her allegiance: and no explanations are necessary.

In these places the prominence of the thematic need has cast part of the narrative image into obscurity. We have an example of the reverse process, though a less clear one, in the adventures of Una. The scenes where Una is protected by the lion (iii. 5–9, 19,20) befriended by the satyrs, and helped by Sir Satyrane (vi) seem thematically all to consist of the same material: truth is part of the natural law, and therefore creatures purely under the natural law—wild beasts and half-human beings—though far from the means of grace and instruction, will all do homage to it.

# BOOK I: HOLINESS

It is a beautiful and orthodox piece of Spenserian mythology, and one in which his view of the world is most sadly different from ours. But it is hardly central to Book I and thematically it hardly needs to be developed at such length. As romance narrative however these are among the most delightful passages in the book. And here it is the romantic charm of the image rather than thematic necessity that has brought them in. The picture of these shaggy furry creatures performing their glad homage to the delicate maiden is the source of poetical delight. Thoughts of the relation between nature and theological truth are not entirely absent, but they have retired into the shadow and are only seen at a closer look.

So it is not only that a single image may comprehend within itself more than one theme, and a single theme proliferate into an extended series of images; it is also true that the relation between theme and image varies. Thematic intention no doubt controls the whole, but that does not mean that it is all set in an even light; sometimes one aspect is illuminated, sometimes the other. And it is just this play of light and shade that formal exposition often seems to obscure. I have at times spoken of the naïve reader who will see *The Faerie Queene* only as a fairy story in Hazlitt's sense. We might now invoke a different figure whom I will call the simple but instructed reader—one who is not immoderately addicted to footnotes and commentaries, but who has a general sense, both instinctive and informed, of the way that mythical and romantic poetry works. Such a reader quite naturally makes the adjustments of his vision that I have been suggesting, knows naturally when to rest on the image and when to explore the theme, how closely to pore into what lies in the shadows of the picture. Here I am trying to do little more than make his unanalysed procedure explicit; and it is only necessary to do that because a critical habit derived from modern realistic literature has rendered such ability less common than it was.

Some of the most celebrated and significant episodes of Book I do not stand in need of commentary—or not of any that I have to offer. They may be briefly mentioned however, to show how various in kind they are. Each book of *The Faerie Queene* contains what Professor Lewis has called an allegorical centre; it is also likely to contain at least one formal allegorical set-piece, often in a rather archaic manner; also passages of some human and dramatic intensity. The allegorical centre of Book I is plainly the House of Holiness in canto x. There was a faint suggestion for it in Ruggiero's sojourn in the house of Logistilla in *Orlando Furioso*. But we noticed how little interested Ariosto was in the regeneration of his hero and how quickly he sent him off on new adventures. Everyone has noticed that in most fiction virtue and order commonly get a slighter and less adequate rendering than disorder and evil. Spenser is among the poets whose positives can be as powerful as his negatives; and in the House of Holiness, where thematic intention decisively takes charge, the image is fully equal to it. These scenes where the characters are all 'abstract' personifications of the virtues achieve exactly the serene and tranquil beauty that is required. It is not a mere static picture, for Dame Caelia and her daughters enter into active relation with the Red Cross Knight. His stay appropriately culminates in the anagogic vision of the New Jerusalem; but since we are still after all in an earthly romance and the decorum of romance forbids that we should remain too long or too exclusively in this rarefied air, Redcross is told like Plato's philosophers that he must return to the world of action; and to bring us back appropriately to the romance material, the dragon-fight, he is told like any other knight of his lineage and his future deeds.

The formal set-piece is the procession of the Seven Deadly Sins, pageant-like and emblematic in the medieval manner.[1] Brilliant and characteristic as these descriptive pageants are they are only one of Spenser's modes of presentation. They are rightly admired by everyone, but they should not be allowed to obscure the presence of others. The deadly sins are presented with an abundance of pictorial detail—sometimes coarse and disgusting, which should be enough to dispose of the 'dreamy beauty' theory of Spenser's style. But they are quite undramatic.

---

[1] The closest parallel that has been cited is Gower's *Miroir de l'Homme*. (*See Works*, Vol. 1, p. 407.) It was a medieval commonplace, but perhaps we are saying little in saying this. The illustrations to Ripa's *Iconologia* show the sins personified in much the same way.

They do not do anything, or enter into any significant relation with Redcross, and they are in no way central to the action as the house of Holiness is. We may contrast with this stiffly stylized representation the sombre and splendid scenes of Duessa's visit to the Underworld (v. 31 seq.), with all its shadowy horror. It is of course deeply affected by the sixth book of the *Aeneid*. A still greater contrast is the Despair episode (ix. 33 seq.). The description of Despair is more original and more profoundly felt than the grotesque heraldry of the House of Pride, and in Despair's argument with Redcross a powerful dramatic rhetoric is developed, illogical but none the less psychologically true for that. This effect is not particularly frequent in Spenser, and it is quite unlike the merely pictorial representation of Lucifera and her followers.

## Chapter VIII

## BOOK II: TEMPERANCE

Whenever Book I was written, whether at the beginning of the enterprise or, as I think more likely, after Books III and IV were well advanced, Book II must surely have been fairly close to it. The two books are constructed on the same lines and the parallelism between them is so marked as to be evidently deliberate. Each has a single knight, a single quest, and incidents in thematically close relation to the virtue of which the knight is champion. In each the knight succeeds in his initial adventures, then suffers a sore trial and gets into difficulty from which he is rescued by Arthur, goes through a period of purgation and instruction, and finally meets the ordeal which is the consummation of his quest, and triumphs over an enemy. Book II is the simpler in structure, for we follow Guyon's adventures almost all the time, while in Book I the interest is divided between Redcross and Una. Book II is simpler in thematic content too; necessarily so, for it does not deal with the mysteries of faith, but with moral discipline and moral action—neither *quid credas* nor *quo tendas*, but *quid agas*. The scene of action is always the world, the temptations are those of ordinary earthly experience, and the means by which they are overcome are not revelation and grace but reason and self-command. Yet this very simplicity leads, as we shall see, if not to a moral ambiguity at least to an uncertainty about where some of the imagery is leading us.

In this book we have little difficulty with Spenser's claim to follow Aristotle; Temperance is certainly one of the Aristotelian virtues (*Eth. Nic.* 3. 10–12). But Spenser's rendering of it seems to owe more to Aristotle's Continence (*Eth. Nic.* 7. 1–10) than to temperance itself; or perhaps he makes a fusion of the two. The temperate man is so well-ordered that he does not feel the temptations of passion or desire; the continent man feels them but resists them. Strictly the latter is Guyon's case, though he does not seem to feel any of the temptations very strongly. Guyon alone among the major knights has no lady. He wears the image of the Faerie Queene on his shield, but it is never suggested that she is his lady in any other sense but that she is his sovereign; and the attachment to Medina is so faintly noted as to make almost no impression. Even in an allegory one can hardly have a love affair with the Golden Mean. Guyon's companion is a palmer who represents Reason, thematically appropriate, but a slightly inconvenient attendant for a hero of romance. There is a difficulty about Temperance too; since it is a virtue that consists chiefly of *not* doing things the liveliness of action and imagery must occur chiefly among its opponents. And we know what is liable to happen in this situation, even when there is no doubt about where our moral sympathies should lie; we have seen it in many works of fiction, not least in *Paradise Lost*. Book II contains some of the finest and most powerfully imaginative passages in the whole of *The Faerie Queene*, but Guyon remains a colourless hero and there is neither a heroic trial nor a radiant climax to his quest, only a witch trussed up amid the ruins of her garden.

Cantos i to vii present various exempla of Temperance and its opposite, mostly powerful and all allegorically simple. The opening connects this book with Book I through Archimago's attempt to embroil Guyon with the Red Cross Knight. This fails, and Guyon's proper adventures begin with the episode of Mordaunt and Amavia and the babe with bloody hands. We first hear of Acrasia and the Bower of Bliss. It is through Acrasia's wiles that Mordaunt has been entrapped. He has been rescued from her by the faithfulness of Amavia his wife, but has been killed at the fountain by the long-range effects of her enchantment. Its mode of operation is left obscure (i. 55), but this is an obscure psychological region, and there is an appropriateness in the murky light by which we see it. The power of perverse sensuality may apparently be overcome, but its secret consequences may endure, and the mere contact with purity, symbolized by the fountain, may bring them fatally to light. These consequences may be fatal to others too, as we see in the suicide of Amavia and the baby's hands stained with its mother's blood. This is a powerful statement of the theme at the opening of the book, and it not only sets Guyon on his quest, the destruction of Acrasia, but balances the ambiguous power of the Bower of Bliss at the end. It is not developed further, and it does not need to be; its function is to make the power of Acrasia immediately dangerous and real.

Canto ii is a frigid piece of allegory with an explicitly Aristotelian base, on the doctrine of the Golden Mean. Of the three sisters Elissa represents defect, Perissa excess, and Medina the just balance. Not much is built on this unpromising foundation, and not much could be. It is worth noting that there is a strong element of merely social morality here, of the minor sort. The two unsatisfactory sisters are more tiresome and ill-mannered than anything else, and the rectitude of Medina is correspondingly pallid and uninspiring. Spenser slips back here towards naïve allegory of a weak and schematic kind. Braggadocchio who steals Guyon's horse in canto iii can at a pinch be taken as an example of intemperance too; but this incident is mainly an Ariostan piece of 'interweaving'; it serves to introduce Belphoebe, with a passage of pictorial splendour that whets the reader's curiosity; and both characters are to appear again in later books. Cantos iv and v are devoted to various exempla of anger, Furor and Occasion, Pyrochles and his attendant Atin or Strife. They are vigorous and direct, and while they are perfectly explicit allegory they stand on their own feet as romance adventures.

The sixth canto introduces us to Phaedria, the seductive lady of the Idle Lake, where Guyon deserts his Palmer and is briefly distracted by her wiles. But I will postpone discussion of this episode and take it in connection with the Bower of Bliss, as part of Spenser's general treatment of sensual pleasure. As we reach this middle part of the book the imaginative intensity greatly increases. After the diversion with Phaedria the picture of Pyrochles (vi. 41 seq.) vainly trying to quench the flames of his fury in the lake comes with great force. And this is succeeded by the domain of Mammon in canto vii. It corresponds roughly to the passages of Orgoglio and Despair in Book I. Again Spenser has passed from relatively simple allegory to a richly integrated imaginative conception, in which it would be vain to ask whether the theme or the images came first. Each has its own life and the two lives are perfectly at one. Again there is a finely dramatized debate between the hero and his antagonist (vii. 8–20), and the realm of Pluto is unrivalled, as Hazlitt has said, for its "splendid chiaroscuro and shadowy horror". There are differences from the situation in Book I. Red Cross is really endangered by Orgoglio and Despair. Guyon never seems to be in danger from Mammon, and if he faints at the end it is not that his personal virtue has been shaken but that he is exhausted by long dwelling in a life-destroying atmosphere. The strength of the Mammon scenes partly depend on this; they depart from the conventional pattern of temptations presented and overcome to the subtler horror of a poisoned ambience, an air that suffocates while it repels. Mammon is not even the conventional tempter, for after showing Guyon the sombre splendid halls of Pluto he shows him, without attempting to disguise it, the Garden of Proserpine, which is a sort of Hell. Mammon is what he is; he can believe in nothing but his own desires, can do nothing but show them as they are, and then, if Guyon is unpersuaded, let him go into the upper air again.

Swooning after his season in hell, Guyon is about to be despoiled by Pyrochles and Cymochles when he is rescued by Arthur (canto viii). Then he is led in canto ix to the House of Alma or Temperance, for instruction and restoration, as Redcross was led to the House of Holiness. The castle of Alma is both the allegorical set-piece and the allegorical centre of Book II. It represents the proper constitution of the body governed by temperance, and its antiquated physiological psychology is a relapse into a more primitive kind of allegory than that which is most typical of Spenser. To pass from the passions and the temptations of the world to architectural and anthropomorphic representations of the teeth, the nose, the moustache and the digestive system is a shock to the modern reader. Critics have not been wanting who have found the whole thing ridiculous and banal, from Hughes in 1715 who complains that "the Allegory seems to be debas'd by a mixture of too many low Images", to Grierson in our own day who describes it simply as 'dreadful'. It seems of course a piece of naïve medievalism, and Legouis is astonished that something which "really belongs to the thirteenth or early fourteenth century . . . should have been thus patiently built up in the age of Shakespeare, Marlowe and Bacon".[1] However, there is something like it in Du Bartas; it is imitated by Phineas Fletcher; and those who cannot away with it lack sympathy, rightly or wrongly, with some part of Spenser's imaginative constitution. Moral allegory may correspond to our notion of the dignity of Spenser's theme; but not for the first time we must remind ourselves of the emblematic variety of the art of Spenser's day, in which geography, cosmology, times and seasons can be allegorized, side by side with the constituent affections of the human soul. So why not physiology too? No one can accuse Spenser of wanting grandeur where it is required; but he is utterly remote from any neoclassical notion of continuous decorum; and there is a kind of readers (of whom I am one) who come to find these intermittent naïveties a part of Spenser's charm. To use the Coleridgean terms, Fancy as well as Imagination has its place in this world, and no one who has learnt to read the language of Spenser's fancy would be without Guyon's meeting with Shamefastness, or the personifications of foresight, understanding and memory in the closing stanzas.

It is in the chamber of memory that Arthur and Guyon find the chronicles of British and Elfin kings that are given in Canto x. This is dull to modern readers, but it is a characteristic element in the romantic epic and a characteristic part of Spenser's design. Its historical bearing has been discussed in Chapter VI. The idea comes from Ariosto's genealogical glorification of the Estensi, but the material is wholly British, ultimately from Geoffrey of Monmouth but eclectic in detail and carefully put together from a number of sources.[2] Needless to say it has nothing to do with

---

[1] E. Legouis, *Spenser*, 1929, p. 72.

[2] C. A. Harper, *The Sources of the British Chronicle History in Spenser's Faerie Queene*, Philadelphia, 1910. (Abstracted in Works, II, pp. 449 seq., and in notes to canto x.)

temperance; it belongs to another aspect of Spenser's design. It is one of the elements in this kind of poem that appealed to its age and cannot be revived for ours; it would of course have assumed a more obvious importance if we had the whole structure with its climax at the Faerie Queene's court.

The heart of Book II is in the treatment of the pleasures of the senses. Spenser's Temperance is concerned with anger, riches and worldly honour as well, but these cause no real conflict in Guyon's breast; the only inclination he has to wrestle with is the inclination to sensual delight. We may begin with looking at the episode of Phaedria and the Idle Lake in canto vi; and here we can observe again an element of merely social morality, as in the house of Medina. Elissa is a surly prude and Perissa a vulgar hoyden, but they are neither of them positively evil; and in the same way Phaedria is a silly flibbertigibbet, but no worse; and it is hard to resist the feeling that Spenser treats her with a good deal of indulgence. Certainly Guyon gets off very lightly for his brief holiday from the strict path of temperance. Phaedria becomes tiresome in the end, but she has a kind of dotty charm, and her island is genuinely enchanting (vi. 12–14). It is here that the influence of Tasso begins to make its appearance. Guyon abandons his Palmer on entering Phaedria's boat just as Rinaldo abandons his shield-bearer in similar circumstances (*G.L.* XIV. 58); and Phaedria's exquisite song is imitated from the song sung to Rinaldo by a nymph, one of the creatures of Armida, (*G.L.* XIV. 62–64; *F.Q.* II. vi. 15–17).

The song is unambiguously beautiful; like many lyrics it expresses a mood that cannot last, but if we were entirely to reject its invitation to present pleasure we should also be rejecting one of the happiest tributary streams of the lyrical poetry of Europe. And here I find it impossible not to observe an incipient divergence between Spenser's theme and the image in which it is embodied. It has happened earlier in Spenser's work. The May eclogue of *The Shepherd's Calendar* is a debate in the manner of Mantuan in which the diversities of shepherd life become openly symbolical of ecclesiastical controversy. Piers signifies the Protestant and Palinode the Catholic, and the

shepherds' idle May-games become images of Catholic cere-
monial and a worldly external churchmanship.

> Pal. Sicker this morowe, no lenger agoe
> I sawe a shole of shepheares outgoe
> With singing, and shouting, and iolly chere:
> Before them yode a lusty tabere,
> That to the many a horn-pype playd,
> Whereto they dauncen eche one with his mayd.
> To see those folk make such iovysaunce,
> Made my heart after the pype to daun•e:
> Tho to the greene wood they speeden them all,
> To fetchen home May with their musicall;
> And home they bringen in a royall throne,
> Crowned as king; and his queene attone
> Was Lady Flora, on whom did attend
> A fayre flock of faeries, and a fresh bend
> Of lovely nymphes. (O that I were there
> To helpen the ladies their Maybush beare!)
> Ah! Piers, bene not thy teeth on edge, to thinke
> How great sport they gaynen with little swinck?
>
> Piers. Perdie, so farre am I from envie,
> That their fondnesse inly I pitie:
> Those faytours little regarden their charge,
> While they, letting their sheep runne at large,
> Passen their time, that should be sparely spent,
> In lustihede and wanton meryment.
>
> (19–42)

The position taken by the author is not at all in doubt. Piers
is his spokesman. Yet the picture painted by Palinode is in itself
delightful, and is such as Spenser himself in other places delights
in. There can be no suggestion that he is secretly on Palinode's
side; yet it is Palinode whom the imagery tends to support. The
poet is certainly saying one thing, yet his poem contrives to
suggest something rather different. And I think that an honest
interpretation must take note of this and not merely take a short
cut through the poetry to the moral and religious position of the
historical Spenser. The case of Phaedria is not unlike. She
represents the temptation to idleness and time-wasting; at first
charming she becomes in the end tiresome, and Guyon rejects
her with disgust. But the imagery tends to reveal something

else—it reveals at least an imaginative delight in that which is
being rejected.

These contrary tendencies confront us far more obstinately in
the climactic scenes in the Bower of Bliss. Perhaps we can edge
our way into this difficult question by means of the sources.

The main outline of Book II seems to be derived not from
Spenser's usual authorities in romance, but from Trissino—
Books IV and V of *L'Italia Liberata*.[1] In Trissino a party of
knights set out in search of a wicked enchantress called Acratia
who has imprisoned some of their companions in her beautiful
garden. Spenser has not only given his enchantress the same
name, he appears also to have accepted many suggestions of
detail from Trissino. On their way the knights come to a healing
fountain, sprung from the tears of a woman, on the very spot
where another woman has been killed by Acratia's charms. This
seems to be the suggestion for the Mordaunt and Amavia
episode. There is a minor enchantress called Ligridonia, corresponding to Spenser's Phaedria; and the knights are guided by a
wise old man bearing a considerable resemblance to the Palmer.
The lay-out of the gardens is similar, including some of the
details such as the ivory gate and the wanton boys and maidens.
Acratia is a true Circe; and Spenser's Acrasia also owes something to Ariosto's Circe-figure, the enchantress Alcina. Like
Alcina Acrasia turns her lovers into beasts. But both Acratia and
Alcina have one characteristic that does not belong to Spenser's
Acrasia; beneath their specious beauty they are hideous and
deformed, and when they are captured their actual foulness is
revealed. Spenser cannot continue to follow Trissino and Ariosto
here, for this motif has already been pre-empted for his Duessa.
Also there is another influence at work, that of Tasso.

Rinaldo's captivity with the enchantress Armida and his
liberation by Carlo and Ubaldo (*G.L.* XIV, XV, XVI) is similar
in outline to the Trissino story, and when we come to the garden
itself the flat verse and the cold thin descriptions of Trissino could
afford no inspiration; so as everybody knows Spenser turned
for his Bower of Bliss to the enchanting sensuous loveliness

[1] *See* C. W. Lemmi, *The Influence of Trissino on the Faerie Queene*, P.Q. VII (1928).
Not quite conclusive, but it seems convincing to me.

of Tasso. Much of the description in his canto xii is either imitated or directly translated from cantos XV and XVI of the *Gerusalemme*. The scenery, apparently natural but really exquisitely disposed, the pool with the two nymphs bathing, the rose-song, and the behaviour of the enchantress with her lover, are all from Armida's garden. De Selincourt writes that here "he has no need to change the spirit of his model", and Castelli drily comments that Spenser "seppe copiare il suo modello". But these remarks are not quite just, and they do not give us a sufficiently accurate view of the relation between Tasso's Garden and Spenser's Bower.[1] The disposition and accompaniments of the central scenes are after all different in Spenser, and if his Bower of Bliss is an imitation it is at least a creative imitation. But more important, we can hardly say that Spenser did not need to change the spirit of his original. Both the antecedents and the consequences of Armida's enchantments are quite different from Acrasia's, and the atmosphere of the Bower ought therefore to be different from that of Armida's garden. We may come to think that Spenser has gone dangerously far in borrowing from Tasso—dangerously that is for the integrity of his own purpose.

Armida is not hideous beneath her outward beauty, she is really beautiful. She is not even particularly wicked; her only crime is that she stops Rinaldo getting on with the First Crusade, and that is hardly a crime since she is a pagan and acting out of loyalty to her own side. When Rinaldo is recalled to duty by his companions they do not destroy the garden; Armida does it herself in despair. Rinaldo has an extremely bad time in excusing himself for leaving her; what we see behind Armida is not the figure of Circe but that of Dido. And the tender-hearted Tasso cannot even let her suffer Dido's fate: when all her enchantments have failed she submits, amid the ruins of captured Jerusalem, using the words of the Virgin to the angel of the Annunciation, and offers herself not only to Rinaldo but to the Christian God.

So Spenser has taken the delectable imagery that belongs to the redeemable Armida, and conflated it with the stories of the

---

[1] *See* Robert M. Durling, "The Bower of Bliss and Armida's Palace", *Comparative Literature*, VI, 4 (1954).

really hideous, irredeemable enchantresses Alcina and Acrasia. Tasso's is essentially a love-story. Armida is passionately in love with Rinaldo, and he with her, except that he loves his duty more. Landscape in the romantic epic is essentially sympathetic landscape, constructed on the pathetic fallacy. So the scenery Spenser is borrowing for the Bower of Bliss is really a landscape of love, not a landscape of mere sensual corruption. Hence the shock, and the sense of contradiction that many readers have felt between the loveliness of the Bower and its sudden wanton destruction. It has been stated most plainly by Miss McMurphy: "Why does he feel it necessary to destroy the Bower of Bliss? If Acrasia is to be bound, if we are to see her as alluring as ever, but conquered, why mutilate the mere physical, sensible scene of her enchantments, powerless if its tutelary genius is subdued? This seems like a strain of image-breaking Puritanism overcoming the artist".[1]

So far, mere confusion of sources; a crude mechanical explanation that in reality does not explain. Spenser has chosen these different elements and combined them into his own new whole. The real thing that needs explaining is why these apparently inconsistent elements lie side by side in *The Faerie Queene*, not where they came from. It can be argued that there is no inconsistency. The first duty of an enchantress is to be enchanting. If the Bower of Bliss were not lovely there would be no temptation. And this is true, as far as it goes. Two courses would be possible for the narrative. The Bower might look lovely, Guyon might be wholly enchanted by it at the start, and gradually find out that it was false. This is what happens to Ruggiero in Alcina's garden, but clearly it does not happen in *The Faerie Queene*. Guyon knows from the start that Acrasia is the enemy and her garden evil. The other course would be to give a hint of the Bower's falseness all along—thematically speaking to show that we willingly deceive ourselves with a pleasure that we half know not to be real pleasure. This is more nearly what Spenser does, and Professor Lewis in his admirable discussion of the Bower of Bliss relies largely on this argument.[2] Since I am going to

---

[1] Op. cit., p. 36.
[2] *The Allegory of Love*, 1936, pp. 324–33.

disagree with some of his conclusions may I first acknowledge the debt that all students of Spenser must feel to his general thesis here; sexuality can be sterile and life-destroying, or fertile and life-enhancing; Spenser knows this, and shows the first in the Bower of Bliss and the second in the Garden of Adonis; and those who cannot see the difference between the two have misunderstood their author or have not looked very hard. But in the course of making this argument good Professor Lewis has involved himself in a denigration of the Bower of Bliss that leaves me unpersuaded. The Bower is made by art, but it is by no means clear that to Spenser art is bad. The ivy round Acrasia's bathing pool is artificial ivy made of gold. As inheritors of Ruskinian ideas about truth to material, we see this as horrid; but it is far from evident that Spenser saw it so. The nymphs bathing in the fountain are degraded by Professor Lewis to sluts having a vulgar romp;[1] and this is utterly false to the spirit of the passage, as it is to the place in Tasso from which the scene is derived. Professor Lewis writes as though their provocations cancelled out their beauty; but Spenser does not. Venus Anadyomene and the morning star are the similes he finds for them. And when Professor Lewis argues that the Bower is not even a place of honest sensuality, but of inactive, lascivious *looking*, scopophilia, he is surely wrong.[2] Acrasia's brow is wet with pearly drops "through languor of her late sweet toil" (78). I do not suppose that the toil referred to is watering the garden.

No; for all we can say to make Spenser's intention clearer the obstinate beauty of the scene remains unchanged. The enchantress is bound with all her charms unabated; the Bower with all its mazy loveliness is suddenly and abruptly defaced; and we are shocked. When we come to describe and analyse this sense of shock it is easy to put it badly. It would certainly be absurd to say that Spenser was secretly on Acrasia's side. Professor Lewis has finally disposed of that notion, if it was ever held in quite such a crude form. An anonymous writer has put it as follows: "We have only to read, with an advised ear, the passage of most sustained and various beauty in *The Faerie Queene*—the adven-

---

[1] Ibid, p. 331.
[2] Ibid, p. 332.

ture of Sir Guyon in the Gardens of Acrasia—to be certain that Spenser's heart was not in his morality. When, as in this episode, it came to a struggle between his morality and his sense of beauty, his sense of beauty, very properly, triumphed".[1] This is a little better, but still not good enough, unless by morality we mean moralizing, and unless we are to give an absurdly small extension to the concept of the 'heart'. Spenser's conscious, rational moral position is not ambiguous. It is perfectly clear; and a large part of anything we can mean by his heart went into it. But his sensibility was in imperfect accord with it, and this is shown by the fact that the image has assumed an independent life that in part works against the theme.

I think we can deduce something from this about the nature of Spenser's genius in general. There is a kind of mind whose sensibility instantly obeys the monitions of its conscious judgement. It is generally approved by our moral tradition. I remember the case of a young Nazi who was laughing himself sick at a Marx Brothers' film, but instantly ceased to find it amusing when he discovered that they were Jews. His opinions were unfortunate, but the obedience of his sensibility to his rational will would certainly have been praised by all Christian-classical moralists, including Spenser. Spenser himself however was not of this type. There are those for whom beauty associated with any kind of moral dubiety at once ceases to be beauty. But for Spenser beauty is always beauty, whatever its tendency. His moral principles are clear and well-established, received for the most part from religion and the civil tradition; but they are not co-extensive with his poetry. The poetry is too wide for them. His heart was very much in his morality; but it was in other things too. Much that is poetically important in *The Faerie Queene* is morally indifferent; and some things that are poetically important tend to run counter to the morality that is consciously invoked.

I should not put it any more strongly than that, but I think it is important to say that much. Since the immediate conformity of the sensibility to the moral imperative is generally approved in our culture there is a strong critical inclination to make the

[1] TLS, Feb. 27th, 1930. Quoted in Works, II, p. 371.

poets conform in this way. I think we should be more willing to recognize unresolved tensions. It is one of the missions of the poet to retain them. It is not what Milton meant, but perhaps that is one of the reasons that they are better teachers than Scotus or Aquinas. Professor Lewis's learned and sensitive exposition of Spenser would banish this moral tension altogether. For him the nymphs in Acrasia's fountain become vulgar and trivial because they are showing off their sensual charms. For Spenser they did not; nor did they for Tasso. Indeed I believe there is an unresolved moral tension at the heart of the Christian romantic epic. On the one hand there is a rational and world-denying morality; on the other there is the blaze of earthly glory and erotic ecstasy. And the second can never be put wholly to the service of the first. It is not in the nature of the romantic epic to do so, even if it were possible. For the romantic epic is an encyclopedic poem, a microcosm of the actual condition of humanity; its parts, as Tasso says, "are joined and knit together with a kind of discordant harmony"; and even the best earthly life can hardly expect more. If we try to eliminate all the discords and see only the music of the spheres we see the poem as something that it is not.

We are often told nowadays that a poem should enact its morality, whatever that means. It means I suppose that imagery and plot should entirely support the stated moral theme, or adequately take its place if there is none stated. What is enacted in the final part of Guyon's adventures seems to me partly discordant with what is stated; and I do not think we should be unwilling to recognize this. But if any reader is entirely happy about the destruction of the Bower of Bliss and thinks that Spenser was so too I would not try to persuade him.

## Chapter IX

# BOOK III: CHASTITY

The unity of *The Faerie Queene* is a unity of atmosphere; and when we come to Book III "contayning the legend of Britomartis or of Chastity", finding it presented in the same form as I and II, the same verse, the same chivalric manners and incidents, we naturally assume that we are in for a book of the same kind. When it turns out that we are not, the commentators are apt to see mere deficiency. They speak of "Spenser's confusion" in the plan of Book III, of his long and numerous digressions, of his carelessness of form. Whatever valuation we may place upon it the formal difference is apparent. Books I and II each comprise the definite quest of a single knight, self-contained, concluded within the book, and clearly related to the presiding virtue. All this disappears in Book III. Britomart is the titular heroine, but she drops out of sight in canto iv and does not reappear till canto ix. There is no quest. Britomart's final ordeal and achievement in the House of Busirane is not the result of a deliberately undertaken quest, but a fortuitous adventure not heard of until xi. Other heroines, Amoret, Belphoebe and especially Florimell divide the interest with Britomart, and there are several interpolated tales, one of considerable length.

But clearly this way of looking at Book III as an accidental divergence from the pattern of I and II is wrong. What we have here is a romance on the Ariostan interwoven pattern, where it is absurd to look for formal unity of action, or even a single dominant theme. Furthermore, the book is not self-contained and all the principal stories continue into Book IV, some even into V. In spite of separate publication III and IV must be taken together. Whatever their formal titles, their main subject-

matter is the central one of the romantic epic—love; and love in
a setting of adventure and chivalry. Here Spenser could say with
Ariosto:

> Le donne, i cavalier, l'arme, gli amori
> Le cortesie, l'audaci imprese io canto.

This would hardly have been a suitable introduction to Book I
or II. And as was suggested earlier I am strongly persuaded that
III and IV substantially belong to the earliest layer of the poem,
the design to 'overgo Ariosto' referred to in Harvey's letter.

The moral atmosphere in Book III is also markedly different
from anything in I or II. In fact there is much less moral atmosphere. The two earlier books are full of characters who are
personifications of moral forces, and are labelled as such—error,
despair, faith, hope and charity, fury and its occasion, strife and
intemperance. In Book III, except for the Mask of Cupid in xii,
such characters are few. The principal persons could not possibly
be labelled by single abstract nouns. We have moved several
degrees round the allegorical circle, away from naïve allegory,
through allegory proper, towards the free-moving romance of
types, in which allegorical significance is fluctuating and
uninsistent. If it were not for the title of the book and the
expectations established by the two earlier ones, one would
hardly have suspected Britomart of being the champion of
chastity; or that chastity, in however special a sense, was the
theme of the book as a whole. Since I seem to be in a minority
in saying this I had better try to substantiate it.

One of the striking features of the book is its free acceptance
of violence. We are not quite among the "open manslaughter and
bold bawdry" that the severe Ascham condemned in Malory;
but we are sometimes not far off it. Unprovoked personal combat is frequent—for the sheer love of fighting and the sheer love
of glory. Here Spenser accepts this norm of romance behaviour,
without much considering its moral implications. The first thing
we notice about Britomart is her fiercely emulous spirit, which
often provokes the reflection that the overthrower of Guyon,
Marinell, Paridell, and later Artegall himself, though she is in
other ways the very embodiment of faithful love, would be

likely to prove an unrestful companion. In ix and x we have the bawdy novella of Paridell and Hellenore, told with a rich appreciation of its comic potentialities, a considerable degree of cruelty towards the old cuckold Malbecco, and only the slightest and most conventional moral condemnation. At the end of canto vii is the cynical little tale of the Squire of Dames who found only three women proof against his blandishments and only one of them for honourable reasons. These are both old fabliau motifs; and they are curious constituents for a tale of chastity.

We have spoken in an earlier chapter of the extremely un-allegorical conception of Britomart. In ii where we hear of the beginning of her love for Artegall after seeing his face in the magic mirror she is simply a romance-heroine in love. And the love is *amour-passion*, eros, turbulent and distressful. A considerable part of this passage is adapted from the pseudo-Virgilian (in fact Ovidian) *Ciris*,[1] and the lines in the original (223 et seq.) describe a more or less lawless passion. Yet the purity, honesty and single-mindedness of Britomart are never in doubt. This is the place to discuss the character of Britomart and the conception of chastity that we see through it.

The name Britomart is not Spenser's invention, Britomartis was a nymph of Diana, and sometimes confused with her. She is mentioned in the *Ciris* among the passages that Spenser uses. Spenser no doubt, by a fanciful etymology means by her name simply the martial Britoness; but a lingering suggestion of the goddess Diana survives through her name and becomes a part of her character. The remote origins of the warrior-maiden are to be found in Homer's Amazons and the Camilla of Virgil, but there is no need to look so far. These warlike heroines were prominent in the Italian epics, and Ariosto's Bradamante is obviously Spenser's original. The spirit in which Ariosto conceived this type of character is seen in the opening stanzas of *O.F.* XX, which Spenser imitates at the beginning of his second and fourth cantos in this book. The woman of active power and achievement such as Ariosto celebrates here was much admired in the Italian Renaissance, as Burckhardt has noted. She was

[1] First noted by Warton, and fully discussed by M. Y. Hughes in *Virgil and Spenser*, Univ. of California, 1929, pp. 348–58 (Works II, pp. 330, 334–57).

called a *virago*, and the term implied no shadow of disapproval. Lord Julian in the third book of the *Cortegiano* declares that "if you will consider the ancient histories . . . and them of later dayes, ye shall find that virtue hath reigned as well among women as men: and that such there have been also that have made war and obtained glorious victories, governed realms with great wisdom and justice and done whatever men have done". An English poet thinking on those lines must inevitably be celebrating the virtues of Queen Elizabeth; and Britomart accordingly is also a type of the Queen.

Of these the Bradamante element is plainly the most important. And Bradamante in the *Furioso* is also the lover of Ruggiero. Their mutual devotion, continually frustrated by accident and the exigencies of war, is one of the main continuing threads of *Orlando Furioso*, as the Britomart-Artegall story is of *The Faerie Queene*. The passages of Britomart's anxiety and jealousy over Artegall, which do so much to make her the most rounded and human of Spenser's characters, are directly imitated from Ariosto. So are the places where her shining hair falls down and her sex is revealed. There is a greater delicacy in Spenser's handling of the character, but the conception of a lovable femininity beneath the swashing and martial outside is the same. And Bradamante is taken by the allegorizers of Ariosto as the type of faithful and honourable love, conjugal love (Toscanella); and even of *pudicizia* or chastity (Porcacchi). Evidently Spenser conflated these ideas, so far as they are separate, and Britomart, conceived primarily as an individual woman, spirited and brave, passionate yet controlled, warm-hearted and faithful, becomes the type of chastity—but chastity not as abstinence, chastity as active, honest and devoted love. This is not what chastity usually means, it is something more; and there can be no doubt Spenser chooses to give it this fuller and more generous meaning.

Britomart's virtue is essentially active; but besides her powers and achievements we always notice the dignity and courtesy of her bearing. It is important that having taken on the manly rôle she can hold her own in male society with an easy and amicable equality, as we see in her relations with Guyon,

Arthur and the Red Cross Knight. She represents one of the
earliest appearances in literature of woman as the companion
and equal of man. Spenser gives this prominence; but it would
be a mistake to make it more than one component of his feminine
ideal, or Britomart's kind of virtue as more than one element of
Book III, in spite of its titular pre-eminence. The story of
Florimell occupies as much of Book III as that of Britomart; she
is also a heroine of chastity, in a different mode. Yet she is the
antithesis of almost everything that Britomart represents—
fugitive, helpless, constantly threatened, like Britomart only in
that she too is in search of her only possible love. She retains
faint traces of an Ariostan original—some of her adventures are
modelled on those of Angelica; but the whole conception of the
character is different. Angelica's impudent caprices set the whole
plot in motion, and they are acts of her will. Florimell is only
the hapless object of desire. We see her hardly escaping from the
grisly forester, from Arthur, from the witches' son, from a
monster, from the lascivious old fisherman, from Proteus;
always in love with Marinell, the one man who does not want
her, always in flight from importunate and unwanted lusts. It is
a living picture of the inevitable desirability of beauty, and its
helplessness when unallied with any other qualities. For Florimell is beauty and desirability alone. She has no other qualities,
besides purity and constancy. She is timorous and passive, her
only activity is flight. Yet she too is one of Spenser's heroines.
Her character is so little salient that it can only be defined by the
creation of the false Florimell, the hollow simulacrum of all that
Florimell represents. The allegory of false beauty against true
is less conventional than it appears at first. Spenser is deeply
imbued with the Platonic feeling that outward beauty is the
index of inward, that a beautiful body reveals a beautiful soul.
Sometimes by perversion or enchantment we can have the one
without the other. But for Spenser this is not the normal
situation. Beauty is really beautiful and is the proper object of
desire. And even without personal strength or effectiveness, as
a mere passive lovely image held up for our contemplation, it
has the power to move action and to command the course of
a tale.

Florimell's mishaps follow one of the time-honoured traditions of romance, active from the beginning to the radio serials of today. In the story of the twin sisters Amoret and Belphoebe Spenser has created a new myth of his own. Begotten by the action of the sun without human father, they are a twin symbol of the nature of woman *per se*, without the accidents of human generation. Amoret brought up by Venus, Belphoebe by Diana, each takes on the nature of her protectress. But they are not goddesses, they are girls; and each illustrates both the fulfilments and the dangers that such divinely one-sided courses of development must incur when embodied in human flesh. Belphoebe's story continues into Book IV, where we learn that in spite of her beauty, her graciousness, even her charity, her way of life leads to insensibility; and the insensibility to a piling up of unrecognized feeling, which breaks out in a proud jealousy. But more of that in its place. The picture we have in Book II is an enchanting human version of the virgin huntress. Amoret, on the other hand, bred for love alone, falls into the opposite excess, although she loves faithfully and is loved by Scudamour, her true knight. This is difficult ground, and the situation can only be presented allegorically and allusively in the Busirane episode at the end of the book. Both have to change. Belphoebe has to learn pity and tenderness for her lover the squire Timias, and Amoret has to be rescued from the tortures of the house of Busirane, whose significance we shall consider in a moment.

Britomart is set aside from the others, by the mode in which she is presented as much as anything, for she is a far more fully realized, fully dramatized character. Florimell, Amoret and Belphoebe are far from allegorical abstraction; each is tenderly and humanly appealing in her own way. Each represents a distinct type of femininity, one of the possibilities of womanhood, and each therefore has her own kind of love-relation and is subject to her own kind of perils and obstructions. It is as if the idea underlying their interwoven stories is that of differing temperaments, yet with the possibility of a norm for love, a right and natural development. Whatever the thematic implications of their adventures, they are not distinctly moral ones. We are rather in the realm of erotic psychology, as in the *Romance of the Rose*—though more directly and circumstantially concerned with the actual tribulation of flesh and blood. We may include all this in "Spenser's conception of chastity" if we will; but the real essence of the book is to be an anatomy of love, to portray its enemies, its perversions and its right course. Viewed in this light the unideal or cynical episodes have their place. There is no difficulty about the Malecasta incident in canto i. It retains vestigial hints from Ariosto of a more dubious tendency, but it simply serves to show up the straightforward purity of Britomart at its most vigorous. The long novella of Paridell, Malbecco and Hellenore is different. It is a story of successful seduction, with a great deal of shrewd characterization. Paridell's "I take no keep of her . .. She wonneth in the forrest there before" is a roughly realistic bit of observation on the fate of the deserted wanton. Yet Spenser is quite unconcerned to turn it to the ends of edification; Hellenore gives every sign of thoroughly enjoying her abandonment to the satyrs. I recommend those who have heard too much of the 'maidenliness' of Spenser's imagination to re-read canto x, 44–51. When Marinell heard the disobliging tale of the Squire of Dames he laughed 'full hartely'. In the assumption that we are reading an allegory of chastity in any ordinarily expected sense, these incidents are highly incongruous. But if we see the book as an anatomy of love—not love in the 'Platonic' manner, but sexual love between men and women—then they are natural and appropriate. For Eros is not to be confined in any particular moral sphere; he haunts the slums and alleyways as well as the heights. And Spenser's idealism is never of a kind that shirks the actual facts of the case.

Like the earlier books this one contains its allegorical peaks; and I have kept them for separate discussion. Book III has its centre in the Garden of Adonis, and its great set-piece in the Mask of Cupid. But the Mask of Cupid is only the heraldic exfoliation of the whole spirit of the House of Busirane. It looks simple, but Amoret's connection with it implies, I believe, a delicately veiled thematic content which I must now try to expound. The episode at the House of Busirane in III. xi and xii is one of the greatest of Spenser's set-pieces—among the greatest because it is dramatic as well as pictorial. The splendour, luxuriance and expressiveness of the imagery is completed by the presence of Britomart through whose eyes it is seen, Britomart observing and active through it all. There are abundant literary precedents for the whole series of scenes and actions. The scene where Britomart comes to the aid of Scudamour, and the castle guarded by fire, have an analogue in *O.F.* II. 34 seq., and a more definite one in Tasso's *Rinaldo*. The tapestries that Britomart inspects owe something to those that Bradamante sees in the Rocca di Tristano (*O.F.* XXXIII). Forerunners of the Masks of Cupid are found in Ovid's *Amores* and in Petrarch's *Trionfo d'Amore* and *Trionfo della Castità*. Spenser may even be re-working his own earlier *Court of Cupid*. But the result is a new and powerfully individual whole. We are equally far from personified moral commonplace and from the charming shadows of the *Romance of the Rose*. Spenser's Venusberg is filled with haunting and compelling images, and they in themselves are neither good nor evil—or good and evil are inextricably intermixed. It is a panorama of passion that is displayed, isolated from moral censorship. The figures in the tapestry room are equally divided between the joy and the ferocity of love; and it is not till stanzas 47–49 that we discover why the atmosphere of enclosed menace is so strong: this is a temple where passion is not only celebrated but made the object of idolatry. Beyond in the next room it is the monstrous and destructive forms of love alone that are portrayed. They prepare us for the pageant in the twelfth canto.

The processional maske with the figures of Fancy, Desire, Fear, Hope and Grief at first recalls the medieval manner, but the conception is far more energetic. As Cory has written, "Here we have all the elements of an elaborate psychology of love, separated, conceptualized, personified and made astonishingly vivid as these personages pour through the halls of the lustful wizard." Spenser's sense of the tragic destiny of passionate love is far more intense than is usual in the allegorical tradition. Behind the figure of the god come Care, Unthriftihed, Change, Disloyalty and Death. Then there is the horror, quite original with Spenser, of Amoret's torture.

# BOOK III: CHASTITY

But this brings us to the difficult question about the whole episode. Why should Amoret and Scudamour, innocent and faithful lovers, be afflicted by the torments of the horrible Busirane? So far as his house, its décor and its pageantry are a detachable spectacle, its bearing is not obscure: it is a visual allegory of obsessive and torturing love. For Professor Lewis Busirane is courtly love, the villain hero of his study. Well, yes; but something more extensive than courtly love as a mere system or convention. Busirane is *amour-passion*, love as it is in Racine or Proust; *Venus toute entière à sa proie attachée*. And it is not easy to see why a happy pair of lovers, blessed by the gods, should become his prey. We must look forward to the passages in Book IV where the earlier course of their love is revealed. The wooing of Amoret in the temple of Venus need not concern us now, except to note that all obstacles are overcome, Scudamour smilingly claims his right, Venus favours his pretence and laughs upon him "with amiable grace" (IV. x. 51). We have already learnt in IV.i that subsequent dangers were overcome and the pair were to be married. It was actually on their wedding day before the bride was bedded (IV. i. 3) that Amoret was stolen away by Busirane and his crew, who enter under the guise of "that mask of love that late was showen". So the terrifying pageant that Britomart witnessed at Busirane's house actually made its appearance at Amoret's wedding and became the agent of her captivity. There is no question of Amoret's being disloyal to Scudamour or being possessed by another love; there is no doubt that her love for Scudamour is a blessed and happy one. Neither of the lovers is to blame in any way. Spenser has so often been seen as the moralist of love that his subtlety as the psychologist of love has sometimes been neglected. Scudamour and Amoret are true lovers, but they are by nature purely erotic lovers; and Eros in itself, besides its sweetness, contains an element of threat and fear. True lovers smiled upon by circumstance are not always immediately happy. They may meet the conflicts of voluptuousness and timidity, fear and desire. It is only otherwise by the conventions of romance, and Spenser has far more to say about the nature of love than his outward obedience to the conventions of romance

175

would suggest. Passion, even when ratified by the gods and sealed by marriage can be torturing and terrifying—until it is qualified and completed by friendship, fidelity, active affection and endurance: all the qualities that Spenser sums up in Britomart's chastity. The scholastic definition of love is "a fixed direction of the will"; and however incomplete that may be it is an essential part of the true definition. It is this active and courageous constancy that Britomart displays, and that she typifies when, as here, she is functioning allegorically. That is why Scudamour, the merely erotic lover, is powerless to rescue Amoret, and Britomart must become the saviour from the divisive perils of a passion that is only passion. She becomes the friend of Amoret, is present when the two are brought together;[1] and so completes one of Spenser's most reticent, delicate and perceptive pieces of allegory.

The allegorical core of the book is the Garden of Adonis in Canto vi. It follows the charming mythological account of the birth of Amoret and Belphoebe, and its narrative *raison d'être* is that it is the place where Amoret is nursed. But the thematic intention extends beyond the narrative function. It has little to do with moral or erotic allegory; the theme is cosmological. The Garden is mythologically the place where Venus meets Adonis; and it is also the garden of generation where all living things are formed and re-formed after they have disintegrated. It reminds us that the Venus who presides over *The Faerie Queene*, whatever relation she may bear to the Uranian Venus of Platonic myth, or the earthly Venus, goddess of love's delight, is also the Lucretian Venus, (closely related, if we may be anachronistic, to the Freudian Eros), the power of generation and fecundity in the whole living universe. The thought of this passage has given a good deal of trouble. It is hardly to be reduced to an orderly sequence of ideas, and I believe with Denis Saurat that the attempt to read it as a systematic essay in

[1] Unfortunately the completion of the story is spoilt by one of the worst loose ends resulting from the unfinished state of *F.Q.* The reunion of the lovers originally took place at the end of III. Spenser later cancelled these stanzas, prolonged their separated adventures in the interest of a protracted Ariostan design—and then forgot to insert the cancelled reunion in the appropriate place. This is undoubtedly at IV. ix. 39. With a little adaptation the stanzas can be put in there and the defect made good.

natural philosophy is bound to fail.[1] Even when Spenser is
borrowing ideas from the philosophers it is idle to look for
philosophical rigour in his thought. He works by vision, image
and action; for him the formal notions of philosophy are only a
species of metaphor, and take their place in a series of imaginative tableaux, not in a logical structure. We are certainly
wrong to imagine that when Spenser borrows images from
Lucretius, as he does, he is adhering to Lucretian atomism and
materialism. We should be equally wrong in falling into the
more popular error of supposing that because he borrows
Platonic images he is an orthodox neo-Platonist. Both kinds of
imagery are used in the Adonis passages; but Spenser's use of
them, and of places from Ovid that have also been laid under
contribution, is to make a loose synthesis guided by feeling
rather than a tight doctrinal web. He uses philosophical ideas in
a poular and exoteric way; indeed all those that he employs here
are commonplaces in the general thought of the time.

Stanzas 8 and 9 of this canto form a prelude to the Garden
passage by celebrating the sun as 'the great father of generation',
and the earth as ministering 'matter fit' for his formative power.
In 29–35 the Garden is shown as the seed-bed of all living
creatures, who are clothed with fleshly weeds by Genius and sent
out into the world; to return to the Garden when their course is
run, remain there for a thousand years, and then go back to a
new incarnation. The idea is familiar from the myth of Er in
Book X of Plato's Republic; Spenser might also have found it in
Ovid; and the concept of the earth spontaneously generating an
infinitude of living forms is very close to Lucretius. Stanzas
36–8, with their idea of the indestructibility of matter and its
continual replenishment are again a positive echo of Lucretius I.
The first extract suggests a Platonic notion of immaterial forms
embodying themselves in material weeds; the second suggests
a purely material cycle of causation, in which the 'naked babes'
are not platonic ideas but the pre-existing 'seeds' of living
creatures. If we are to choose it is the second that is the more in
harmony with the general purport of the passage. We should

[1] Denis Saurat, Literature and Occult Tradition, 1930, pp. 184–200. On the
whole controversy see Works II, 340–53.

probably not press too hard upon them, but look on them as alternative metaphors for the strictly indescribable cycle of generation. Stanzas 39–42 deal with *tempus edax rerum*, a traditional lament, but one which seems to apply to the phenomenal world rather than to the Garden its seed-bed where all things are perpetually renewed. The thought is that the Garden, as part of the natural process, is not a changeless paradise; it too, though always renewing itself, is subject to Mutability— an aspect of this part of the poem that connects it very closely with the Mutability cantos themselves. As it is, the Garden is blissful enough:

> Frankly each paramour his leman knows,
> Each bird his mate, ne any does envie
> Their goodly meriment, and gay felicitie.

And this leads on to the final picture of the shady natural bower in the middle of the Garden where Venus comes to lie with Adonis her lover and "reap sweet pleasure of the wanton boy". This is yet another metaphor, a mythological presentation of the same process of generation; for Adonis though a mortal never perishes; he is "eterne in mutabilitie". He is called "the Father of all formes"; and this has led to a puzzle about how Spenser intends us to interpret his myth. There are those who would say that Adonis must represent matter, substantially unchangeable though impressed with numerous forms. I find it very hard to believe that Spenser would be so extravagantly untraditional as to make the male represent matter, the female form. Nor do I think this necessary. Surely Spenser is using 'form' here in a popular, not a philosophical sense. He means merely 'shapes', not Platonic 'forms' or ideas. Adonis is simply the father of all the shapes that living creatures assume. Nor need we suppose that he is 'form' and Venus 'matter'. The concept is not an analytical one. Their joyful union is simply a symbol of the eternal process of birth, decay, death and rebirth that pervades the whole physical universe. Venus is divine, and Adonis is quasi-immortalized. "Man is in love, and loves what vanishes. What is there more to say?" This is the truth, if we remain within the individual human consciousness. If we expand our range to the whole cosmic process, the same facts indicate a continual glad renewal. And this is what the Garden of Adonis is about.

There are those who have seen the Garden of Adonis and the Bower of Bliss as good and evil paradises, in some sense rivals to each other. They have been disturbed by the surface similarity between the central scenes in each, and feel that Spenser has not sufficiently distinguished between them. It is Professor Lewis who has deployed the most elaborate argument against this.[1] He makes much of the artificiality of Acrasia's Bower: rightly, for it is emphasized. But I doubt if this was unambiguously bad in the eyes of Spenser and his contemporaries. It is true that Venus's bower in the Garden is "not by art/But of the trees' own inclination made". Yet surely the radical distinction is simply that the Garden is a place of fertility. The Bower is a pleasure-ground, and nothing more. The Garden is a seed-plot. The Venus that Spenser worships is not only love, but the Lucretian genitrix of all things; and as long as genesis, not merely sterile and self-enclosed pleasure, is the result, Venus can "reap sweet pleasure of the wanton boy" without reproach. Nor need we interpret the fertility literally: we are not told that Adonis gets children on Venus: it is enough that we know that some kinds of love are fruitful and life-enhancing, and some sterile and life-destroying. The natural world knows only the former; the complexities of knowing the latter as well are reserved for human kind alone.

[1] *Allegory of Love*, p. 324 seq.

*Chapter X*

## BOOK IV: FRIENDSHIP

Complaints about the formal deficiencies of Book IV have been even more vocal than those about Book III, and indeed it departs even farther from the plan announced in the Letter. There is no quest; there is no single knight. Cambel and Triamond who give their names to the whole are the heroes only of an episode that is not central and has no general consequences. The illustration of the· virtues of friendship seems faint and fluctuating at first sight, and the attempt to find an orderly narrative structure seems more completely doomed to failure here than in any other part of *The Faerie Queene*. The attempt has nevertheless been made by Notcutt,[1] presumably on the principle of achieving a general victory by defending the least promising case. But for all its resourcefulness and ingenuity the effort is in principle mistaken. Notcutt draws attention to some elements of design that are certainly present; the balance between Ate at the beginning and Concord near the end of the book, and the central position of the recognition scene between Britomart and Artegall. But the alleged symmetry can only be demonstrated by considerable wrestling of the real proportions; and no part of *The Faerie Queene* is to be defended on these inappropriately formal lines. Manifestly the book is like its predecessor a series of Ariostan cantos. Regarded in this light it develops in a perfectly lucid fashion, and its main stories are all continuations of those in Book III. The adventures of Britomart and Artegall, Amoret and Scudamour, Florimell and Marinell, the false Florimell, and Belphoebe and her squire are all carried on from the earlier book.

What we have then is obviously a sequel to Book III; but

[1] Notcutt, "The Faerie Queene and its Critics", *Essays and Studies XII* (1926).

as usual no reliable deductions can be made about dates. Presumably the two books were not far apart, as both narratives and characters retain their continuity. Yet there has been a change of plan. The reunion of Amoret and Scudamour, placed at the end of Book III in 1590, is removed in 1596, and their continued search for each other forms one of the main motifs of Book IV. This is in accord with the Ariostan principle of delaying the conclusion of a narrative line by interweaving it with others—a principle which is observed throughout the book with considerable fullness and address. The main threads are carried forward, varied by two interpolated tales, those of Cambel and Triamond (ii, iii) and Amyas and Placidas (vii, viii, ix); and as usual there are descriptive and allegorical halting-places. Transitions are skilfully handled. The only respect in which the book deserves the strictures made upon it is that the two interpolated tales are neither of them of the highest Spenserian quality.

The moral atmosphere too is much the same as that of Book III. The formal allegorical personifications are rather more numerous—Ate, Concord, Slander, Care, and the *Romance of the Rose* figures in the Temple of Venus. But most of the stories have moved away from allegory towards romance with a merely typical significance. And it is mainly erotic romance; the recurrent thematic interest is still love. The announced theme is Friendship, and this brings up the question of how far the book is really about friendship at all, and how Spenser conceived that quality. It is a little difficult to think of friendship as a 'virtue' if the word virtue is given its ordinary modern significance. Aristotle whom Spenser is supposed to be following describes it doubtfully in the Ethics as 'a kind of virtue' and as 'something that goes along with virtue'.[1] But if we think of virtue in the extended sense in which a drug or a herb is said to have its special 'virtue', Spenser's idea of friendship is easier to understand. Friendship is a power, a principle, an attractive force that may exhibit itself in personal character, but also in the goings-on of the universe, on a variety of different planes. That it is not seen simply as a personal quality is sufficiently shown by the fact that there is no one hero who stands as its embodiment.

[1] Eth. Nic. VIII, 1.

181

We normally think of friendship as a personal *relation*; and as such of course it occupied a conspicuous and honourable place in the values of Spenser's time. It is hardly necessary to refer to its importance in Castiglione, in Sidney, and in the view of life of Shakespeare's youthful heroes. It is equally honoured, as we have remarked, in Ariosto. It would be idle to hunt out Spenser's sources for anything so universally diffused. All the lights he casts upon it were commonplaces and had been for centuries; all could be found in a book of such general currency as Cicero's *De Amicitia*, besides innumerable other expressions in romance or sententious literature. The most obvious fable of friendship in Book IV is the story of Amyas and Placidas, which has a medieval original. There is the less conventional and less noted, but steady and beautiful friendship of Britomart for Amoret, and the general comradely ideal displayed in all the relations between the worthier knights. But in the general conduct of Book IV a wider conception of friendship is to be found, and one that goes beyond the word's normal semantic range. In canto i the figure of Ate is conspicuous. She slanders Amoret and Britomart, sows suspicion in the heart of Scudamour and brings about potential discord between the lovers. The story of Cambel and Triamond is mostly occupied with internecine strife. In the first four cantos there is an inordinate amount of squabbling and fighting. Even the meeting of Artegall and Britomart (vi) begins with a stern contest. And in all cases throughout the book it is the function of the good characters to restore peace. Glauce, the Squire of Dames, Cambina, Britomart and Arthur all act in this way. And here friendship is no longer a relation; it is the pervasive force of good will, restoring the normal harmony in all human relations. This has in the end its allegorical embodiment in the figure of Concord at the gate of the Temple of Venus (x), placed antithetically to Ate at the beginning; and the name concord is perhaps more ordinarily appropriate to the thematic content of the book than friendship itself. We see Concord not as a virtue or as a relationship but as a cosmic principle; a cosmic principle to be further illustrated in the picturesque and amicable rout of the marriage of Thames and Medway (xi). The highest form of this cosmic principle is love. The book of Friendship is starred with the reunions of lovers, and the Temple of Venus, less inappropriately than it seems at first, forms its allegorical centre.

In a book like this where formal allegory disappears or runs underground for long stretches together we cannot go straight to the thematic content. The allegorical short cut is never the proper way to read Spenser and here it is hardly possible. As with a pure romance we must focus on the shifting pattern of the image itself and let the theme arise naturally from it. The early cantos present the normal desultory course of knight-errantry and encounters by the way. In the first canto we have one of the lovely scenes where Britomart unbinds her hair and reveals her womanhood. Like all these scenes it has its original in Ariosto, but it has its special function here in putting an end to an unseemly contretemps about the possession of Amoret. Then, as Britomart and Amoret go on their way they are joined by another group of characters—Ate and Duessa, Blandamour and Paridell. Blandamour claims Amoret, is overthrown by Britomart; and she and Amoret go off. The remaining group is joined successively by Scudamour and Glauce, Ferraugh and the snowy Florimell, the Squire of Dames, and finally by Cambel and Triamond, Canacee and Cambina. There are several quarrels, realignments, uneasy reconciliations that we need not follow in detail. At first they seem episodic and rather pointless, but gradually it becomes apparent that we are observing a series of exempla of true and false friendship. It is an Aristotelian principle that the best kind of friendship can only subsist between the virtuous;[1] and so it is here. Though Paridell and Blandamour seem to be comrades they are always breaking out into quarrels and there is no steadiness in their relation. The false Florimell is a cause of strife. And all this discord springs from sheer shallowness and inferiority, distinct from the deliberate malice of Ate and Duessa. On the other side we have the constant and harmonious relationship of Britomart and Amoret, of Cambel and Triamond and their ladies, securely founded on character and disinterested affection.

This leads to the previous history of Cambel and Triamond

[1] Eth. Nic. VIII, 3.

(ii. 30–iv. 3), a longer and more developed exemplum of strife and harmony restored. It is not one of Spenser's most brilliant episodes. Wind has remarked on the story of the three brothers whose souls successively migrate into each other's bodies, and has found it typical of one element in Renaissance syncretist mythology, the 'infolding' of several natures into one.[1] He has also remarked, justly, on the poetical ineptitude with which it is handled. The contest between Cambel and the thrice-powerful Triamond is an unduly prolonged spell of walloping and carving, redeemed only by the apparition of Cambina as peacemaker (iii. 28). The incident seems to be compounded of a passage from Natalis Comes on the Caduceus of Mercury and its power of restoring harmony; a passage from the *Odyssey* (IV. 219) on Nepenthe, the drink of forgetfulness; an acknowledged citation of the magic fountain from which Rinaldo drinks in Ariosto; and surely, a recollection of the deities and allegorical beings who appear in chariots in pageants and court spectacles. In this sudden outburst of allusive and spectacular mythology, wonderfully typical of Spenser's eclectic harmony, the story comes to life. Otherwise it is scarcely memorable and scarcely worthy of the charming invocation of Chaucer at its opening (ii. 32). The theme of all this first part of the book is summed up in the opening stanzas of iv, which reflects on the instability of friendship 'without regard of good', and the equal impermanence of enmity that springs not from evil but only from 'occasion'.

We then pass to the tournament for Florimell's girdle. This is the usual chivalric mêlée, to us a rather tedious interruption of the narrative, to the earlier readers of the romantic epic an intrinsically interesting part of it. It extends through most of Cantos iv and v, and in the general economy of the story it serves to bring Britomart and Artegall together in combat, unknown to each other since both are in disguise. The fighting over, the interest passes in the second part of Canto v to the beauty contest for the prize of the girdle—once the possession of Venus, then that of the lost Florimell. The girdle would seem to have been suggested by the Cestus of Aphrodite in Homer (*Iliad*. XIV. 214), or the girdle of Armida in Tasso (*G.L.* XVI. 24–5), except that

[1] Edgar Wind, *Pagan Mysteries in the Renaissance*, 1958, p. 171 seq.

its properties are almost opposite. Theirs was to excite passion, that of Florimell's to restrain 'loose affection', and to be un-wearable except by a chaste woman. This is typical of Spenser's way of taking a motif from earlier literature or mythology and turning it to his own quite different purpose. Here, after the prolonged knightly scuffling, the ghost of an allegorical inten-tion makes its appearance. The girdle falls off the waist of the false Florimell, and many other ladies try it with the same result. It will fit only on Amoret, less dazzling in beauty than the snowy maiden, but a tender, chaste and faithful lover. The tone of the contest is not however an exalted one. The Squire of Dames laughs loudly at the ill success of the earlier contestants (v. 18, 19), and the other knights follow him. We are nearer to the realm of a sceptical worldly chivalry than to the 'Platonic' idealism that is often presented to us as the uniform temper of Spenser's mind. In the following scene the false Florimell is passed from hand to hand, ultimately taking by her own choice Braggadochio, the least worthy knight of all; and the party breaks up in general discontent. The moral situation is always clear, but the tone is that of shrewd comedy.

This leads to the recognition scene between Britomart and Artegall in vi. It does not bring their story to an end, but the train of events that starts with Britomart's vision of Artegall in the magic mirror here reaches a climax. The whole relationship of Britomart and Artegall is modelled on that of Bradamante and Ruggiero in Ariosto, but there is no exact imitation. The anagnorisis in O.F. XX is not preceded by a fight; it is at the end of their·adventures that the two lovers meet in combat (O.F. XLV). Spenser's scene conflates the two, and is affected also by the duel of Tancredi and Clorinda in G.L. III. We can see here how Spenser handles the material of the romantic epic. He is soaked in its spirit, easily familiar with its material, can take one of the major Ariostan themes and handles it with com-plete freedom in his own way. His scene occupies the whole of canto vi and is far more developed than the brief and hastily broken-off recognition in Ariosto. The handling is extremely skilful. Both Scudamour and Artegall have cause of resentment against the unknown Britomart. Scudamour encounters her first and is overthrown. Artegall then takes on the combat (the raw collocation of ferocity and beauty owes a good deal to the spirit of Tasso) and it rages until he shears off the front of Britomart's helmet and her lovely face and her shining hair are revealed. We have had similar scenes before, at Malecasta's house, at Malbecco's, at the castle in IV. i. All these revelations are imitated from Bradamante at the Rocca di Tristano (*O.F.* XXII. 79); but in repeating them Spenser builds up a fine effect of dramatic irony; we as readers have come to expect what the actors in the story are ignorant of. Artegall's amazement and veneration (vi. 21, 22) are validated for us by the cumulative effect of earlier discoveries of Britomart's beauty. The transition from enmity to love and the necessary change in the whole attitude of Britomart are not easy to manage. While the two lovers are still doubtful and confused Spenser with great art introduces the interest of Scudamour and his anxious inquiries about the fate of Amoret (34). This interposes a diversion for Britomart's modesty and pride; and by the time she has replied to Scudamour we are prepared to find her a woman instead of a warrior, to find that affection and peace has imperceptibly established itself among them all.

It is an instance of the dream-like quality of *The Faerie Queene* that after this vivid and strongly felt encounter they all repair "unto some resting-place that mote befall". It is well provided with feasting in bower and hall; yet it is never particularized; we do not know what or whose it is. It just appears from nowhere because some place is needed for Artegall to complete his wooing of Britomart. In Ariosto the reconciled lovers set off for the precisely indicated Vallombrosa—

> così fu nominata una badia
> ricca e bella, nè men religiosa
> e cortese a chi unque vi venia.

But Spenser is no more allegorical here than Ariosto. Britomart and Artegall in other places are the embodiments of their respective virtues, but no one here finds that Chastity is being reconciled with Justice. The two lovers are completely and happily themselves. And there could be no better example of

true friendship between man and woman than the final passage
where Britomart, against her affections and desires, yet allows
Artegall to go off and complete his quest. He is a man and must
fulfil his obligations and Britomart is a good enough woman to
see it.

The continuation of Amoret's adventures in vii is quite without thematic implications. It is simple romance-adventure, and
in typical Ariostan fashion it leads into the next tale, for
Amoret's fate becomes entangled with that of Aemilia. This
brings us to the story of Aemilia, Amyas and Placidas, but not
directly, for the episode of Belphoebe and Timias intervenes
(vii. 36–viii. 9). Belphoebe's coldness, her jealousy of Timias
and his ultimate recovery of grace is no doubt a part of what is
called the 'historical allegory'. A better way of putting it is that
it is a personal allusion, to Sir Walter Raleigh's loss of favour
with the queen.[1] However that may be, it occupies a perfectly
fitting place in the thematic economy of Books III and IV.
Amoret, the twin-sister who has been bred for love, has to be
educated in love and be rescued from its perils by Britomart. So
Belphoebe, the virginal sister, unapproachable, dangerous and
solitary, has to learn tenderness and fellow-feeling. And it is a
little wild natural creature, a bird, that brings her to do so. The
tale of Amyas and Placidas is an adaptation of the well-known
French romance of Amis and Amiloun, described by Pater in
*The Renaissance*. It is a self-contained tale, again an exemplum
of true friendship, parallel to the story of Cambel and Triamond
earlier on. It affords an opportunity for Arthur to appear in viii
as reconciler and peacemaker, a rôle that he continues in ix,
where he subdues the quarrels arising from false friendship. All
this time Scudamour and Amoret have been parted by an evil
fate and estranged by slander; their reunion postponed from the
end of III should be inserted at ix. 39. Throughout this book the
unions of lovers recur as the supreme symbol of friendship—
Cambel and Cambina, Triamond and Canacee, Artegall and
Britomart, Timias and Belphoebe, Amyas and Aemilia,
Scudamour and Amoret, and Marinell and Florimell at the end.

[1] The historical circumstances are recounted in A. L. Rowse, *Raleigh and the
Throckmortons*, 1962.

It is consistent with this theme so often repeated that the Temple of Venus (x) should be the allegorical centre of Book IV. Yet at first it is hard to see it so. We have seen the idea of friendship extended to include the general principle of harmony in the universe. But the Temple of Venus does not on the face of it represent this kind of cosmic love. In spite of the borrowing of a hymn to Venus from the opening lines of *De Rerum Natura* it hardly seems to be the Lucretian life-force that is primarily celebrated here. In essence the whole canto is the medieval allegory of courtship, in the *Rose* tradition. The old enemy Danger appears; the maidens in the temple, Shamefastness, Cheerfulness, Modesty and the rest are familiar figures from the love-allegories, and the object of Scudamour's quest is to woo and take away his Amoret. Yet merely by placing it in his book of Friendship Spenser is setting romantic love in a wider context. What is evil about 'courtly love' in the conventional sense is the worship of it as an exclusive duty, love turned to idolatry. Here the romance and the courtliness remain, but there is none of the brooding confinement of the Venusberg. At the gate of the temple sits Concord, holding apart the two brothers Love and Strife. This is a new twist to a frequent Renaissance allegorical theme. The idea of necessary strife as the motive power of the universe, held in check by concord and amity, is one that the Renaissance inherited from a number of late classical sources. Ultimately it goes back to Empedocles.

> It is well known that in the fables of the Greeks Harmony was born from the union of Mars and Venus: of whom the latter is fierce and contentious, the former generous and pleasing. . . . Empedocles calls the force effective of good by the name of love and friendship . . . and the destructive force he calls pernicious strife.[1]

So Plutarch, in a passage that Spenser must have known, since he uses the same work in other places. Most commonly Venus herself is identified with concord. Spenser is giving his own turn to an honoured theme; and his Temple of Venus, for all the dominance of courtship and erotic allegory, does from this point

[1] *De Iside et Osiride*, 48. Quoted in Wind, op. cit., p. 82.

of view turn out to be also a temple of cosmic harmony. It surpasses in beauty not only the temple of the Ephesian Diana but also the temple that Solomon "that wise king of Jurie framed/With endless coste, to be th'Almighties see" (30). The analogy from sacred history can hardly be accidental; here for a moment the Queen of Love is brought into relation with *l'amor che move le sole e l'altre stelle.*

Besides the figures from erotic allegory the temple contains pairs of lovers, and the famous friends of antiquity such as Hercules and Hylas, David and Jonathan, Orestes and Pylades— some of whom, we might observe, were friends who were also lovers. The hymn sung in the temple (44–47) is the Lucretian invocation to *alma Venus*, both the power of harmony and the power of generation and desire. The goddess herself is veiled; the mystery of her form may not be revealed, because she is the hermaphrodite Venus and "hath both kinds in one". Wind has remarked that the pseudo-Orphic pantheon of the Renaissance is filled with divine hybrids, with the idea of the gods reconciling opposite natures in a single harmony.[1] It is something of a surprise, after these cosmological and mythic overtones, to come to the gentle figures of the old love-allegory when Scudamour finds his Amoret seated in the lap of Womanhood and attended by Courtesy, Cheerfulness and the other maidens. When Scuda-mour offers to take her away from them (53, 54) he boldly invokes the symbolism of his own shield, says it is right that Cupid's man should have Venus's maid, and that it is ill for the service of the goddess to be performed by virgins. With perfect gentleness and delicacy Spenser is celebrating completely natural 'pagan' love, maintaining its connection with the great pervading forces that move and govern the natural world, yet maintaining also the romantic tenderness that the ancient world had never known, and that had been the civilizer of the heart of Europe ever since the twelfth century.

So much in Spenser seems a happy accident that it would be easy to regard the marriage of Thames and Medway in the next canto in this light. It is almost certainly a re-writing in some form or other of the *Epithalamium Thamesis*, an early poem of

[1] Op. cit., p. 164, 172 seq.

Spenser's now lost. It appears in the narrative as a continuation of the story of Florimell and can be looked at as a mere decorative interpolation. Its peculiar charm lies in the mingling of the grandiose roll-call of mythological persons with the homely and intimate geography of England and Ireland. Yet thematically it is perfectly appropriate. This happy riot is a symbol of concord and amity in nature, as it were a splendid pictorial celebration of joyous harmony, seen as a natural force, not merely a human habit. And it is not without its effect on human life, for Marinell happens to come to the wedding, and it is there that he overhears Florimell's plaint and finds his heart softened.

Friendship, then, as a human relation, with love as its most intense and refined form; and friendship, love, concord, whatever we care to call it, as the moving principle of the universe—these are the themes of Book IV. Spenser the moralist is very much in abeyance here; we see rather Spenser the celebrant of the laws of life, and they are above all rich, genial and loving. Those who deny them through quarrelling and falsehood are overthrown; those who resist them through austerity or insensibility are overcome; and Venus smiles on the bold lover who proposes to take away her favourite child.

## Chapter XI

# BOOK V: JUSTICE

Structurally Book V is a return to the pattern of I and II, with a single quest and a single knight embodying a definitely conceived virtue. The story of Britomart is continued and that of Florimell concluded here, but the form and spirit are quite different from those of Books III and IV. The plot is far less intricate and varied, the fortunes of Artegall are followed pretty continuously throughout, and there are no interpolated tales. This simplicity has its attractions, and there is a good structural reason for it here, after the complexities of the preceding books. Yet Book V is the least liked of all *The Faerie Queene*—and not without cause. Invention and narrative power are weaker, the verse is often flat, the peaks of allegorical or pictorial concentration are lacking. The thematic material is less deeply felt than in I or III; it is largely social and political, and the historical allegory for the first time becomes quite inescapable. Violence, unjust disposition of the world's goods, communism, and the position of women are the social themes of general application. The specific political ones are rebellion in Ireland, the trial of Mary Queen of Scots and the struggle of the Netherlands against Spain. Such political subjects are always likely to be ephemeral unless they are seen as types of the general human situation, or become so by their own nature and importance. Spenser's themes do not achieve this. There might have been the feeling of a profound religious conflict or a great national drama behind the romance-images of this book; but in fact there is not. There are some vivid episodes and exempla, but for much of the time we are contemplating a thin allegorical covering over a somewhat distorted version of particular historical events.

The titular virtue.of the book is Justice; but it is justice in a strictly limited sense—confined entirely to its practical and external operations. Justice might be conceived as an internal constituent and governor of the soul, or in the Platonic way as the harmony of the soul resulting from the right balance of its elements. This cluster of ideas is dealt with if anywhere under the head of Temperance in Book II, and there is no trace of it here. Artegall's quest is a military and political one—it is to free Irena's lands from the usurpation of a tyrant. In the course of it he functions as a judge, deciding causes and righting wrongs; and he exists largely in his actions. He has no inner life, and his deeds are not symbols of anything in the inner life. It is not true to say that his operations are purely political, for several of his cases occur in the private sphere; but they are legal rather than moral, and after the whole book has been read it is the political parts that remain most clearly in mind.

This makes difficulties for the modern reader and they had perhaps better be faced at the start. Spenser is executing his allegorical decorations on one of the blackest pages in English history. He was the defender of a hateful policy in Ireland, and if his own position is not quite at its most hateful extreme, it is not far off it. He did not recommend the actual extermination of the Irish peasantry, but that is about all that can be said; he deprecated even the slight mitigations of repressive savagery favoured by Burghley and the Queen. Artegall's central quest is the liberation of Irena; and heavens knows what Ireland his Irena signifies, for it seems to exclude the entire population of the land. We cannot but feel that the position is false from the start. Allegory must appeal to an existing moral community; it has little power of conversion or persuasion and is at its strongest on the great moral and emotional commonplaces that endure through a whole civilization. Particular political issues are never in this class; and in the present case the moral community on which Spenser depends has long since rejected his claims. In his attitude to Ireland he is largely the creature of his age and it would be idle to expect him to display a humanitarianism that is quite alien to his historical situation. His attitude towards rebels is near enough to that of the authoritarian governments of our own day to make us realize that he is occupying a recurrent political position. But we are accustomed to find Spenser's themes based on something better than the wisdom of political expediency. It is possible that he is not even up to the best of his own place and time in this respect. There is a note of assertive polemic in parts of this political allegory that suggests something less secure than the steady deep-rooted convictions of most of *The Faerie Queene*.

Having said so much we can look at other difficulties that are less well grounded. Justice is not a popular virtue in our age and a more or less conscious resentment against some of its classical forms is one of the current social derangements. Only a very reduced conception of justice is at all generally accepted nowadays—the egalitarian one; and that is precisely the view that Spenser did not hold. The legitimacy of the punitive function is now very widely doubted; and Spenser is quite clear that justice is impossible without it. In these ways he is out of sympathy with the general current of feeling in our place and time—though in sympathy of course with a far larger and more general current of feeling in other places and other times. It is easy to see that in specific political cases Spenser is not living up to the insights that his Christian and classical training could have given him. He could have found plenty of persuasion towards clemency, generosity and mild government if he had wished to look for them. But in his general interpretation of justice, though it is incomplete, he does not fall short of orthodoxy. The outlines of the Aristotelian conception of justice —or rather of part of it—are faintly discernible. Justice is divided into distributive and corrective.[1] Distributive justice is not egalitarian; it is giving every man his due and more is due to the better man. Justice results in a hierarchy, and Spenser is very clear about this. Corrective justice in Spenser is not as in Aristotle, the redistribution of goods that have been falsely assigned;[2] it is concerned with punishment and the 'correction' not of a state of affairs but of the wrongdoer who has brought it about.

The earlier cantos—up to iv. 22—consist of various exempla

[1] *See* Eth. Nic. V, 2.
[2] Eth. Nic., V, 4.

of justice in action. Artegall rights wrongs, represses violence and decides causes. Distributive or civil justice is fairly prominent, as when he settles the property case between the two brothers (iv. 1–22). The concern with the right distribution of the world's goods includes an open attack on contemporary evils in the episode of Pollente and his daughter Munera in ii. We can regard Pollente as representing extortion in general, and Munera as the omnipresent Lady Meed, a familiar symbol of lust for gain since Piers Plowman. But it is probable that there is a quite specific reference to the much canvassed evils of monopoly and bribery. Whatever corruptions Spenser may have lent himself to in Book V obsequiousness to authority is not one of them. This is an attack on one of the obviously present abuses of royal and aristocratic prerogative. It is at once followed by a consideration of what is almost its polar opposite—the set of opinions represented by the communist giant "who all things would reduce unto equality". The tone of somewhat confused indignation that pervades the argument (echoed by several of the commentators) suggests a contemporary target. Egalitarianism has always presented a strong minority report in the committee of Western values. Its exponents in Spenser's day were the Anabaptists who had established a community at Munster in 1534 and attracted unfavourable attention in England in 1575. The question is eternally recurrent, and that is why Artegall's conversation with the giant (ii. 30 seq.), in spite of a good deal of confused thinking on both sides, is one of the liveliest episodes. It would I think be idle to try to discover the exact nature of the giant's operations, or exactly where his arguments and Artegall's meet—the whole effect is rather like that of an unscripted discussion on the Third Programme—but the general axis of the opposition is clear. The giant looks back to some supposed state of primitive equality and stability and he is a doctrinaire and a planner. He proposes to return everything to that state, and to keep it there. To this Artegall opposes a philosophy of stability-in-change very like that of the Mutability cantos. But there are difficulties. The giant's complaints of degeneration from primitive perfection, here regarded as erroneous and heretical, are remarkably like those advanced by the poet himself

in the long philosophical Proem to this book. And Artegall's
reply is self-contradictory. He first says that there has been no
change (35, 36), and then that if there has it is still contained
within the circuit of the divine order (39–42). The fact is that
Spenser is uncommonly inept at set dialectic. His method is the
poetic one; and the essential of the poetic method is that its
effect depends on the process, not on the conclusion reached. A
rejected argument may be as poetically powerful as an accepted
one. The whole question of stability and change is plainly a
source of distress and perplexity to Spenser, and the debate with
the giant dramatizes this condition. Artegall has no real answer
to the uncertainties and inequalities of the changing world. He
recommends an acceptance of things as they are, as necessarily
a part of the divine will. What evidently angers Artegall is that
this political and metaphysical doctrinaire is willing like
Dryden's false Achitophel to appeal to the passions of the
ignorant rabble; and Talus is called in to put an end to the
question by pushing the giant off the cliff. It is the willingness
to settle what is after all a real debate by these brutal and
summary methods that casts a faintly malodorous cloud over
this and some other parts of Book V.

The other part of justice, the corrective, becomes more
prominent in the later cantos, though it is present throughout.
Artegall is a deposer and slayer of tyrants, (Sanglier, Pollente,
the Soudan, Grantorto) but he is also a suppressor of rebels (the
giant's rabble followers in ii, Malengin in ix). We need not
refer again to the feeling of the Elizabethans about order and
subordination, and the almost universal literary and aristocratic
contempt for the mob. Spenser's is an extreme case of this. It
enables him to identify Artegall's justice with Lord Grey's
harshly repressive policy in Ireland, to look on the miseries of
the Irish without pity and to see them simply as a rout of thieves
and murderers to be violently suppressed. This is plainly one of
the corruptions of imperialism, though not a necessary one; and
it is probably the strains and the degradations of his experience
in Ireland that account for the harsh severity of his idea of
corrective justice. Spenser clearly believes that if people are
disturbing civil order and making a nuisance of themselves the

proper thing is to beat and kill them until they stop; if necessary kill them all. We have been too close to these practices, on too huge a scale, in recent years to be other than horrified; but if we survey the political history of humanity Spenser is of course in a comfortable majority.

All this is embodied in the person of Talus, the iron man, the automaton with a flail. If Artegall is Justice Talus is evidently the Law, especially the executive power of the law—the police, the militia, the soldiery. To Spenser he represents necessary power, but the symbolism is unlucky; to moderns he is apt to appear a conscienceless robot whom Artegall employs to do his dirty work for him—though he does call him off when the slaughter has gone far enough. To be fair we must I think look a little more closely. In the opening stanzas of canto iv Spenser emphatically asserts the necessity for an unflinching executive power.

> For vaine it is to deeme of things aright,
> And makes wrong doers justice to deride,
> Unless it be performed with dreadless might.
> For powre is the right hand of Justice truly hight.

Any Lord Chief Justice, however humane, from Spenser's day to our own, would be obliged to agree. This is what Talus signifies. He is an automaton and made of iron because it is not his business to consider equity or mercy. These are in Artegall's sphere; he is merely the instrument of Artegall's decrees; he punishes when he is told to and stops when he is told to as well. This too much recalls the SS man and the kind of defence offered in the Eichmann trial. But we are wrong to make this association. The reason that the defence "I was only obeying orders" cannot be adequate is that there are some orders no man ought to obey. But Talus is not a man and this is allegory. Talus symbolizes only the swift and complete execution of the decisions that Justice has made. There is nothing to complain of, morally or juridically, here; and Spenser shows great insight and discretion precisely in making Talus an insentient robot, not a human being. If the decrees of justice were made with the greatest possible wisdom, insight and clemency, and the execution of them could then be carried out, immediately and completely, without further human complicity, the world would be a better place than it is. Any blame that attaches to the operations of Talus must fall back on Artegall; and what leaves us disgusted or unsatisfied is that so often *Artegall's* decisions seem harshly mechanical, lacking in insight and clemency. Yet it is idle to pretend that Spenser's Justice is not confronting a real problem. We have seen so much of the appalling corruptions of power in recent years that for us the whole field of executive authority is enveloped in confusion. There are many who deny the legitimacy of punishment altogether. Politically speaking the very words 'police action' stink in the nostrils. Yet we all know that without penal authority the operation of justice is a mockery. How much slaughter and misery in the Congo might have been avoided by an early application of the old, crude, outmoded colonial whiff of grapeshot? Yet by the standards that the best collective wisdom of the nations now profess it would have been impossible to employ it. This is taking us far from Spenser; but it is intended to suggest that in our present state of mind we cannot see the operations of Talus objectively. We do not deny the facts, but we feel that Spenser ought to have been more embarrassed by them.

It is quite clear that he was not embarrassed by them. He is an unhesitating exponent of the necessity for swift and relentless punishment. This is a point of view that is not in itself disreputable; and there is more to be said for it than is commonly said today. It is true that by making Talus an automaton Spenser avoids the profoundly disturbing question of how far this punitive function can be undertaken by a fully human being, without corrupting both the nature of the action and the character of the executant. But this is a problem with which the human conscience had hardly begun to concern itself in his day. It is also true that the rendering of Artegall—and behind it Spenser's conception of justice—is in fact corrupted by the identification with Lord Grey in Ireland. Spenser's motives were not personally dishonourable; he was not supporting an established tyranny. On the contrary; Lord Grey was in disgrace, his policy discredited, and Envy, Detraction and the Blatant Beast at his heels. It was an act of considerable political courage for Spenser

197

to write as he did. But the fact remains that in his political allegory he was defending something indefensible, and that this necessarily affects his moral allegory too. There have been many honest and humane men since Spenser's day whose ethical conceptions have degenerated in the atmosphere of a colonial campaign. Guerrilla warfare and political intrigue are not a soil in which an adequate conception of justice can be expected to grow.

To turn to other matters. The structure of the book is simple; it falls into three parts. There are the early cantos, occupied with various exempla of justice in action; then comes the long Radigund episode in iv, v, vi and vii; then the remaining cantos, largely political, concerned with the Armada, the trial of Mary Queen of Scots, and events in the Low Countries, Ireland and France. The Radigund story tells at length of Artegall's subjection, through a mistaken impulse of pity, to the Amazon Radigund, his reduction to woman's status, and his ultimate liberation by Britomart. It is a good story, though neither a sympathetic nor an edifying one; and Spenser's reasons for introducing it are not quite clear. Some political reference to the prepotency of Mary Queen of Scots may be intended, and Spenser may be reinforcing the arguments of Knox's *Monstrous Regiment of Women*. This is not firmly established, but seems likely. Outside this special context Spenser seems by no means hostile to the woman of character and authority. His conception of Britomart and of Queen Elizabeth herself forbids him to be so. But as so often in Spenser a virtue is mimicked by its opposing vice. The duel between Britomart and Radigund (vii. 27 seq.) may be the struggle between Queen Elizabeth and Queen Mary; it is certainly a struggle between the proper kind of womanly authority, strong yet loving, exacting yet respectful of the rights and duties of others, and the improper kind, tyrannical, greedy and unscrupulous. Radigund owes something to Ariosto's Amazon queen, more perhaps to his Marfisa, but the tale as a whole is not like anything in Ariosto. It is an unpleasing history of a man's subjection to a cruel woman, and the more unpleasing because it is linked with the Spenserian idea of justice. Artegall is betrayed into Radigund's power by an impulse of pity and admiration for her beauty; and we are left in no doubt that he was wrong (v. 17); justice has no business with such tender extenuations of its rigour. As a juridical principle this is sound; but thematic material in the romantic epic must after all be controlled by what is possible and sympathetic in a hero of romance. What is appropriate to abstract justice may not be appropriate to a gentle knight. This is only one instance of the besetting difficulty of Book V.

With the political material of the closing cantos the narrative temperature is decidedly lowered. Much of this part of the poem is competent and workmanlike verse and no more; some of it is a good deal less. Most of the historical allusions are clear and unmistakable, others have acquired a high degree of traditional probability. The killing of the Soudan who plots against Mercilla is usually thought to refer to the defeat of the Armada (viii). The hunting of Malengin or Guile in ix is a brilliant allegorical evocation of the spirit of guerrilla war and its exponents. Spenser is quite untouched by pity for the wretched Irish rebels who are typified in the person of Malengin; but this is perhaps no more than normally human for one who has actually lived among this kind of disorder. The trial of Duessa or Mary Queen of Scots (ix. 38–50) is an exceptionally fair and plausible piece of dialectic; and here the political atmosphere did not forbid the humanity of divided sympathies. The operations on behalf of Belge against Gerioneo (Philip of Spain) and his seneschal (Alva), the meeting with Burbon (Henry of Navarre), are adequate, poetically undistinguished, and self-explanatory. We should add that even here where the political allegory seems most consistent it is impossible to make a precise historical identification of Arthur and Artegall; the several activities of Leicester, Essex and Lord Grey are adapted and conflated. Finally in xii Artegall kills Grantorto and frees Irena. This is historically proleptic and does not correspond to anything that had actually occurred. Grantorto is probably best identified with the Pope, since it was Catholic intrigue that English power was chiefly contending with in Ireland. In the closing stanzas where Artegall is attacked by Envy, Detraction and the Blatant Beast he becomes unambiguously Lord Grey, and Spenser is giving an open expression of sympathy with his discredited patron.

# A PREFACE TO *THE FAERIE QUEENE*

In any other book we should wish to discuss at more length the pictorial episodes and the allegorical centre. Here they are unimportant and undeveloped. There is a welcome return to pure romance in iii, where we have the tournament for Florimell's wedding. The unmasking of Braggadochio and the restoration of Guyon's horse are humorous and charming; and the confrontation of the real and the snowy Florimell, the disappearance of the simulacrum in the face of the true beauty, is a brilliant and beautiful relapse into the spirit of Books III and IV. Britomart's sojourn in Isis's Church at the beginning of vii looks as though it were meant to come to something but it hardly does so. Both on the level of image and on that of theme it remains rudimentary and somewhat confused. As if half-aware of this Spenser introduces Mercilla's house in ix, as another attempt at an allegorical core. Mercilla is of course Queen Elizabeth in the aspect of a just and merciful ruler; but Spenser brings little imaginative conviction to his task. Neither the house nor its ruler is impressive—or they do not impress us in the way that was intended. Some writers have seen a contradiction between Spenser's independent and retired character, his dislike of court life, and his glorification of the Queen. But I doubt if there is a contradiction. The fact is that Spenser has very little aptitude for political flattery. The *idea* of queenly grandeur and grace arouses his enthusiastic admiration; when it comes to anything more specific he is willing to go along with the spirit of the age; but he is rather lost and tongue-tied and soon passes on to more congenial themes.

*Chapter XII*

## BOOK VI: COURTESY

After the harshness of Book V Book VI is a delectable return to the most sympathetic side of Spenserian romance. In his legend of Justice Spenser had the task of versifying a given train of political events and justifying a consciously held policy. The demands of a legend of Courtesy are met in a different way. Most chivalric romance is in some sense a romance of courtesy, and with only the slightest thematic adaptation Spenser is free to ride with a loose rein, to follow his invention and his natural bent. The *fiorita vaghezza* is more appropriate here than the *semplice gravita*, and accordingly the book becomes Arcadian and pastoral in its setting. The plot is wayward, episodic and interwoven in the Ariostan manner of Book III. There is a central knight and there is a quest—Sir Calidore in pursuit of the Blatant Beast, but they are only on the scene at the beginning and the end; Calidore disappears in iii, reappears in ix, and does not remember about the Beast again until the last canto. In between we have the story of Calepine and Serena, adventures of Arthur, Timias and others. There are no great descriptive set-pieces, no grand castles or temples. The setting is the forest or a pastoral countryside; and special prominence is given to wild or simple or sequestered beings; and since the poet is no longer on his historical dignity there can be an element of naïve inconsequence that suits him well. Yet Spenser's Arcadia is never an unadulterated idyll; there is violence and sadness in this world, and they are at least as likely to prevail as gentleness and peace.

Courtesy is in itself an attractive virtue. Spenser's conception of it includes sincerity, contrasted with 'fayned showes'; gentleness, contrasted with disdain and pride; and an element of spontaneous charm—the truly courteous "so goodly gracious are by kind". Professor Lewis's pages on this virtue in *The Allegory of Love*[1] catch the spirit of the sixth book with such fullness and happiness that it would be futile to follow him. I shall confine myself therefore to a few special points that still seem to require exposition. There was of course an elaborate, almost scholastic literature of courtesy in Spenser's day. The Italian courtesy-books were well known in England, and there were many translations and adaptations. Spenser seems to have known Guazzo and Castiglione; but he has not really made very extended use of this kind of material. The argumentative and expository nature of these treatises is hardly reflected at all in Book VI. There are places in Spenser when he feels the need to argue out the nature of the quality that supplies his theme; but this is not one of them. There is an older tradition of 'gentillesse' derived from Provence and France, running through medieval romance literature, which had its rules and its casuistry too, but expressed itself chiefly in actual exempla and a pervading chivalrous tone. Spenser is so imbued with its spirit that he hardly needs to seek out scholarly authority for his conceptions. It is not necessary to look up an encyclopedia to find out what a gentleman is. But there is one paradox that seems a somewhat troubling one to the poet. It is the relation of courtesy to courts and gentleness to gentle birth.

There is a contradiction in the treatment of courtesy and the court. In the Proem the virtue is referred to as 'Princely courtesy' and Queen Elizabeth is its pattern. In the first stanza of canto i the two words are brought together, etymologically and in fact:

> Of Court, it seemes, men Courtesy do call,
> For that it there most useth to abound.

But there is nothing courtly in the atmosphere of the legend; the forest, the fields, a hermit's hut, a shepherd's cot provide the setting, and in the speech of old Meliboee (ix. 25) the court is a place of vainness and idle hopes. It is true the passage is borrowed from Tasso, but it is Spenser who borrows it, and the feeling is very close to that of *Colin Clout's Come Home Again*.

[1] pp. 350–3.

This double attitude towards the courtly life goes very deep with
Spenser, even if we allow for a certain amount of routine
flattery. On the one hand the glorification of England requires
what Northrop Frye has called the centripetal gaze, directed on
the monarch. It was not possible in Spenser's age to see a nation
except as embodied in its ruler. And this involves the conception
of a hierarchy with the Queen at the centre as the fountain of
honour and virtue. It is not mere routine for Spenser to see the
world in this way; it is built into the major structure of his poem,
and his imagination delights in this plan where everything is to
be focused in the end on Gloriana and her court. Yet conflicting
with this is the love of retirement, the private virtues, contemplation and seclusion. Professor Lewis points to this duality
when he contrasts with the idea of 'courtly Spenser' the equally
appropriate 'homely Spenser, rustic Spenser'. The court as an
ideal is well enough; the actuality is something different; and
the alternative to the life of honour and emulation is felt both
by the Red Cross Knight and Sir Calidore. But it is felt as something of a temptation. This is common enough outside Spenser;
indeed it might almost rank as a commonplace. Sidney himself
passed two years in retirement at Wilton and caused concern to
his friends by doing so.

The explicit statement, then, connects courtesy with the court,
the setting and the tone of feeling with the life of sequestered
simplicity. When Spenser says that courtesy grows "on a lowly
stalke" he only means, I think, that it occupies a modest rank
among the virtues. There is no strong suggestion, in spite of
what is sometimes said to the contrary, that courtesy is a
democratic affair, or that its origin is in a native human gentleness as against the gentleness of birth and breeding. The humble
life of the hermit is the deliberate retirement of one who has
been a knight and lived an earlier life of chivalrous endeavour;
the delightful Salvage Man, though nourished in the wilds and
unable to speak an intelligible tongue, proves that he must be of
'gentle blood' by his kind usage of Serena; the lovely Pastorella
is really no shepherdess but a knight's daughter. The only
exception to the linking of gentleness with gentle birth is the
old shepherd Meliboee. Spenser may be said to leave the

question undecided; and it is possible that in this ambiguity he is
following Castiglione, for in the first book of the *Courtier* this
very matter is debated. Count Lewis of Canossa lays it down
that the ideal exemplar of courtesy must be of noble blood,
while Lord Caspar Pallavicin maintains "that we all had one
self beginning, and one should not be more than another".[1]
However that may be, both are agreed in a point that seems very
close to Spenser—that the capacity for true gentleness and
courtesy is something inborn. "Truth it is, whether it be
through the favour of the starres or of nature, some there are
borne indeed with such graces, that they seeme not to have been
borne, but rather fashioned with the very hand of some God,
and abound in all goodness both of body and mind."[2] Calidore is
of this favoured race, and for that reason, though the book
abounds in examples of kindness, gentleness, serviceableness,
as against harshness, inhospitality and pride, it is not an allegory
of moral effort but of unsought natural grace. Perhaps we may
even suppose that in an allegorical romance gentle birth could well
symbolize not its literal self but this happy endowment of nature.

Sir Calidore has been traditionally identified with Sidney, and
it is surely in the image of Sidney that most readers will wish to
see him. A plausible case has also been made for Essex. For-
tunately this does not matter. There is no book in *The Faerie
Queene* where historical identifications are of less importance.

The Book falls into three parts; first some exempla of
courtesy in the actions of Sir Calidore; then, from iii. 25 on the
varied and interwoven adventures of Calepine and Serena,
Arthur, Timias and Mirabell; last, from ix to xii, the story of
Pastorella and the sojourn of Calidore among the shepherds.
There is little formal allegory and the few overtly allegorical
characters are not prominent. After the rather plodding thematic
purpose of V it is a welcome return to the freedom and lightness
of romance. After fighting with Maleffort and Crudor and
taming Briana, Sir Calidore meets the young Tristram and in
response to his entreaties makes him a squire (ii). Again what
looks like an incident on the theme of "a man's a man for a'

[1] Castiglione, *Il Cortegiano*, Hoby's translation, Everyman edn., p. 34.
[2] Ibid, p. 32.

that" turns out to be otherwise. Tristram is reproved for fighting with a knight when he is only a simple woodsman, but in reality, of course, he is a king's son. This marks a first influence from Malory; the early history of the young squire is taken from the *enfances* of Tristram of Lyonesse in *Morte d'Arthur*. It is followed by the rescue of Priscilla and her wounded knight, and concluded by the charming and indulgent episode of Calidore taking Priscilla home, and telling fibs about her escapade to her father, to save her from getting into trouble. I do not know what Guyon or Artegall would have said about this; one is glad that they were not present. The interest then shifts to Calepine and Serena, and Calidore goes off in pursuit of the Blatant Beast.

There is no need to follow these adventures in detail, and it would be absurd to look for formal allegorical significance in them. The affairs of Calepine and Serena become intertwined with those of Arthur and Timias, though Arthur is not important in this book. It is Spenserian romance at its most free and delightful, directed always by the general theme of gentleness and courtesy contrasted with harshness and brutality. Naturally the lovers are parted. Sir Calepine goes in pursuit of a bear who has carried off a baby. Having defeated the bear he is left with the baby, and there is a charming picture of his awkward attempts at looking after it (iv. 23–25). He travels on—

> And evermore his lovely little spoile
> Crying for food, did greatly him offend—

until he meets a lady weeping in the forest. She is Matilda, an honourable dame whose one sorrow is that she has no children. To which Calepine replies, in effect, "Ah well, if that is the trouble, that you haven't got a baby, as it happens I have one about me at the moment. I should be only too pleased. . . ." So he bestows it on her and all ends happily. The element of tender absurdity in this episode adds a characteristic note to Book VI. Meanwhile Serena is being protected by the Salvage Man. He is one of the most finely imagined of Spenser's woodland creatures (the whole sequence can be compared to Una's reception by the satyrs) and he occupies a prominent place in the narrative from canto iv to canto viii. He is evidently

Spenser's conception of primitive natural virtue. He is naked, unarmed, swift and active, and quite fearless; savage to his enemies but fiercely devoted to anyone to whom he has given his loyalty. He utters only "soft murmurs and confused sound of senselesse words, which Nature did him teach"; mostly he communicates by signs; but he is instinctively gentle and humane. We do not know what lies behind this figure, but apart from ancient Golden Age tradition, Spenser's world was full of travellers' tales, some harsh but some idyllic, of primitive life; and the wild man of the woods was a common element in masques and pageants. He is of gentle blood, but this can only be by the code of his own tribe; there is no suggestion that he is an ordinary gentleman in reduced circumstances. He is a genuine wild man, and he is a happy instance of Spencer's wish to see the natural world as innocent and good.

That he could also see the primitive world as bad—not merely as *selvaggio*, but as savage in the ordinary modern sense—is witnessed by the horrifying episode of Serena and the cannibals (viii. 38 seq.). Its tone is markedly unlike that of the rest of this book. If the Garden of Adonis and Temple of Venus are the great examples of lovely and happy sensuousness in *The Faerie Queene* this is the great example of sensuous beauty juxtaposed with cruelty and horror. The anthropophagous appetite combined with scopophiliac lust is peculiarly horrible, and Spenser makes the most of it. The whole episode is carefully composed. The luscious description of Serena's naked beauty is evidently adapted from that of Olimpia exposed to the orc (*O.F.* XI, 67 seq.), and the intended sacrifice of a captive is apparently suggested by a late Greek romance, *Clitophon and Leucippe*. The voluptuous cruelty is indeed that of the cannibals and not of the author; but the masterly painting and the obvious imaginative delight in the situation bring us close to Ariostan sensuality, or the faintly perverse Tassonian collocations of feminine loveliness and violent death. The passage should be read again by those who over-emphasize the 'maidenliness' of Spenser's imagination.

The interpolated tale of Mirabella punished for her scorn of love is again in another mode. Some have suggested that it is a re-working of Spenser's early *Court of Cupid*; and it may well be.

It is certainly a reversion to medieval love-morality and to the medieval kind of erotic allegory.

We now approach the essential passages of the book— Calidore in the shepherd's country. This occupies something the same place in *The Faerie Queene* as the episode of *Erminia fra i pastori* in the *Gerusalemme Liberata*, and was influenced by it, though not by it alone. Calidore in pursuit of the Blatant Beast comes to a pastoral land and is constrained to forget his quest and his knighthood and live among the shepherds. The princess of the shepherd girls is the beautiful Pastorella; Calidore falls in love with her and at length wins her favours and displaces her rustic lover Coridon. The land is to all intents and purposes Arcadia, the Renaissance poetic Arcadia where all that was imagined of the Golden Age is fused (by Elizabeth's courtiers no less than by those of Lorenzo de' Medici) with a lingering sense of actual rural happiness and simplicity. The shepherdess who is no shepherdess, Pastorella and her setting, remind us of the Perdita and the Bohemia of *The Winter's Tale*; and with reason, for both look back to the same original. It is Longus's romance, *Daphnis and Chloe*, probably mediated in the same way in both cases—through Greene's *Dorastus and Fawnia*. The influence of the pastoral parts of Sidney's *Arcadia* is also felt; indeed it is there that some critics would find the source of the Pastorella story. The feeling of a lost rural retreat from a life of strenuous achievement reminds us of Tasso, and Meliboee, Pastorella's putative father, is modelled on Tasso's old shepherd. The lines in which he describes his modest contented life, his experience at court and its vanity and emptiness (ix. 20–25) are imitated from the *Gerusalemme* VII. 14–18. When Calidore wrestles with Coridon we seem to have a reminiscence from a speech of Lord Caspar Pallavicin in Castiglione; "In our country of Lumbardy these matters are not passed upon, for you shall see the young gentlemen upon the holy days come daunce all the daye longe in the sunne with them of the countrey, and passe the time with them in casting the barre, in wrastling, running and leaping. And I believe it is not ill done".[1] Other literary parallels have been cited. But we know

[1] Everyman edn., p. 97.

from *The Shepherd's Calendar* how widely Spenser was read in pastoral literature, and the search for particular originals is not ultimately illuminating. He is distilling the essence of all the Arcadian poetry that had delighted him for so long, and he does it far more successfully here than in his formal pastorals. In *The Shepherd's Calendar* he often seems to be producing a diploma piece with all the elements of scholarly pastoral conscientiously reproduced. Here, in spite of the dense literary soil from which it springs, the whole sequence grows as naturally as a wild flower.

Tasso was reproved by the rigorist critics for inserting a pastoral episode in a heroic poem; but such an interlude gains a peculiar poignancy from being a half-stolen diversion from sterner and more melancholy concerns, and Spenser is careful to preserve it so. The unmixed literary Arcadianism of Sannazaro, for example, is far less affecting. When Meliboee has finished his encomium on the shepherd's life Calidore wishes that his lot had been the same, but is doubtfully answered by the old shepherd that each has his own destiny to pursue. Nevertheless he gains leave to rest his barque "which hath been beaten late/ With stormes of fortune and tempestuous fate". At the beginning of canto x we are reminded that he is leaving his quest and his promise. Yet he is hardly blamed for it, for he is pursuing a true happiness and peace, enough to cure him for ever of any delight in 'false blisse' or 'painted show'. And before the quest is called to mind again Calidore is shown a sight that raises the pastoral vision to a still higher pitch.

Wandering about the fields one day he comes upon a fair hill, surrounded by woods and a river. It is Mount Acidale, the haunt of Venus. There Colin Clout is piping (Spenser himself in his old pastoral disguise), and a hundred naked maidens are dancing before him. In the middle of their ring three more maidens are dancing, and in the very centre of the circle is yet another damsel, more beautiful than all. This is quite unlike the great set-pieces in other parts of the poem, but it is one of the most exquisite passages of *The Faerie Queene*. It is the only one in which the poet introduces himself into his poem; and the girl in the centre of the dancing circle is his own love. We know

from the eightieth sonnet of the *Amoretti* that the six books of
*The Faerie Queene* were completed during the time of Spenser's
courtship, and the note of happy love in the legend of Courtesy
suggests a close connection with that period. The calculated
breach of epic decorum is beautiful in itself. Nothing but a strong
and personal impulse could have been allowed to break the
objective surface of the poem, and this delicate piece of waywardness is a beautiful tribute to his future bride. But its significance
is more than biographical and there is perhaps more than a
mythological compliment implied in placing his own lady in the
midst of the Graces' dance. As soon as Calidore discovers himself they all vanish, and leave Colin Clout mourning their disappearance. Professor Lewis has explained the Graces as
inspiration, the poet's inspiration, that comes unsought and goes
away again, no one knows why. The Graces as figures of
classical myth have caught an overtone from Grace in the
Christian sense—an unlooked-for visitation of the divine. If that
is so, the fourth maid around whom they are all dancing is the
source and centre of gracious inspiration: all is derived from
love, and the whole rhythmic action springs from and is offered
to Colin's love and Colin's own beloved. The dance and the
music become among other things the symbol of Spenser's art;
and an apology to Gloriana for the predominance of the fourth
maiden has to be inserted (x. 28), since it is to Gloriana that
the poem is formally devoted. We may write this off as a piece
of required flattery if we will; and that is what it is almost bound
to seem to modern taste. I doubt if it was so in Spenser's eyes.
The imagination of his day is so accustomed to making parallels
between different loves on different planes that it was quite
possible, without hypocrisy or indecorum, to associate the
formal devotion and the private affection in this manner.

The complex symbolism of the Graces in Renaissance
iconography has been studied by Wind.[1] It is impossible to say
how much of this was present to Spenser's mind. The neo-
Platonic refinements almost certainly were not, and there is no
overt sign of them here. But the primary source for the allegorical mythology of the Graces is a passage of Plutarch, followed

[1] Op. cit., p. 31 seq.

later by Servius, Boccaccio and others. More to the point, it had been already paraphrased, either by Spenser himself or one of his circle, in the gloss to the April eclogue of *The Shepherd's Calendar*:

> The Graces . . . otherwise called Charites, that is thanks, whom the Poetes feyned to be the Goddesses of al bountie and comeliness, which therefore (as sayth Theodontius) they make three, to wete, that men first ought to be gracious and bountiful to others freely, then to receive benefits at other mens hands curteously, and thirdly to requite them thankfully; which are three sundry Actions in liberalitye. And Boccace saith, that they be painted naked (as they were indeede on the tombe of C. Julius Caesar), the one having her back towards us, and her face fromwarde, as proceeding from us: the other two toward us, noting double thanke to be due to us for the benefit we have done.

They are, then, as Colin explains to Calidore, the bestowers of all gracious gifts, and the fountains of civility and courtesy, dancing in a round to show the continual circle of gracious action. The Graces are the attendants of Venus, and by placing his own mistress in the centre of them Spenser makes her more than another Grace, no less than a type of the Goddess of Love herself. In other places Wind has shown that for the neo-Platonists the Graces were the triadic expansion of the power of Venus;[1] but here Venus is replaced by his own beloved, and Spenser is seeing the whole cycle of benefits and gracious deeds springing from his love as their source; and that love identified with the love that is the motive power of the Universe. More than a mythological, a metaphysical tribute. But that would only be speculation. It is rarely possible to say how much of the riot of syncretist allegorical fancy that was abroad in his day is to be read into Spenser's pictures.

No sooner is the lovely vision on Mount Acidale completed than it is succeeded by calamity. The shepherd idyll is broken up, the land ravaged by brigands, Meliboee killed, and Pastorella carried off into captivity. From then on we have the usual romance story of rescue and restoration, including the Daphnis and Chloe motif by which Pastorella's origin is revealed and she

[1] Op. cit., pp. 39, 42, 74, 158 seq., 168.

is restored to her true parents. It ends with a restoration it is
true, but it is a sad one. It is a revelation of the precarious
status of grace and beauty and innocent happiness in a world full
of evil. Spenser is the least sentimental of writers; he never sees
these resting-places as more than islands of tranquillity in the
middle of a turbulent sea. Something must be allowed for the
unfinished state of his poem, but he is not on the whole the poet
of the happy ending. He is too sadly aware that there are no
permanently happy endings in this vale of tears, and the consciousness of it seems to grow upon him as *The Faerie Queene*
advances. After the return of Pastorella Calidore goes on the
interrupted quest of the Blatant Beast, achieves it after a fashion,
but it is doubtful and impermanent victory; and we cannot forget
that Meliboee is dead and Arcadia destroyed.

The significance of the Blatant Beast has been much discussed.
His origin is in the Questing Beast of Malory, who was pursued
by Sir Palomides; and doubtless other sinister beasts of scripture
and legend have contributed. Ben Jonson told Drummond of
Hawthornden, on the alleged authority of a paper given by
Spenser to Sir Walter Raleigh, that the beast represented the
Puritans. Certainly in xii. 23–25 he is found ravaging monas-
teries and despoiling churches. This has been felt as inconsistent
with Spenser's own supposed Puritanism; and certainly he cannot be supposed to have any particular tenderness for monas-
teries. On this there are two things to be said; one, pointed out
by Professor Lewis, is that in a Protestant allegory specifically
Catholic institutions are themselves allegorical; when a hermit
or a monastery is mentioned we are not to see Spenser as
pronouncing either for or against solitude or the conventual
life. The Beast is at any rate a symbol of violence and spoliation.
Secondly, if Spenser was in any real sense a Puritan, he was
certainly not so in the sense of the Marprelate fanatics; and his
own kind of ideal, moderate, reforming churchmanship could
only have made him their enemies. So there is no obstacle to
accepting Jonson's identification; but clearly it is only part of
the meaning of the Beast. Historical allusion apart the creature
has usually been identified with Slander, and this is the rôle he
plays at the end of Book V. But he is probably something more

—the force of malignity and settled ill-will, always abroad in the world and never finally subdued. It is notable that Calidore does not kill him, but only binds and muzzles him, and the book ends with an outspoken declaration of his raging dominance in Spenser's own world.

## Chapter XIII

## THE MUTABILITY CANTOS

The Mutability Cantos first appear in the 1609 Folio of *The Faerie Queene*, printed by Matthew Lownes, with the title "Two Cantos of Mutabilitie: which, both for Forme and Matter, appears to be parcell of some following Booke of the Faerie Queene, under the Legend of Constancie. Never before imprinted". They have no other authority, and the question has been raised whether they belong to *The Faerie Queene* at all. But the arguments to suggest that they do not are very weak. Those who object that they would be a long digression from any possible story and that they contain no human characters can hardly have examined the existing body of the poem with very close attention. Stanza 2 of canto vi announces that the lineage of Mutability was found recorded in the annals of fairyland; stanza 37 includes an apology for turning from the heroic theme to Irish hills and rivers. These are obvious indications that the cantos were part of the poem that we know. The "legend of Constancie" may be an editorial conjecture, but the numbering of the cantos vi, vii, and viii can hardly be so. What editor would arbitrarily number discovered fragments in this way? But minor quibbles and rejoinders fade into insignificance beside the rich magnificence with which these cantos claim their kinship to the rest of *The Faerie Queene*. What we have here seems to be the allegorical centre of a yet unwritten book. There is no compelling evidence as to date; but what there is suggests that it was late. In fact the Cantos seem rightly to occupy their traditional position after Book VI; and there is every reason for accepting Lownes's moderately worded statement exactly as it stands.

The Cantos have always attracted much attention both because

they contain Spenser's most splendid and majestic allegorical
pageant and because their implied philosophy of fixity and flux
seems to come very near to the centre of his poetic belief. By
what may or may not be chance, the theme of the Mutability
Cantos seems to follow naturally on the ending in which the
shepherd's land is ravaged, the Blatant Beast, captured but not
destroyed, is destined to break loose again, and no human
felicity is secure. But these later Cantos remove the question of
change and decay from the region of human society and its
happiness to the cosmological plane. They describe an attempt
made by the Titaness Mutability to make a rebellion against
the stable order of the Gods—that is against Jove himself.
Mutability was first one of the subordinates of Jove, but
aspired to absolute rule, like Satan, and has changed the face of
all earthly things (vi. 6 and 7). She mounts an attack on Cynthia
—first attacking one of the lesser powers, again like Satan
(10–13). Summoned by Hermes to Jove in council, she appears,
defies him, appeals to Nature, and a day is appointed for the
cause to be heard, at Arlo-hill near Spenser's Irish home. This
leads to a digression on the Irish rivers; we have the story of
the nymph Molanna, daughter of the River Mole. It is charming,
and it throws light on Spenser's attitude to Ireland—a lovely
idyllic country spoilt by violence and revolt (55); but it is not
otherwise connected with the Mutability theme.

In canto vii the gods assemble on Arlo-hill under the presi-
dency of 'great dame Nature'. She is veiled, and her beauty
and majesty cannot be described (5–10). Mutability pleads her
cause: the elements Earth, Air, Fire and Water are subject to
her sway. Then she summons her witnesses, the Seasons
(28–31), the Months (32–44), the Hours, and Life and Death.
After this lovely pageant Mutability continues her speech, and
describes change in the planets and the spheres. Then, surprisingly brief and cryptic, comes Nature's judgement (58–59).
Mutability's case is dismissed, on the grounds that, though she
appears to rule everything, changelessness is the necessary
ground against which change must work. Two surviving stanzas
of canto viii show how heavy the sway of Mutability yet is, and
the only ultimate escape from it is to raise the cause to a higher

sphere than that of Nature. They close with a prayer to the Lord of Hosts for the peace of his eternal Sabbath.

The theme of the Mutability Cantos is by no means an unprepared appendage; it is one that has occurred very frequently in Spenser's work. The Garden of Adonis passage also discusses change, decay, regeneration and changelessness, and the substratum of argument there is very close to that used by Nature in her judgement. In the proem to Book V the poet himself speaks of change in the planets and the spheres, in exactly the same terms as Mutability does. The communist giant and Artegall argue on the same theme in V. ii, and Spenser either makes complaints against change or borrows them from others in *The Ruines of Time*, *The Ruines of Rome* and *The Visions of Petrarch*. No doubt the subject was a commonplace, but Spenser recurs to it often and obviously with deep feeling. It is connected with his melancholy and his reverence for antiquity. Looking back on his work as a whole it seems appropriate, almost necessary, that it should become the basis for a substantial chapter in his allegory. Change and its operations were a haunting cause of distress to him; and if we consult the passages where he treats of it we find little formal consistency and no philosophical resolution. Spenser speaking in his own person has many times employed most of the arguments of Mutability. She is presumptuous and her works are deplorable, but she is not a liar; indeed in the debate no one attempts to contradict her. The communist giant (whom we are clearly asked to disapprove of) revolts against the achievements of Mutability and proposes to return everything to its primitive state. And Artegall (whom we are clearly asked to approve of) contradicts himself hopelessly in reply. First he contradicts the world-picture given by the giant (which is also that given by Mutability herself), and says that there has been no change (V. ii. 35, 36); then he says that if there has been it is all part of the Divine will (39–42). The Garden of Adonis is certainly under the sway of Mutability, for it is a perpetual cycle of birth, death and regeneration; a cycle which here, however, seems benign in its operations. Yet if it is so, it is hard to see why Time should be the enemy of the Garden, though it may be of the 'fleshly weeds' in the phenomenal world. What we seem to see here is a fascinated circling around an insoluble perplexity, rich in metaphor and poetical casuistries, but not leading to a conceptual solution. It is possible that the Mutability Cantos themselves achieve no more. It may be that they simply give the mystery its richest and most complete expression. It may be that they do something more, imaginatively and poetically, if not with dialectical sureness.

Many attempts have been made to examine the thought of both the Mutability and the Adonis passages by examining their sources. Spenser naturally drew from earlier cosmological poets, and from the philosophers as mediated by them. But *Quellenforschung* is less illuminating here than in other contexts. Sometimes there is no light, but rather darkness visible. When we are led back by source-study to Spenser's originals in romance we are moving in one and the same world and are made conscious of the *genre* to which his poem belongs. When we trace his philosophical ideas to their source we are apt to be led outside his imaginative world altogether, and to misconceive the way in which he uses philosophical material. Even more than most poets he uses it eclectically and unscrupulously. Passages from a materialist natural philosophy may be used as images in a complex vision of quite a different kind. Idealist metaphysics no less suffer the same fate. Spenser is not a conventional 'Platonist' any more than he is a Lucretian atomist. He is Spenser, and he is writing a poem; and the status of a metaphysical doctrine within a poem is quite different from its status in a philosophical treatise. Some poets, like Dante, have a powerful command of regular dialectical exposition, and use it both as an imaginative instrument and as a tool intended to be effective in the world outside. Spenser has little of this power. His arguments are usually weak, considered in themselves. He would perhaps be a greater poet if they were stronger, but these local weaknesses do not much affect the standing of his poem as a whole. The arguments are only present as elements in an imaginative vision; and it is a vision in which the poet can blend, as a metaphysician could not, a philosophy of nature with a philosophy of spirit; just as in the ethical sphere he can blend a tenderly human romantic naturalism with an uncompromising religious apprehension.

This is by way of preliminary caution. Greenlaw has argued for a strong Lucretian influence both here and in the Adonis passage,[1] and it may well be admitted. The lines on the generation of all things from the earth and the indestructibility of matter in III. vi seem to be borrowings from the Lucretian philosophy of nature, though they could have been found elsewhere. Greenlaw goes on to present Mutability herself as an Epicurean-Lucretian naturalist, expounding a doctrine of metaphysical scepticism and purely material causation. He goes rather far with this, for after all Mutability is primarily mutability. But it is the case that the changes she prides herself on are mostly physical declinations from some supposed ideal order; and she is scornful of all belief in what we cannot see (vii. 49). A rather complicated debate among the commentators has followed.[2] Greenlaw appears to suggest that because Spenser expounds this philosophy dramatically he has in some sense made it his own. To this it is replied that Mutability is the enemy both of Spenser and the Gods, and that her case is rejected. This is true, and it would be absurd, as Greenlaw himself concedes, to saddle Spenser with the arguments of his devil's advocate. But it is also true that they are much the strongest arguments in the debate, that they remain formally uncontradicted, and that whatever their juridical fate or Spenser's private opinions, they stand as an element in the poem. It remains to be seen what other elements are set against them.

To make brutally short work of many detailed inquiries, we can distinguish two opposing lines of argument. One is a philosophy of cyclical change by which things "turn to themselves again" —the cycle of the Garden of Adonis by which the naked babes are clothed in fleshly weeds and sent out into the world "till they again return backe by the hinder gate", to start out on their course again after a thousand years' sojourn in the Garden. This answers Mutability by admitting change within the cycle, but

[1] "Spenser and Lucretius", SP 17 (1920). (Works III, p. 340).
[2] See Works III, pp. 340–52; and VI, 389–432.

seeing the cycle itself as eternal and unchangeable. It is almost vain to ask where Spenser actually derived this way of thinking, so we cannot hope to make it more precise by consulting a specific source. He displays the idea very indistinctly, and he might have found it anywhere. In the myth of the Republic X, in the diffused Platonism of Boethius, in later neo-Platonism or in some version of the doctrine of Pythagoras—there is a particularly likely one in Ovid, *Metamorphoses* XV. The great advantage of this vaguely entertained notion of metempsychosis is that it permits Spenser to do what all his temperament and natural convictions impel him to do—to give full measure, sometimes joyfully, sometimes sadly, to the changeful variety of the phenomenal world, and yet to see it contained in an eternal design. The second line of argument against Mutability refers only to the eternal design. It is that all created things are moving towards a final consummation when "none no more change shall see". For this Spenser could have found authority in Plotinus or his Renaissance disciples; but of course he needed no authority outside his own Christianity.

The form of the Mutability episode is dialectical. Besides being a vision it presents itself as an argument, even a juridical argument. We must now turn to examine the credentials of the contestants and their testimony. I think we should be wrong to see the Titaness as wholly evil. As human creatures we must often lament her power; she is a rebel, and we know Spenser's feeling about rebels. She presents certain analogies with Satan, and it is hard not to read some of the feelings that attach to that cosmic revolutionary into her case. She has broken the laws of Nature, of Justice and of Policy, and our subjection to her is a curse—a curse which seems to be connected with the Fall (vi. 6). But she is as tall and beautiful as any of the gods and goddesses (27); Jove is moved by her lovely face and addresses her with some tenderness, first as "fair Titan's child", and then as "thou foolish gerle" (31–39). Although we are told that she has broken the laws of Nature, she is willing to appeal to Nature; and her appeal is permitted. It would seem that she cannot be entirely a rebel against the natural order after all. The polemic against her in 6 is spoken from the point of view of battered humanity: within the larger cosmic order she has her honours and her rights.

She is in rebellion against Jove and the gods. And who are they? It has been suggested that they are a collective representation of divine power and that Jove is simply God. This imaginative transposition is common enough in Renaissance literature; but here it is surely impossible. Mutability and Jove are opponents in a law-case; the Titaness, if not rightly the eqʾial of the gods, at least moves on the same plane. Together they submit their case to the judgement of Nature, who is clearly the superior power. The gods are among other things the planetary deities, and as such, the symbols of natural laws, or rather of the particular administration of natural laws. Mutability claims to rule over them, and her claim is never refuted. It cannot be. Spenser does not accept the traditional distinction between a changeless, incorruptible heaven and a shifting sublunary sphere; he is too near the coming scientific revolution for that. Already in the proem to Book V he has lamented change and unsteadiness in the heavens; and no one attempts to answer the arguments in vii. 49–55. But if the claims of the Titaness cannot be refuted, they can be transcended. And so they are, twice: first in the judgement of Nature, and again in the two stanzas of the eighth canto. The judgement delivered by Nature is so brief and so cryptic that we cannot be certain of understanding it, or even of how much there is to understand. We must first consider what Nature is in herself.

The goddess Natura has a long history in medieval and Renaissance tradition. Spenser derives her from Chaucer and Alanus de Insulis (vii. 9)—unless the citation of Alane is only a sly reference in the Chaucerian manner to an authority who in fact has not been consulted.[1] Traditionally and in Alanus she is God's vice-gerent in the phenomenal world; as such she is the guarantor of order and stability, "still moving, yet unmoved".

[1] Which who will read set forth so as it ought
   Go seek he out that Alane where he may be sought.

Alane may be sought in Migne's *Patrologia*, or in a translation by D. M. Moffat, or abstracted and described in C. S. Lewis's *Allegory of Love*. The description of Nature is in Prose I of *De Planctu Naturae*, but the seeker will not find any very close resemblance to Spenser.

But as Dame Nature she embodies something of the idea of the Great Mother, a creative as well as a regulative principle, as we see by her pavilion made of spontaneously growing trees, and the flowers that spring beneath her feet (8, 10). Above all, she is mysterious. No one knows whether her form is male or female; no one has seen her face. Metaphysically she is closely related to the neo-Platonic emanations from the One—the World-Soul, or that activity of the World-Soul that is called Nature in Plotinus. In vii her garments are compared to those of the Lord at the Transfiguration. Spenser is sometimes surprisingly free in transitions between secular and sacred imagery, but such a comparison is not made idly. What does it mean in the metaphysics of Christian romance? 'The gods' in such a context are all lesser aspects, separated and personified for imaginative purposes, of the all-embracing power of God. That Nature can be brought, even if it is only by way of simile, into such close contact with one of the divine persons shows that she has a more integral and intimate participation in Divinity. The gods are natural laws, rivals of Mutability but in some degree affected by her power. Nature is the whole ontological principle on which all natural laws must rest—if we may reduce Spenser's radiant presentation of the goddess to this dim abstraction. It is this being—looked at from above the agent and deputy of the ineffable Godhead, looked at from below the creating and governing principle of all earthly life—who pronounces the final judgement against Mutability.

As we have said, she does not counter any of Mutability's arguments any more than Jove does. But she passes beyond them. All things change, as Mutability has alleged,

> yet being rightly wayd
> They are not changed from their first estate;
> But by their change their being doe dilate:
> And turning to themselves at length againe,
> Doe work their own perfection so by fate.
>
> (vii. 58)

We may if we like take this as the cryptic answer of a mysterious veiled goddess, not to be questioned too much. But let us suppose for better or worse that the words have a discover-able meaning, and begin with the easiest. All things change, but "turn to themselves again". In the Spenserian context this can only mean one thing: it must refer to the doctrine of cyclical birth, death and rebirth that we have met in the Garden of Adonis. We tentatively proposed a Platonic source for this; and here another one suggests itself. Spenser may have been draw-ing on a rendering of Plato's original, Pythagoras. The Mutability Cantos contain several echoes from Ovid's *Meta-morphoses*, especially the long discourse in the fifteenth book where Pythagoras is represented as expounding his philosophy. From verse 145 onward he elaborates the doctrine of metem-psychosis, the soul remaining the same through an eternal flux of changing material embodiments. We have a useful gloss to the spirit of the Garden and of Nature's speech in the following:

> Nec species sua cuique manet, rerumque novatrix
> ex aliis alias reparat natura figuras:
> nec perit in toto quicquam, mihi credite, mundo,
> sed variat faciemque novat, nascique vocatur
> incipere esse aliud, quam quod fuit ante, morique
> desinere illud idem, cum sint huc forsitan illa,
> haec translata illuc, summa tamen omnia constant.
>
> (*Met*. XV. 251–258)

Nothing retains its own form; but Nature, the great renewer, ever makes up forms from other forms. Be sure there is nothing perishes in the whole universe; it does but vary and renew its form. What we call birth is but a beginning to be other than what one was before; and death is but cessation of a former state. Though, perchance things may shift from there to here and here to there, still do all things in their sum total remain unchanged.

> utque novis facilis signatur cera figuris
> nec manet ut fuerat nec formas servat easdem,
> sed tamen ipsa eadem est, animam sic semper eandem
> esse, sed in varias doceo migrare figuras.
>
> (ibid. 169–172)

And, as the pliant wax is stamped with new designs, does not remain as it was before or keep the same form long, but is still the selfsame wax, so do I teach that the soul is ever the same, though it passes into ever-changing bodies.

# A PREFACE TO *THE FAERIE QUEENE*

This I take to be the sense in which things turn to themselves again; and this is the first transcendence of the indubitable truths uttered by Mutability. But Nature goes farther than this, for in preserving their estate and returning to themselves all things "dilate their being" and "work their own perfection". Nature sees the cycle of incarnations as progressive, like the Vedantists, or as Toynbee sees the cycles of history: progressive towards the final changeless union of all things with God. Others better informed than I will have to say what immediate authority Spenser might have had for this doctrine of fused physical and spiritual evolution. But its tendency is that of neo-Platonism; the old Pythagorean metempsychosis transformed by the conviction that the soul is a teleological category, that the cycle of birth and rebirth is the soul's striving to realize its own true nature. Then it will be reunited with the One, unalterably. This is the second transcendence; and the final union is no more than hinted at by Nature:

> But time shall come that all shall changed bee,
> And from thenceforth, none no more change shall see.

In the two stanzas of the eighth canto Spenser makes this last transformation more explicit. After doing full justice to the heavy and the weary weight of all this unintelligible world, he concludes not with poetical philosophy but with an act of devotion:

> But thence-forth all shall rest eternally
> With him that is the God of Sabbaoth hight:
> O that great Sabbaoth God, grant me that Sabbaoth's sight.

On that note *The Faerie Queene* ends.

## Chapter XIV

# THE WHOLE IN THE PART

### I

As usual at the end of a literary study, there is no specific conclusion to be drawn. If any illumination has been achieved it has been dispersed through the course of the discussion. But I will attempt by way of finale to bring some of the threads together, and to show that *The Faerie Queene* is more of a whole, more 'complete in itself' than has generally been maintained. Since the main purpose of this book has been to see the poem as an example of the romantic epic, it will be appropriate to ask how far it partakes of the general characteristic of its kind and what are its elements of individuality and novelty.

The essence of the romantic epic is in its material. This is the material of chivalric romance, but re-handled in an age when chivalry has become a remote legend. Yet it is a legend still in a sense in touch with the life of the day. In this Spenser is entirely at one with his Italian predecessors. At the court of Queen Elizabeth as at the court of Ferrara chivalric manners still constitute an aristocratic social ideal, and the adventures of knight-errantry are still a source of literary delight. There is the fusion of a deliberate and indulged archaism with a surviving or a revived ideal of conduct, and the poles between which the romantic epic moves are at one extreme an imaginative game, at the other the fashioning of a noble person in virtuous and gentle discipline. The emphasis naturally varies in different writers. Spenser is least close in spirit to Ariosto, for whom the whole machinery was a matter of ironic and sometimes burlesque artistry. In some ways he is nearest to Boiardo, who shares with him a genuine homesickness for a knightly past. In others he is nearer to Tasso, who reforms his historic and legendary material according to the religious pressures of his own age. But all are alike in using their knights, ladies and magicians, their military encounters and enchanted gardens with a sophisticated aware-ness of their obsolete quality and a deliberate turning of the material to various contemporary ends. Their matter is not given, like that of the primary epic, nor even dictated by an overriding national tradition; it is to some extent arbitrarily chosen, playfully or gravely eclectic, at the same time popular and literary. We should hardly call the romantic epic an artificial form, in the sense of something mechanically contrived; it has grown in response to a real taste. But the taste is not one of the primary human needs; it is the result of a great deal of secondary elaboration.

The immense attraction of this kind of material to the writer was that it permitted so much variety and freedom of treatment. The stock of romance motifs was so large and it had had so many accretions from history, from classical epic and from mythology that almost any kind of fiction, from the pious apologue to the erotic novella, can find a place within the boundaries. Spenser has availed himself of all the freedom that he met with in his predecessors. It is worth emphasizing this for it is often suggested that he gives us a spare and Protestant version of his luxuriant Italian exemplars. I have tried to indicate throughout the variety of Spenser's tone and manner, and there is no need to recapitulate. I believe he has suffered from an excessive stress on his religious and didactic purpose; and a current tendency to insist on his community of spirit with Milton is also over-worked.[1] He is not really very like Milton; the sparsely-furnished grandeurs of Milton's epic belong to a very different world from the crowded and infinitely varied pageant of *The Faerie Queene*. Spenser shares with the Italian writers the tendency to become encyclopedic in scope, to include extremes of experience and feeling, to reduce to the same picture-plane images drawn from very different depths and different levels.

In one respect he is like Ariosto and Tasso but has surpassed

[1] E.g. "Blake is a poet in the tradition of Spenser and Milton." H. Bloom, *The Visionary Company*, 1962, p. 1.

them. This is the pictorial element. We are continually haunted in reading the Italian writers by reminiscences and suggestions of Renaissance painting, but these elusive parallels are far stronger in Spenser. There is a paradox in this, for Spenser can have seen very little, if any, of the great Italian pictorial art; such acquaintance as he had with the visual mythology and the iconographical symbolism of his time must have been almost entirely from emblem-books, tapestries and court pageantry. Yet Botticelli's *Primavera* and *Birth of Venus* seem far closer to Calidore's vision on Mount Acidale than to the elegant verses of Politian with which they are really connected. Bellini's *Allegory* in the Uffizi might be taking place on the outskirts of Spenser's Temple of Venus; Giorgione's *Tempestà* surely occurred in some corner of Spenser's forest. Una among the satyrs should have been illustrated by Piero di Cosimo, the Garden of Adonis by the Bellini of *The Feast of Gods*, and the marriage of Thames and Medway by the Raphael of the *Triumph of Galatea*. These no doubt are fanciful or personal associations; they are made only in order to suggest how fully, for all his Englishness, Spenser shared in the general spirit of Renaissance art.

To return to the conventions of the romantic epic—there is much in Spenser's organization of his material that is quite new. The internal structure of the books is capricious—sometimes continuous, more or less episodic narrative, sometimes Ariostan interweaving. But the self-contained character of each book (except for III and IV which partly run together) has no parallel in the Italian poems. At first sight this looks like a merely external device of construction, but on a closer acquaintance it is seen to give a very different quality to the whole poem. In Ariosto there are no real internal divisions; it is a long breathless gallop from first to last. In Tasso all (or nearly all) is subordinated to the needs of a unified epic structure. Spenser's poem is composed of parts each with a certain unity of its own. This offers the opportunity for a real sequence and development of thematic interest, as I shall try to suggest in a moment. For it is of course by its thematic content that each book is given its separate integrity. As far as material and incident are concerned, much would be interchangeable between one part and another;

but however loosely or intermittently the allegory may be pursued, the idea of Temperance, or Justice, or Courtesy or whatever it may be, does control and dominate each book. This thematic arrangement makes it possible to organize the medley of motifs and episodes in large blocks, each with its distinctive tone and colouring. And this is something quite different from either the Ariostan or the Tassonian form. In spite of incompletenesses and loose ends *The Faerie Queene* does by this means arrive at an authentic form of its own. It is characteristic of Spenser that this formal principle is given by his theme, not by the sequence of his images. Without implying any lack of invention or narrative vitality it is true to say that Spenser is a more thoughtful poet than either Ariosto or Tasso. Not because he has serious moral intentions that extend outside his poem (though of course he has), but because it is his thought that dictates the real form of his work; dianoia, not the demands of narrative sprightliness or neo-classic convention.

II

The unifying factor among the books—Arthur's quest of Gloriana—is largely ineffective as a narrative device. The loves of Artegall and Britomart provide a stronger narrative thread than those of Arthur and the Faerie Queene. We cannot tell how far this is due to the incomplete state of the design. If we had the reunion in Cleopolis, above all if we had Cleopolis itself and not merely a few scattered allusions to it, no doubt the whole sequence of adventures would be seen in different proportions. We can only deal with what we have, and in what we have the figure of Gloriana does not appear at all and that of Arthur only in an intermittent and inorganic way. That is in the narrative, on the plane of presented images. If we look behind the image to the thematic content Arthur and Gloriana have a fuller and more continuous significance. The allegorical meaning announced in the Letter is not particularly plausible, nor very well borne out by the development of the poem itself. It is safe to say that nobody actually reading *The Faerie Queene* ever thinks of Magnificence in search of Glory, and as the idea is so faint and uninsistent it hardly seems worth while to inquire whether the glory referred to is earthly or heavenly fame. The real significance of Arthur and Gloriana is that they are the main vehicles of that glorification of Britain that is the great thematic groundswell beneath the diverse surface movements of the poem. But the 'glorification' of Britain is perhaps an unfortunate phrase. It suggests a patriotic trumpet-blowing which is only a very small part of Spenser's intention. 'Idealization' would be better, except that that suggests a sort of discarnate abstraction that is equally un-Spenserian.

The element of dynastic celebration is already present in the Italian epics. Both Ariosto and Tasso offer their works as part of the mythical history of the Estensi, the ducal house of Ferrara, just as Spenser offers his as part of the mythical history of the Tudors. In the primary epic no doubt such historical and genealogical motifs are still living and currently felt realities. In the romantic epics they are a deliberate reconstruction, fancy rather than imagination, half-way between legend and made-up courtly compliment. Ariosto makes his Ruggiero and Bradamante, Tasso his Rinaldo, the mythical ancestors of the house of Este; and no one of course was expected to believe this. And it does not in any sense constitute a national celebration. The duchy of Ferrara was not coterminous with Italy—we cannot say the Italian nation for there was no Italian nation. Ariosto has a deep feeling for Italy, as we can see when he laments her exposure to foreign invaders; but Italy is a geographical or cultural concept, not a nation. Spenser in celebrating Britain has something far more actual and self-aware to deal with. The long-established sense of English nationality, powerfully reinforced by the Tudor settlement and the successes against Spain, gave Spenser a much stronger historical foundation for his poem. And by a happy chance, the mythical genealogy on which the romantic epic relies for its link with a legendary past in his case already existed; it had a status outside his poem. The descent of the Tudors from the ancient British kings, of Elizabeth from Arthur, was attached to a tradition going back to Geoffrey of Monmouth, and was already, as we have seen, part of the political mythology of the age. So that what is mere flattery or complimentary fancy in the Italian epics is something more in Spenser; it is already a real element in the imaginative consciousness of the poet and his contemporaries.

By building on this, by adorning his verse with English and Irish geography and historical allusion, Spenser is going some way towards providing a British mythology, and giving *The Faerie Queene* at least a chance of occupying the ideal epic situation in the tradition of his own country. I do not think that he has completely succeeded. French, British or Celtic in origin, largely translated as it may be, it is the Arthurian legend that is the real British mythology, and it is Malory who has established it. Spenser's Arthur is aside from the central tradition; Spenser is describing the *enfances* of the king that we know, and they are merely his own invention. One does not invent a mythology; and Spenser's Arthur remains a personal imaginative creation, not a true part of the national consciousness. But the effect of having this Arthurian link between the past and the present is to make his poem a more serious and more firmly grounded conception than its Italian predecessors. And it is serious in a way that goes deeper than mere national pride.

The English have always been inclined to see their history as a microcosm of the history of humanity. This may be dangerous —at its worst it can lead to provincialism or *folie de grandeur*. At its best it is ennobling. The real disaster is to see a national history not as a microcosm of the human situation but as the actual historic centre of the human situation. This is the German error, and we have seen its consequences. The English may have come some way towards it at the close of the nineteenth century, but in Spenser's day this was neither spiritually nor historically a danger. Christendom was already torn in two, but the concept of Christendom still existed; and the great spiritual and historical current that carries *The Faerie Queene* along is directed towards conforming the idea of Britain with the idea of a Christian kingdom. Arthur represents both a historic ancestor and a spiritual ideal. The situation that both the great Italian epics inherited from the *chansons de geste*—Christendom embattled against the infidel—has disappeared from *The Faerie Queene*. Its place it taken by the less contingent and more com-

prehensive warfare of good against evil in every relation of life.
Yet the protagonist in this war is a British prince. It is in this
subtler and profounder way that Spenser inherits the tradition
of the Christian epic, and without chauvinism or special pleading integrates it with the intention of his national heroic
poem.

We seem for the moment to have forgotten Gloriana. If
Arthur is the bearer of the historic national consciousness, what
of the Faerie Queene herself? Britain and Fairyland both appear
in the poem, yet Fairyland is also Britain. Is this a mere duplica-
tion and confusion, or can we distinguish between them? I think
we can. Queen Elizabeth, as we have seen, is given two
ancestries—one which links her with Arthur and the ancient
British kings, and one with the purely fanciful history of the
realm of Fairyland. They serve two different ends. The one
embodies the destiny of the historical Britain, culminating in the
actual Tudor rule. The other embodies the destiny of an ideal
Britain, the kingdom of love, of chivalry, of true devotion,
culminating in that idealized version of queenliness that was so
powerful a factor in the Elizabethan imagination. The glorification of the Queen is sometimes court flattery; but it is also
something quite different—a dedication to an embodied ideal in
which the actual Queen becomes the cynosure of a complex
range of erotic, patriotic and quasi-religious feelings that is now
almost impossible for us to realize fully. *Iam redit et virgo,
redeunt Saturnia regna*. . . . The roots of this feeling go very deep
into the mythological past, where ideas of divine monarchy, the
great goddess, the virgin and the destined bride are seen faintly
moving in a remote and shadowy distance. I have never yet
seen a satisfying account of the way this mythic substratum
affects individual poetic creation, though nowadays everybody
talks about it. We should not demand more precision than the
situation allows; and clearly we miss much of the power of much
of our greatest poetry if we remain wholly unaware of this
ancestral presence. The Faerie Queene both is and is not Queen
Elizabeth; Cleopolis both is and is not London. It is London
and its court as they ought to be and are not (Spenser is quite
clear that they are not). It is also London and its court (the

heart of an England seen as the type of all humanity) as they really are in some ultimate depth of the imagination.

### III

One thing that is clear is that Cleopolis is not the Heavenly City. It is sharply distinguished from the Heavenly City, the New Jerusalem, in the episode on the Mount of Contemplation (I. x. 57 seq.) "Yet is Cleopolis for earthly frame,/The fairest peece that eyes beholden can". It follows then that "that soveraigne Dame" who rules it, though spoken of as "heavenly borne", is an earthly governor; and the scene of the whole action is on earth. There is a tendency to make *The Faerie Queene* a more other-worldly poem than it really is. It is a religious poem in the sense that its earthly action is suffused with Christian thought and feeling, but not in the sense that it is occupied with a supernatural quest. It is no *Pilgrim's Progress* and has little affinity with *Paradise Lost*. It is only near the beginning, in the Red Cross Knight's vision of the New Jerusalem just referred to, and at the close, in the aspiration towards the eternal Sabbath, that man's last end enters directly into the theme. Its field is the world and its theme the conduct of life in the sublunary sphere. Its dilemmas and oppositions are ethical, social and erotic. When it engages with cosmology the explanations offered are naturalistic. Of course Spenser is a Christian, of course his whole view of life is contained and bounded by a Christian consciousness, but the sphere of his artistic operation is the natural world, and even his ethics, though their ultimate sanction is outside nature, tend to assume a naturalistic colouring. We can if we will draw a contrast with Dante. The sins punished in Hell or refined away in Purgatory are sins because they are forbidden, and they are equally sins and equally forbidden even when they are steeped in every imaginable human sweetness, as were those of Paolo and Francesca. Spenser rarely exposes himself to this cruel dilemma. The evil in his world is as a rule clearly recognizable by its ugliness. If not it is a deliberate imposture and ultimately unmasked, like the false Florimell. In the case of beauty and sensuous delight we feel (or at least I feel) a struggle to accommodate the naturalistic ethic to the demands of an absolute morality; and poetically speaking the absolute morality wins no more than a doubtful victory. The unutterably clear and poignant human sympathy confronted with an inexorable law that is ultimately beyond human sympathy—that is what Dante shows us in his colloquy with Francesca. Spenser avoids this and wishes to avoid it; his tendency is to show that every true human sympathy can be accommodated to eternal law. But it is the right management and direction of human sympathy that he is mainly concerned with. Eternal law does not find any very clear definition in his pages.

No one in Spenser gives all his heart to an earthly love and then has to laugh at it as unworthy and unimportant in the end, like Chaucer's Troilus. No one in Spenser has to reject or deny the passion that he has lived for, like Malory's Lancelot. And no one in Spenser transmutes his earthly love into a love of a different order, like Dante. This is to say that Spenser has overcome, or is striving to overcome, the desperate medieval split between *amour courtois* and the severity of the Christian scheme of redemption. But this is the theme of Professor Lewis's *Allegory of Love*, and there is no need to repeat what he has expounded so brilliantly. He sees Spenser as the inaugurator of the romance of marriage, against the medieval romance of illicit love. We might add however that except for Artegall and Britomart it is their status as lovers that is important with Spenser's characters, not their status as potential married people. A tender, chivalrous love is the highest human value in Spenser's world; and it is always an uncomplicated unwavering love that looks to its "right true end", to a human and earthly fruition. The delays and deviations in reaching that consummation are the substance of romantic narrative, and Spenser retains much of the procedure of the medieval romance of courtship; but there is never any suspicion of that lingering pleasure in frustration for its own sake that M. de Rougemont has found characteristic of love in the Western world.[1]

It follows from this that there cannot be much of Platonism,

[1] Denis de Rougemont, L'Amour et l'Occident, 1939; (revised 1956).

either of the original or the neo-variety in Spenser's love-morality. Although "Spenser and Renaissance Platonism" is one of the standard themes for commentary I have said little about it for I have found little of the platonic spirit in *The Faerie Queene*. Love may have a heavenly birth, but there is never the slightest suggestion that love of an earthly object should be the stepping-stone to heavenly love. Indeed there is very little about heavenly love in the poem. So much I could see for myself; but there is another reason for keeping away from the subject of Spenser's 'Platonism'. It has recently been studied with such exhaustive learning by M. Ellrodt[1] that to do other than cite him would be an impertinence. It is not possible to summarize his extremely detailed investigation, but the following are the points that are most to our purpose here. There is a large body of diffused Platonism in the literature at Spenser's disposal—dilute philosophical Platonism in Boethius, literary and poetical Platonism in Petrarch, a social and gallant version of Platonism in Castiglione. But there is no evidence that Spenser's acquaintance with Plato himself was more than very moderate, or that he had any acquaintance at all with Plotinus or the Italian neo-Platonic writers, Ficino, Benevieni or Pico—except perhaps in the last of the *Four Hymns*. Platonic-looking expressions are often poetic adornments without real philosophical content, and the superficially Platonic character of many passages in *The Faerie Queene* is not confirmed by real examination. Take for example the invocation of love in III. iii. 1:

> Most Sacred fire, that burnest mightily
> In living brests, ykindled first above,
> Emongst th'eternall spheres and lamping sky,
> And thence pourd into men, which men call Love;
> Not that same, which doth base affections move
> In brutish minds, and filthy lust inflame,
> But that sweet fit, that doth true beautie love,
> And chooseth vertue for his dearest Dame,
> Whence spring all noble deeds and never dying fame.

M. Ellrodt comments on this passage:

[1] Robert Ellrodt, *Neoplatonism in the Poetry of Spenser*, Geneva, 1960.

The opening lines raise an expectation of the Neo-Platonic contrast between love as a desire of contemplation kindled by intellectual beauty, and love as a desire of generation excited by earthly beauty. But from the closing lines it appears that the higher love is conceived as a spur to virtuous action on earth rather than an invitation to fly back to heaven. . . . The love that sent Britomart on her quest for a husband, the love that "afterwards did raise most famous fruites of matrimonialle bowre" is obviously not a desire of intellectual beauty. Yet that same love has been described as "ykindled first above" and contrasted with brutish love. The distinction therefore was not drawn on the metaphysical level, between the earthly and the heavenly Venus, but on the earthly—and Christian—level, between virtuous love and "filthy lust". . . . It is characteristic of Spenser that his conception of love, whenever he echoes the Platonists, should remain either purely ethical when human love is concerned, or purely natural when cosmic love is discussed. To both human and cosmic love he ascribes a heavenly origin, but in *The Faerie Queene* he has no place for "heavenly love" as conceived by the Platonists, love "ad divinam pulchritudinem cogitandam".[1]

To his ethical and natural conceptions of love we must add all that Spenser inherited from the romance tradition of love-poetry and all that he found about him in the English lyric tradition—that tender idealization of sensuousness, the loving appreciation of the unity of soul and body that is one of the great secular legacies of the Middle Ages. A sense of preciousness and fragility in this feeling is perhaps a part of its essence. This often arises in medieval poetry because the love itself is a stolen thing; in Spenser from a different cause. Though love and happiness can be reconciled and both are at home in the natural world there is something in the world that is against them. The Blatant Beast, the brigands and Mutability are always at large; and if Spenser is the great poet of natural happiness he also knows its limits and its lack. Otherwise he could not make it so poignantly beautiful.

IV

In discussing *The Faerie Queene* we always tend to speak of it as a whole poem, and it is continually necessary in the course of special arguments to pull oneself up and recall that it is a

[1] Op. cit., pp. 34–5.

fragment. Of course it is a fragment—six books and the chance survival of part of a seventh out of what should have been twelve. Yet our unguarded way of speaking of it is not mere carelessness; it does correspond to a genuine experience. When we become familiar with the poem we do feel it as a whole. And I do not think that this is merely because we have got used to our half loaf and decide to make the best of it. The poem is unfinished because Spenser died. But I suspect he must have known for some time that his vast project was not likely to be completed. It sometimes happens that a man's life and work tends to round itself off, even when death comes prematurely, according to some plan that was not premeditated and is never consciously entertained. It is perhaps a fantasy, but I cannot help feeling that something of this sort must have happened with Spenser. At all events it is possible to experience a sense of completeness in the poem as it stands.

It begins with the book of Holiness, because for Spenser this is the necessary ground of all human development. A Catholic poet might have put it at the end; Spenser's placing of it as he does corresponds to the Protestant theology of prevenient grace —without it all other activity is worthless. Next comes Temperance, as the first condition of any possible human integrity. It is what divides man from the beasts—the moral control of passion that distinguishes him from the natural world while still leaving him a part of it. These books are self-contained, complete within themselves; they have perhaps greater density and complexity of organization than all the others; yet they are in a sense preliminary to Spenser's main preoccupations.

Then we have Books III and IV, called the legends of Chastity and Friendship, but really to be taken together as the poem's great central area, concerned with Love. It is primarily love between men and women, love in the ideal romantic sense. Whatever Spenser's ostensible subject this is the theme to which he continually returns. The celebration of love, the distinction of its different tempers and varieties, the portrayal of the conditions which foster it, and of its enemies in the heart and in the outer world—it is this that forms the main substance of *The Faerie Queene*. Other human qualities are there as its environment and its support. Love is the active source of value. It is in human life and human relations that Spenser sees the quintessence of love; but it is a quintessence distilled from the force of love pervading the whole universe; the Lucretian Venus or the power of concord that keeps the whole creation together. The Temple of Venus with its romance of courtship and the Garden of Adonis with its life-giving cosmic power are the two allegorical poles on which this central part of the poem turns.

Since man is a political animal the force of concord must be prolonged into the social and political sphere. This is the function of the book of Justice, and it is perhaps the one grave fault in *The Faerie Queene* that the repressive function of Justice is so much more evident than its socially harmonizing power. By now the main lines of Spenser's view of life are laid down. There remains the final enhancement of a spontaneous natural grace. This is celebrated in the book of Courtesy. It is a natural flowering that crowns the whole with loveliness. But the scene of the poem is the world, and no achievement of virtue or beauty in the world is lasting. Everything is subject to change, and this seems at first subversive of all happiness and all good. By submitting to the judgement of nature it is just possible to see this change as life-giving and re-creative. But man can never fully see it so; the weight of mutability presses too heavily upon him. It is only by projecting his mind outside the created world, by seeing it for a moment in its eternal setting, that a resting-place can be found. This takes us a step beyond the ideal naturalism that is the normal temper of Spenser's mind. If the two closing stanzas are the chance breaking-off point of an unfinished poem, there can never have been a happier chance.

This is not the formal design at one time projected. It is not a formal design of any sort. But it is an organic growth with its own kind of wholeness. The legend of St. George is the perfect beginning; Courtesy is the perfect end; the great continued narratives have a mutual coherence of theme, and are grouped as they should be in the middle. Mutability is the perfect epilogue. The real meaning of a form is usually hidden from its creator; and still less can we know by what imperceptible inspiration the poem assumed the form it has. It is not even easy to see the work in its entirety, for we are distracted by the richness of detail. I suspect however that all who come to know it well end by feeling that in spite of a grandiose plan cut short *The Færie Queene* in its actual state fulfils the law of its being.

# INDEX

# INDEX

# INDEX